The French Connection

The French Connection

Robin Moore

BLOOMSBURY

Series editors: Maxim Jakubowski and Adrian Wootton

This paperback edition first published in 2005

Bloomsbury Publishing Plc, 36 Soho Square, London, W1D 3QY

A CIP catalogue record is available from the British Library

ISBN 0 7475 7865 6
9780747578659

10 9 8 7 6 5 4 3 2 1

Typeset by Hewer Text Ltd, Edinburgh
Printed in Great Britain by Clays Limited, St Ives plc

www.bloomsbury.com

Acknowledgments

THE account that follows is a case history of what must qualify as one of the finest police investigations in the annals of United States law enforcement. Almost certainly it represents the most crucial single victory to date in the ceaseless, frustrating war against the import of vicious narcotics into our country. Indeed, this investigation, and the information gleaned from it, eventually has led to the progressive breakdown of Mafia investment and proprietorship in the U.S. narcotics market.

This is neither a clinical study nor an emotional exposition of the ravages of narcotics addiction, of which so much has been written, although more needs to be told. Nor is it populated by the pitiful 'junkies' who should and do frighten the anxious parents who are concerned about American youth. It is a rare view of the murky intrigue among the conscienceless ones who profit from the deadly subversion of dope addicts, young and old. If one parent is jarred by this story, or if one youngster can be saved from disaster out of disgust, then the long, lonely, often dangerous vigils of many police officers will have been rewarded, at least in part.

The detailed information that made this book possible derives from many cooperative sources, all of whom have my sincere appreciation and gratitude. The New York Police Department's tireless Narcotics Bureau, under its former commander Deputy Chief Inspector Ira Bluth, and especially the bureau's elite Special Investigating Unit (S.I.U.) were constantly helpful and patient in supplying details necessary to make the narrative accurate. The Federal Bureau of Narcotics also was of valuable assistance, with its more than five thousand feet of recorded reports and radio transmissions.

The fact that one of the suspects in the case kept a fairly complete diary greatly assisted the author in presenting details not covered by police reports and interviews. The District Attorney's office of Kings County (Brooklyn), New York, particularly Assistant D.A. Frank Bauman, also contributed mightily, making available some twelve hundred pages of court testimony.

But always the primary informants were the two dedicated New York City detectives who stumbled upon, then directed, this extraordinary case to a successful conclusion: Detectives First Grade Edward Egan and Salvatore Grosso. It has been reported to police that even today the international dope-smuggling ring, whose operation was damaged so badly, refuses to believe that one of their own, a 'stool pigeon,' was not responsible for leading authorities to the unraveling of the massive conspiracy. The truth is that the New York police alone, aided by Federal agents, pursued the case to the end without help from a single betrayer.

Speaking of acknowledgments, I could go no further here were I not to make special note of the contributions of my writing associate and friend, Edward Keyes. Ed personally involved himself in every detail of preparing this book, from the essential research, and fieldwork with narcotics officers, to the actual writing and editing.

Together, we are proud to tell this story of The French Connection.

Robin Moore
New York, N. Y.
July, 1968

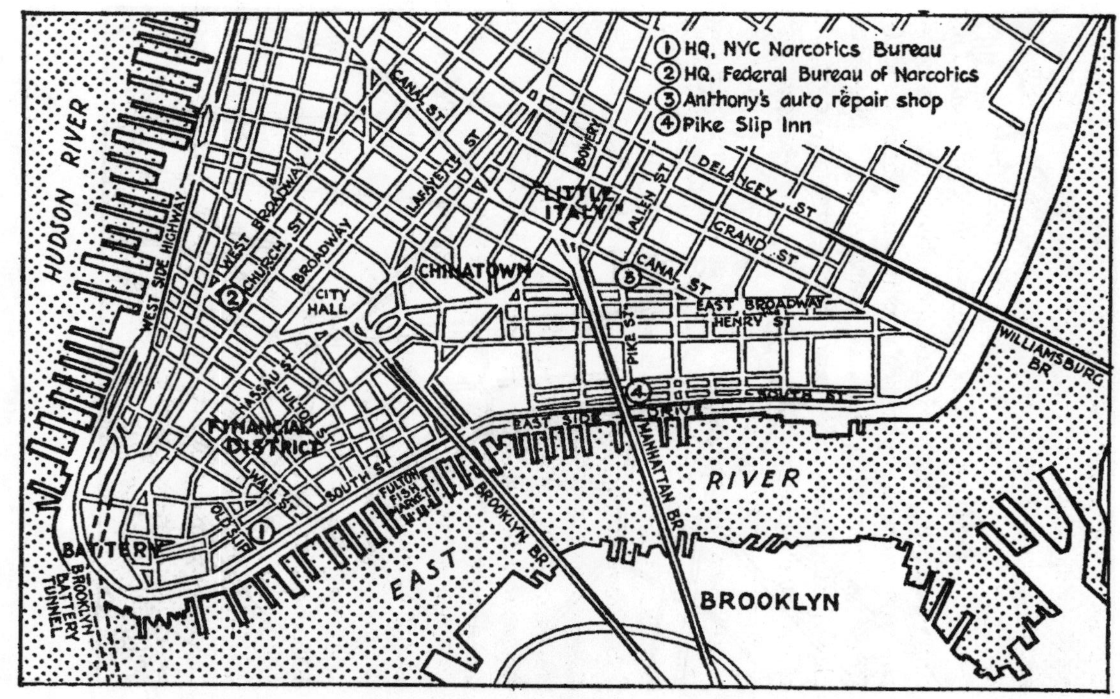
① HQ, NYC Narcotics Bureau
② HQ, Federal Bureau of Narcotics
③ Anthony's auto repair shop
④ Pike Slip Inn
HUDSON RIVER
WEST SIDE HIGHWAY
WEST BROADWAY
CHURCH ST
BROADWAY
CITY HALL
CANAL ST
LAFAYETTE ST
BOWERY
"LITTLE ITALY"
ALLEN ST
DELANCEY ST
GRAND ST
CANAL ST
CHINATOWN
EAST BROADWAY
HENRY ST
PIKE ST
SOUTH ST
EAST SIDE DRIVE
NASSAU ST
FULTON ST
FINANCIAL DISTRICT
WALL ST
SOUTH ST
FULTON FISH MARKET
OLD SLIP
BATTERY
BROOKLYN BATTERY TUNNEL
BROOKLYN BR
MANHATTAN BR
WILLIAMSBURG BR
EAST
RIVER
BROOKLYN

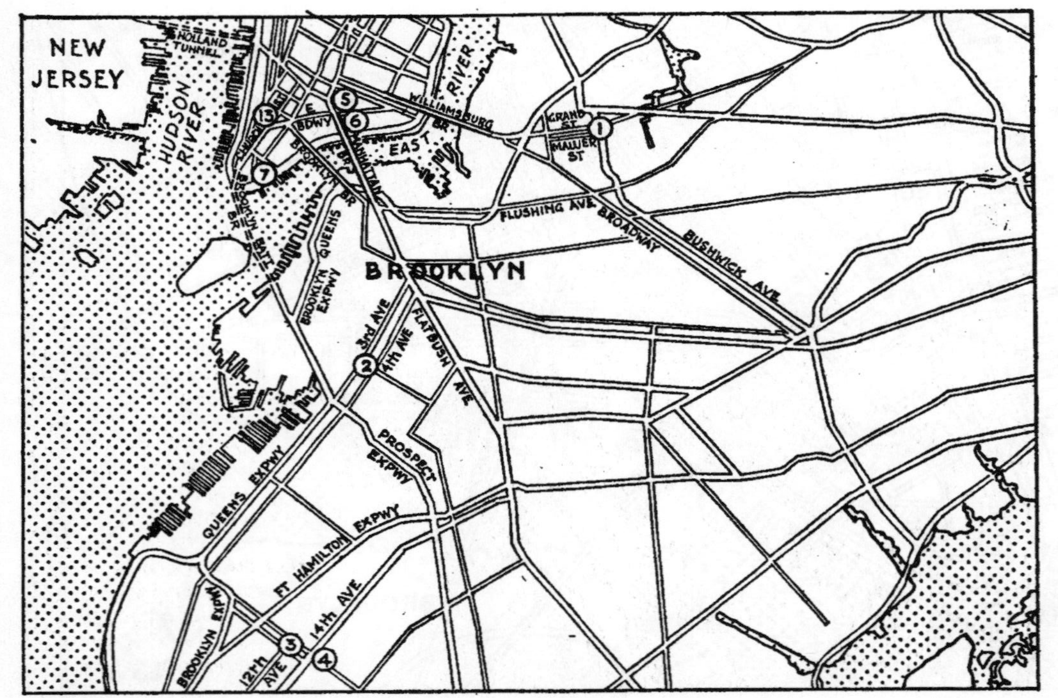
NEW JERSEY
HOLLAND TUNNEL
HUDSON RIVER
EAST RIVER
WILLIAMSBURG BR
E BDWY
MANHATTAN BR
BROOKLYN BR
BROOKLYN BATT
GRAND ST
MAUJER ST
FLUSHING AVE
BROADWAY
BUSHWICK AVE
BROOKLYN
BROOKLYN QUEENS EXPWY
3rd AVE
4th AVE
FLATBUSH AVE
PROSPECT EXPWY
QUEENS EXPWY
FT HAMILTON EXPWY
14th AVE
12th AVE
BROOKLYN EXPWY
1
2
3
4
5
6
7
13

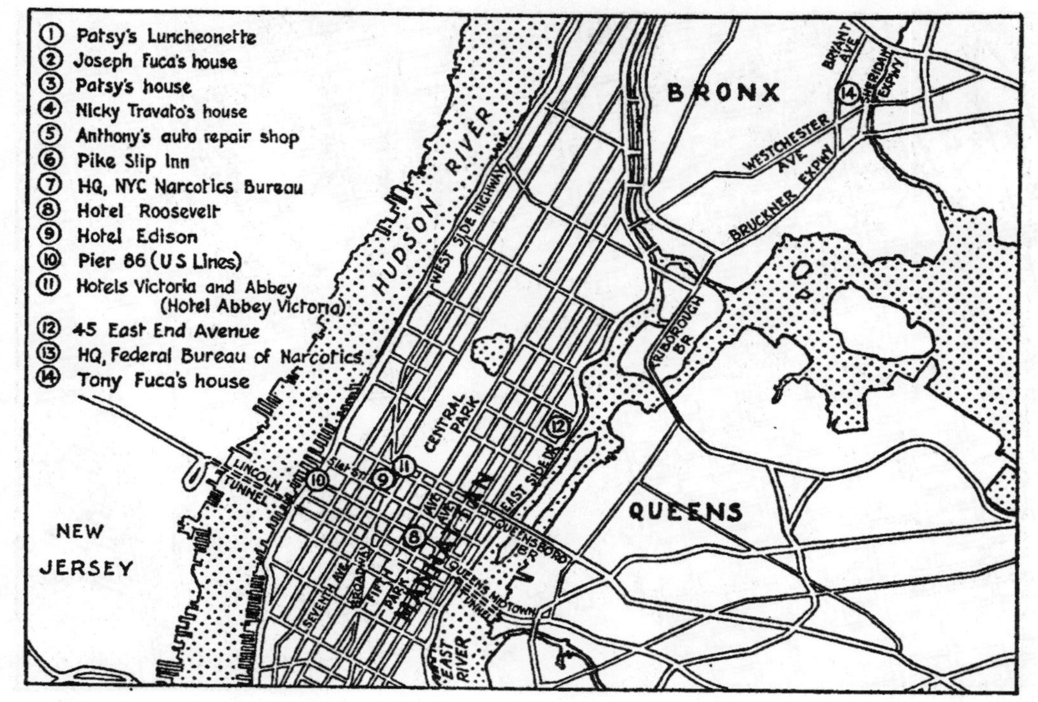

① Patsy's Luncheonette
② Joseph Fuca's house
③ Patsy's house
④ Nicky Travato's house
⑤ Anthony's auto repair shop
⑥ Pike Slip Inn
⑦ HQ, NYC Narcotics Bureau
⑧ Hotel Roosevelt
⑨ Hotel Edison
⑩ Pier 86 (U S Lines)
⑪ Hotels Victoria and Abbey (Hotel Abbey Victoria)
⑫ 45 East End Avenue
⑬ HQ, Federal Bureau of Narcotics
⑭ Tony Fuca's house
BRONX
HUDSON RIVER
WEST SIDE HIGHWAY
WESTCHESTER AVE
BRUCKNER EXPWY
BRYANT AVE
SHERIDAN EXPWY
TRIBOROUGH BR
CENTRAL PARK
EAST SIDE DR
LINCOLN TUNNEL
QUEENS
NEW JERSEY
MANHATTAN
QUEENSBORO BR
QUEENS MIDTOWN TUNNEL
SEVENTH AVE
BROADWAY
FIFTH
PARK
EAST RIVER

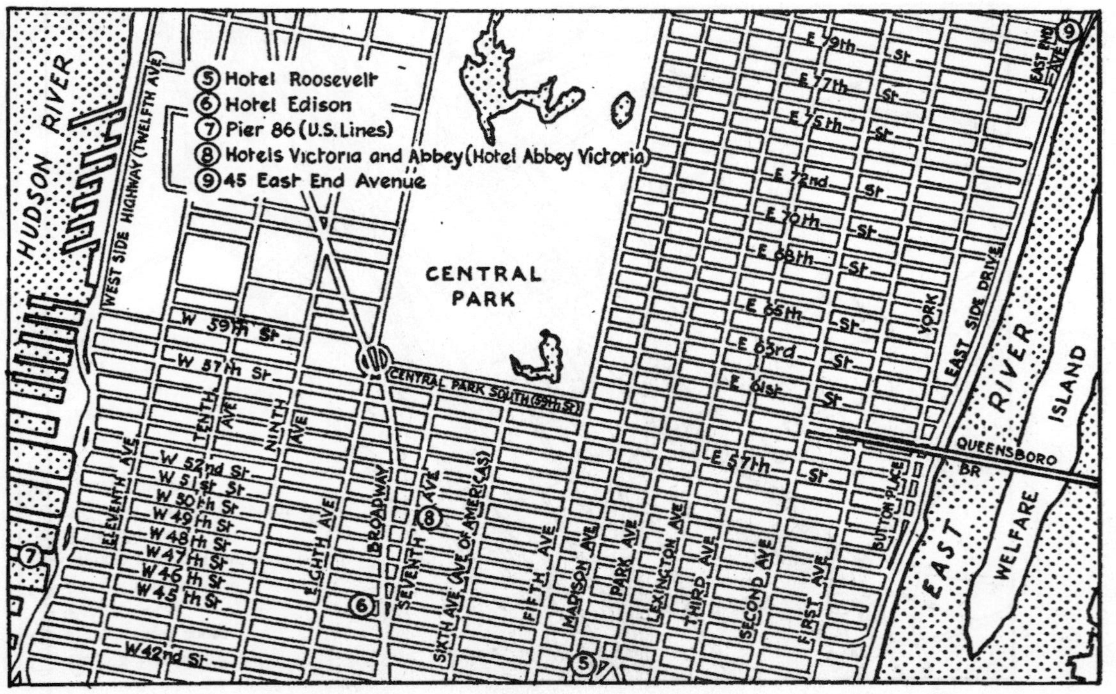

5 Hotel Roosevelt
6 Hotel Edison
7 Pier 86 (U.S. Lines)
8 Hotels Victoria and Abbey (Hotel Abbey Victoria)
9 45 East End Avenue
HUDSON RIVER
WEST SIDE HIGHWAY (TWELFTH AVE)
CENTRAL PARK
W 59th St
W 57th St
CENTRAL PARK SOUTH (59th St)
W 52nd St
W 51st St
W 50th St
W 49th St
W 48th St
W 47th St
W 46th St
W 45th St
W42nd St
ELEVENTH AVE
TENTH AVE
NINTH AVE
EIGHTH AVE
BROADWAY
SEVENTH AVE
SIXTH AVE (AVE OF AMERICAS)
FIFTH AVE
MADISON AVE
PARK AVE
LEXINGTON AVE
THIRD AVE
SECOND AVE
FIRST AVE
SUTTON PLACE
YORK
EAST SIDE DRIVE
EAST END AVE
E 79th St
E 77th St
E 75th St
E 72nd St
E 70th St
E 68th St
E 65th St
E 63rd St
E 61st St
E 57th St
QUEENSBORO BR
EAST RIVER
WELFARE ISLAND

Chapter One

LATE on Saturday night, October 7, 1961, after twenty-seven straight hours on duty, New York Detective First Grade Edward Egan, thirty-one, and his partner, then Detective Second Grade Salvatore Grosso, thirty, decided it was time to have some fun. There was no question where they would go. Comedian Joe E. Lewis was headlining at the Copacabana, and Egan's current romance, Carol Galvin, checked coats at the nightclub.

Eddie Egan was a burly Irish-handsome redhead once known as 'Bullets' to his fellow cops because as a uniformed patrolman he had worn an extra cartridge belt. But his more recent Narcotics Bureau code name was 'Popeye' – after his favorite mode of amusement, 'popeying around,' that is, looking over pretty girls, upon whom he would exercise his Gaelic charm at the merest hint of a blush.

Egan, the off-duty swinger, contrasted sharply with his solemn partner and best friend, Sonny Grosso, a pale-faced Italian-American with large brown eyes. Sonny was a worrier who looked for, and frequently managed to find, the dark side of most situations, unlike the ebullient Egan. They were both six-footers, but Grosso was wiry and at first glance appeared to be slight, even somewhat vulnerable, for a policeman. But Sonny had earned a black belt in karate, and, as a number of hoodlums had discovered, he was definitely not one to underestimate. His code name at the Narcotics Bureau was 'Cloudy.'

The previous evening the two had closed out a narcotics case in Harlem, their beat since 1959. They had arrested three pushers who had been under investigation for several months, had stayed up throughout the night, interrogating, fingerprinting, and booking them, then writing out the endless official reports that are required. Finally, they escorted the prisoners to the old city jail called 'the Tombs' in downtown Manhattan, and then appeared in early court to lodge the formal complaints. It was late Saturday morning before they were finished, but both were too tired to sleep, an occupational hazard among most undercover agents, who live with taut nerves and their senses alert during the long working hours. The two were rabid baseball fans, and because the Yankees were playing the third game of the World Series against the Cincinnati Reds that day, sleep remained far from their minds. They cruised around the city listening to the game on the car radio. Later, after the Yanks' close victory, having come from behind to win in the ninth inning on a home run by Roger Maris, the two felt more inclined to sustain the stimulation of winning than to curb it. They went out to dinner, visited a couple of east midtown bars recommended by Egan for possible 'action,' and at last, fatigued but still restless, they headed across town to the Copa.

It was eleven-forty Saturday night when Egan parked his 1961 maroon Corvair on East 60th Street and he and Sonny stepped into the nightclub – unaware that they were entering upon an odyssey of intrigue and conspiracy that would obsess them night and day for the next four-and-a-half months and would not end finally for a year and a half. It was twenty minutes before the midnight show, and the Copa was filling up. Egan barely had a chance to murmur a smiling hello to Carol, who was disappearing behind coats and hats. She was a beautiful, stately girl, not yet twenty, with short blonde hair; to Egan's eyes she was a double for Kim Novak. He hastily said that he would see her later, and the two went downstairs to the main clubroom, where the headwaiter recognized Egan and directed them to a small table up on one of the raised terraces well in the rear. They ordered a rye and ginger for Eddie, Italian vermouth on ice for Sonny, and sat back quietly to watch the gay night-life scene and perhaps, finally, unwind.

Just as the drinks arrived, Sonny touched his partner's arm and nodded toward a crowded, boisterous table below their perch. The party of twelve really might have been transplanted from the set of a thirties' gangster movie: swarthy, sleek, dark-suited men accompanied by flashy, overly made-up women. The individual at the center of attention would be particularly well cast as an archetypal Hollywood rackets' boss with black, cropped bushy hair, a dark complexion, and a pockmarked face, good-looking in a scowling way. He was about thirty years of age, and overly dapper in a shiny black suit with broad shoulders, a diamond stickpin glittering from a white silk tie against a white shirt with French cuffs. A showy, young blonde with a bouffant hairdo was at his elbow. The man was the host and seemed also to be something of a celebrity at the club. As Egan and Grosso looked on, absorbed, a succession of obviously well-heeled and hard-looking types streamed by to pay their respects. Between times the host sent waiters scurrying with drinks to other tables around the room. During one noisy greeting, Sonny heard someone call the man Patsy.

'He spreads bread like there's no tomorrow,' Sonny observed.

'Interesting,' Eddie commented. 'I make at least two junk "connections" at the table. And I know a couple of those guys who dropped by are in numbers.'

'I've never seen "Patsy" before, have you?'

'No. I wonder how we could've missed him?' Egan's tone was dry.

Throughout the floor show, which lasted an hour and a half, Eddie and Sonny divided their attention between Joe E. Lewis and the table of the big spender. When the lights came up and the orchestra started playing for dancing, Patsy and his retinue arose and went upstairs. The detectives looked at one another, paid their check and followed. The group congregated at the bar in the Copa lounge, where a rock-jazz combo was drowning any conversation. Patsy had ordered nightcaps all around.

Standing near the checkroom while deciding what to do, Eddie and Sonny saw Patsy pull a huge roll of bills from his trouser pocket to pay the bar tab. Sonny whistled: 'Check the bread!'

Egan nodded. 'What do you say we wait and give him a tail, just for fun?'

Grosso shrugged in unenthusiastic accord and, as they went out, Eddie winked apologetically at Carol Galvin and threw her a kiss. They sat for twenty-five minutes in Egan's car near the corner of Madison Avenue, until, at 2 A.M., 'Patsy' and the splashy blonde came down the steps of the Copa alone. The uniformed doorman brought up a late-model blue Oldsmobile compact, and they pulled away toward Fifth Avenue. Driving slowly behind them, Egan speculated: 'I'll lay odds he takes us to Mott Street.'

Patsy drove all the way down Fifth Avenue to its Broadway intersection and turned toward a tenement section of Manhattan that has become infamous in America, the Lower East Side. Narrow Mott Street, where Patsy indeed went, is only eleven blocks long, from Bleecker Street near the edge of Greenwich Village at its northern end, down past the Bowery to Chatham Square in the south. But to the police it long has been viewed as an aorta to the heart of every illegal activity in

New York. Though Mott touches Chinatown, it is mostly in the area known as Little Italy, which for generations has provided a private crime greenhouse for Mafia families.

Patsy did not confine his tour to Mott Street, however. During the next two hours, he made stops on Hester Street, Broome, Canal and Delancey. As Sonny and Egan watched from discreet distances, the Olds pulled to the curb from time to time, and Patsy got out. One or more men would materialize from doorways or out of the shadows of quiet buildings, and they would talk for a few minutes before Patsy returned to his car and drove slowly off. The blonde always stayed in the Olds.

It was nearing 5 A.M. Sunday when the blue compact finally headed east on Delancey Street toward the Williamsburg Bridge to Brooklyn. The two detectives, never far behind in the maroon Corvair, had been active for thirty-two consecutive hours.

Patsy led them off the bridge and into Meeker Avenue beneath the elevated Brooklyn-Queens Expressway. He parked and locked the car. Then the two walked a few steps to a battered white 1947 Dodge, and drove off again. The puzzled detectives followed.

This time the pursuit took them only a dozen blocks. Patsy drove to Grand Street, then west to Bushwick Avenue, turned right a short block and right again on Maujer Street, where he parked just beyond the corner. Egan went past Maujer, made a U-turn and came back and stopped on Bushwick. He and Sonny watched the expensively dressed couple unlock a darkened candy store-luncheonette, called Barbara's, at the corner. While the girl waited outside, Patsy switched on the lights and walked to a small room in the rear, where he filled a coffeepot and placed it on a hot plate. Only then did he return to the street door and motion the blonde inside. The detectives saw her take a gray apron-coat from a wall hook and slip into it, while Patsy removed his suitcoat and pulled on a gray jacket. Patsy then went outside and around the corner to the Dodge to get an armload of newspapers, which he lugged into the store. Then the two set to work fitting together the various sections of the Sunday papers. Across the intersection, the pair of veteran police officers looked at each other in further wonderment.

About 7 A.M., Patsy pulled up the blind masking the glass door to announce that they were open for business. A few customers began to drift in, mostly white-clad medical personnel. Egan and Grosso then realized they were parked in front of St. Catherine's Hospital, which stood on a corner diagonally opposite the luncheonette at the intersection of Bushwick Avenue and Maujer Street. It was a drab area of weather-beaten three-story residential dwellings, but directly across Bushwick there was a modern apartment project with several stores on its ground level, including another luncheonette.

Knowing that they would be conspicuous sitting there in the daylight, Sonny went into the hospital and persuaded a security guard to open an unused ground-floor X-ray room, whose windows offered a good view of Patsy's store. By 8 A.M., Sonny and Eddie were ensconced more or less comfortably, watching the comings and goings around the luncheonette, taking short breaks to nourish themselves with coffee and a Danish or to seek out a men's room.

Patsy and the blonde had been joined in the store by a short, heavyset, dark-haired man wearing a lumber jacket, who appeared to be a helper. Otherwise, nothing noteworthy had happened, nor had any of the three left the premises.

The detectives maintained their surveillance with increasing weariness until shortly after 2 P.M., in their forty-second hour of continuous duty, when they saw the suspects come out of the luncheonette, dressed for the street. Patsy locked up, and he and the girl said goodbye to the stocky fellow who walked the other way on Bushwick, while the couple went around the corner to their car. Egan and Grosso hurried to the Corvair.

They tailed the old Dodge west on Maujer Street, over to Grand and up onto the Brooklyn-Queens Expressway. Patsy sped south, into the Gowanus Expressway toward southern Brooklyn. He exited at 65th Street after about an eight-mile run. In a few minutes the Dodge pulled into a driveway a third of the way into the block on 67th Street. Egan halted his car back at the corner of 67th and Twelfth Avenue.

Sixty-seventh was a neat, sedate, tree-shaded street lined with two- and three-story private houses. After ten minutes, when the detectives felt sure that Patsy and the blonde were settled inside, they turned into 67th and rode slowly past where the Dodge was parked. The house was the right-hand one of a pair of identical attached two-story red-brick houses, built over two-car garages. The common stairway from the sidewalk was divided by a white wrought-iron railing and led to a cement porch and separate entrances. As the Corvair cruised past, Sonny scribbled the address of the house on the inside of a matchbook: 1224 67th Street.

Though seriously fatigued at the moment, they decided the odd situation merited serious investigation after a night's rest. Since when does the proprietor of a luncheonette and newsstand receive red-carpet treatment at one of New York's most glamorous and expensive nightclubs?

Chapter Two

SONNY GROSSO was an aggressive and uncompromising detective, but what private life he would permit himself was restrained and for the most part uneventful. At thirty, he was basically as withdrawn as he had been as a shy child. Introspective and stern, unlike his partner Eddie Egan, the sallow-complexioned Sonny dated infrequently and in fact had never had a really serious romance. Egan was the lover of parties and girls, and if he wasn't always successful in finding a good time the fiery-haired detective invariably found enjoyment in the hunt itself. Grosso, on the other hand, respected women and treated them more seriously, almost with the deference of a gentleman from an earlier era.

Sonny was an only son with three sisters. When his father, a truck driver, died suddenly at the age of thirty-seven, Sonny, the eldest child, became the head of his family at fifteen. He treated his sisters with fatherly care.

Sonny was raised in East Harlem, which he remembers as a shabby but safe and warm Italian neighborhood where everybody knew everybody else and the families were close and reasonably happy. He remembers how his mother, a gentle, indefatigable woman, would leave their tenement apartment 'to get a quart of milk' at the local grocery and not return for two hours because she had to stop and talk along the way with neighbors. To Sonny, East Harlem had always meant a friendly community with big families. The schools were crowded, and streets swarmed with more than enough kids to get up a game of stickball or 'association' (wide-open, one-handed touch football) at any hour of the day. When Sonny was still in his teens, the Grosso family moved across Manhattan to the west side of Harlem to an Irish enclave called 'Vinegar Hill,' where they were suddenly immigrants among immigrants. Despite his dark, brooding Latin features, it did not take Sonny long to assimilate among the bright-faced, garrulous, suspicious Irish: he was quiet, sincere, physically rugged and a good street athlete. After a while, he ceased to miss the old neighborhood.

When he did return to East Harlem after almost ten years, the area had changed radically, and so had Sonny. He was a policeman. After high school at the start of the Korean War he was drafted into the Army, where he spent two years as a radio operator. He was discharged as a sergeant in 1952 after injuring his knee. Then he drove a mail truck for two years, mostly in the Times Square area, still providing the main support for his widowed mother and the younger children. In 1954, he and several friends took the Civil Service Police Academy examination, and out of some 50,000 applicants tested that year Sonny scored among the top three hundred. From the Academy, Sonny was sent on his first assignment to the 25th Precinct in East Harlem. It *was* different: his old neighborhood had deteriorated from a relatively cohesive immigrant community into a vicious ghetto, populated now by a new generation of divisive elements who existed more by muscle and intimidation than by ambition. In a few years, the East Harlem of Sonny Grosso's boyhood had earned the grotesque distinction of spawning as much vice and degradation per square block as any sinkhole in America.

The most serious depravity was the growing illicit sale, and use, of addictive narcotics. Sonny had not before been exposed to the ravages of heroin, and it revolted him. He hated what it had done, and was doing, to the Puerto Rican and

Negro people who now crowded in among those Italians still left in his old neighborhood.

There were still some there who remembered him, and he soon realized that many now looked upon him with unfamiliar mistrust and even contempt. (This, too, was different from the old days, when his father had set a typical standard of proper relations with the police: 'Tell them nothing? Okay. But *hate* them? *No*.') Sonny could not really despise these wretched people in return; only their situation. Drugs, he saw, were at the root of their afflictions but were not the *cause* of their misery. Drugs, or 'junk,' were but a symptom of a deeper disease in their urban society. But in his four years as a patrolman in the 25th, he learned enough to focus his hatred upon this most obvious despoiler, narcotics, and on those who pushed it and profited so inhumanely.

In 1958, Sonny applied and was accepted for a post as detective in the Police Narcotics Bureau. After training downtown, they asked if he would be interested in plainclothes work; he said he would. Where did he think he might do the most good? East Harlem, he replied. And so Sonny was assigned to the Sixth Detective Division, which included the 25th Precinct, and returned again to East Harlem.

Eddie Egan had never thought of being a city police officer before he was twenty-five. He wanted to be a professional baseball player. And he came literally to within an arm's length of making it to the New York Yankees.

Egan learned his baseball the hard way, as most city boys must, in the streets (punchball on the sidewalks; stickball, manhole cover to hydrant in the gutters) and on the debris-strewn lots of Brooklyn with a mushy softball or a taped, leaden 'Rocket.' Eddie's playmates were frequently reminded that he had a temper as fiery as his thatch of auburn hair.

By the time he left high school at seventeen, professional scouts were eying him. And after a two-year enlistment in the Marine Corps, in which he played service ball while growing bigger, stronger and more agile, he was offered a modest contract by the Washington Senators. In 1950 he was traded to the New York Yankees, and with their Class-B Norfolk farm club he was the regular center fielder and batted an impressive 317. The parent organization began to show special interest in him.

The Yankees about that time were starting to search for a bright prospect to be groomed against the inevitable retirement of their aging superstar, Joe DiMaggio. Egan was marked as one of several youngsters who showed promise. Another was a slugging shortstop from Oklahoma who, nineteen years old, had been breaking minor league distance records for home runs – Mickey Mantle.

After the 1950 season, Eddie Egan looked forward to the following spring, when he hoped to be advanced to the Yankees' Class A Binghamton club. And from there – who could tell? That October his dreams were shattered when he was recalled by the Marines. But the doctors learned that he had broken an arm in a training accident during his earlier enlistment and were undecided whether to accept him. They indicated, however, that he might expect to be called up again within three months.

At loose ends, to keep himself occupied while awaiting reactivation Egan passed a competitive exam and became a patrolman with the semiprivate police force of the Port Authority of New York. When January, 1951, passed, without a word from the Corps, Eddie had to choose between leaving the Authority and taking his chances at the Yankees' Florida training camp or holding on to his good job and sweating out his Marine Corps recall at home. He elected to stay on as a cop, and was sure he had made the right decision when that spring the Yankees brought rookie shortstop Mickey Mantle up to the big club and made him an outfielder.

The Marines kept him dangling – they never did call him back – and Egan wound up staying with the Port Authority police for four more years. A truce was reached in Korea, but by then, of course, it was too late for him to dream of a baseball career. But it didn't bother him anymore. He liked being a cop, but didn't like the slim prospects for advancement with the Port Authority. The organization was still so new that none of the senior officers had enough duty time for retirement, thus an ambitious patrolman had little opportunity to climb the ladder of command. So in 1955, having twiced passed tests for sergeant without promotion, Egan took the city police exam and placed 361st out of the almost 60,000 applicants, ten thousand more hopefuls than had taken the tests with Grosso the previous year. Eddie set an ambitious goal for himself: to make detective within one year.

Since the age of twelve, Egan had always considered himself to be very independent. He never knew his real father, and he never had been close to his stepfather, a New York fireman. His mother died shortly before his graduation from parochial school, and he boarded with grandparents. So, he had learned early how to make his own decisions – which he illustrated his first morning as a Police Academy recruit. Reporting an hour early to a gym in Flushing Meadow Park, Queens, he captured three girls hiding in the shrubbery who proved to be escaped prisoners with no less than thirteen felony charges against them.

To set an example for the other rookie cops, the Police Commissioner rewarded Egan by giving him the weekend off. Thus rewarded, Egan attempted to earn every weekend free. He rushed home from the Academy at 4 P.M. each day, changed clothes, and by 6 P.M. was back in Manhattan, either in the perversion-ridden Times Square area or around the Port Authority Bus Terminal, with which he was familiar from his service with the Authority police corps. He only had four hours each night – Police Academy rules require probationary police officers to be home by 10 P.M. – but he knew when and how to look for perverts, prostitutes, purse snatchers and narcotics pushers. His record of arrests, ninety-eight, was so extraordinary that within a month, while still officially an Academy trainee, he was pulled from his class and assigned to a special unit of veteran detectives covering Times Square. But when he refused an offer to become a 'shoofly' (one of the commissioner's Confidential Squad that spies on other cops), even though it probably would have meant sure promotion to detective, Egan was returned to the Academy.

He finally graduated and was sent to a beat in Harlem where, within two weeks, he made thirty-seven arrests, including one which led to the well-publicized indictment and subsequent conviction of singer Billy Daniels in a shooting. He was recommended for detective, and almost a year to the day after joining the department, in the summer of 1956, Eddie Egan exchanged his silver shield for a gold one.

Detectives either are dispatched to precincts around the city or may apply for special assignment squads; such as Burglary, Homicide, Safe and Loft. Egan knew what he wanted while he was still a rookie patrolman: Narcotics. A single personal experience with the bestiality of junk had left him with a permanent purpose in life, to interdict the drug traffic in any way he could.

One day in Brooklyn, while Egan was on his Harlem tour of duty, his six-year-old niece came home late from first grade to find her friends roller-skating. Her mother, Egan's sister, was sitting on the front stoop of their apartment house waiting for the child, and told her to go upstairs and get her own skates. The little girl clambered up the six flights excitedly, threw her plaid schoolbag down on the kitchen table, and ran to her bedroom to get her skates. Four dark, Spanish-looking young men huddled there, staring at her, one clutching her piggy bank. The child screamed. Two of them grabbed her, and a third grabbed her skates from the shelf and proceeded to beat her face and head with them. She slumped to the floor, bleeding and swollen, semiconscious, as the men ran out with her piggy bank. The mother soon found the girl, and in near hysteria she telephoned Eddie who raced out to Brooklyn. In a fury, he tore through the neighborhood, with the help of the local precinct, digging up every known degenerate or suspected felon from the bars and loitering spots. Within two hours the four men were in custody. They were junkies, desperate for a fix. Egan was barely able to restrain himself from destroying them. He never forgot it.

Eddie had been in the Narcotics Bureau for three years when he was teamed with Sonny Grosso. They were different in nature, but they complemented one another: brashness dovetailing with reserve, ingenuity modified by skepticism; and always in common, an abhorrence of the ugly ruin wrought by narcotics. Together, they terrorized the subworld of East Harlem. At the same time, they realized that their enthusiasm was provoking resentment within the Police Department and even within their own bureau. They made too many arrests; they were making certain others look slovenly. Eddie and Sonny shrugged off the sniping. They wanted to do a job.

Late Monday morning, October 9, 1961, after a good night's sleep, Egan drove back to the Williamsburg section of Brooklyn and parked behind St. Catherine's Hospital, opposite the luncheonette at the corner of Bushwick Avenue and Maujer Street. He went into the hospital and identified himself to the chief of security, who gave him permission to use the vacant X-ray room again as an observation point. He didn't explain what or who was to be observed; it was already obvious that many hospital personnel patronized

Patsy's store, and any leak about police surveillance could abort the case before it even opened.

In the middle of the afternoon, Sonny arrived. Most of his day had been spent checking out Patsy. It was supposed to be their day off.

'I think we got something,' Sonny exclaimed, betraying an enthusiasm unusual for him.

'What did you find out?'

'Our friend Patsy's name is Pasquale Fuca. The blonde he was with is his wife. Her name is Barbara. Barbara Desina, it used to be. She's only a kid, nineteen or so according to the marriage license they filed.'

'Yeah, yeah. What else?'

'Barbara has experience. She drew a suspended for shoplifting a year ago. And Patsy' – Sonny's dark eyes gleamed in the pale face – 'he's a sweetheart. He was brought up on suspicion of armed robbery. Tried to hold up Tiffany's on Fifth Avenue! Could have got two-and-a-half to five. But they couldn't hang it on him. Also, downtown they're sure Patsy pulled off a Mafia contract on a guy named De Marco. But it was a clean job. Couldn't touch him.'

'Nice,' Egan growled.

'Wait. Are you ready? I got this from the Feds. Patsy's got an uncle. Guess who? . . . Little Angie!'

Egan blew a low whistle of surprise. Angelo Tuminaro was thought to be one of the bigger Mafia 'Dons' (key leaders), a man who was known to have clawed his way up to and through the high criminal echelons in New York the hard way, knocking over more than one rival en route, although the police were unable to prove it. Tuminaro's wife was Jewish, and her father was powerful in certain Jewish-dominated rackets. Consequently Angelo gained recognition as number-one liaison between the then equally strong Italian and Jewish wings of organized crime. Finally, since 1937, the police were sure, Little Angie had enjoyed the choice responsibility of supervising all heroin traffic into the United States from Europe and the Middle East.

But in 1960 Angie Tuminaro entangled himself in a vice and conspiracy charge with two of the high criminal lords: Big John Ormento, a top-level Don, and Vito Genovese himself, suspected Mafia sub-boss of all United States crime under the deported but still-reigning 'Capo,' or chief, Lucky Luciano. The authorities had managed to arrest all three, but Little Angie jumped bail and dropped out of sight. Now, two years later, he was still holed up somewhere, presumably still calling the important shots in the narcotics racket. Both the federal and city police wanted very badly to locate him.

Egan looked away from the luncheonette across Bushwick Avenue. 'We better go talk to the boss,' he said.

An hour later, Egan and Grosso were seated in the office of Lieutenant Vincent Hawkes, second in command to Deputy Chief Inspector Edward F. Carey, at New York Narcotics Bureau headquarters in downtown Manhattan. They described how they had stumbled upon Patsy at the Copa, his strange tour through Little Italy in the early hours of Sunday morning, and his connection with the missing Angelo Tuminaro. Now they wanted to follow it up.

Hawkes, a tall, lean, balding man of stern demeanor, was known as an exacting but fair commander, and a sound cop. He made a stab at maintaining military detachment. 'All that is great,' he said, 'but you guys work Harlem. You're not supposed to *be* in Brooklyn.'

'Detach us,' Egan quickly requested. 'Let us have a shot at it, at least until we see if there's anything here or not. Everybody wants Little Angie, right? Okay,' he went on, not expecting a reply to the obvious, 'so maybe here's a lead. We deserve it. *We* make this guy, this candy store owner, putting on a big show in a fancy nightclub, with known connections all over him. Then, *on our own*, after working the whole day and night before, *we* tail him downtown and out to Brooklyn and sit on him all day Sunday practically, and who do we come up with? None other than Angelo Tuminaro.' He leaned forward earnestly. 'You got to let us have it.'

Hawkes held up a hand, cutting Egan short. 'Christ, if talk was money! . . .' Outmatched and knowing it, he finally rose. 'Wait here,' he said.

The lieutenant went outside his office and tapped on the adjacent door. A gruff voice said to come in. Even seated at his desk, Deputy Chief Inspector Edward Carey was a massive man, with a round Irish face and huge hands. He had been a police officer in New York for almost thirty-five years, first as a state trooper, then as an investigator for the State Liquor Authority, a city patrolman, then a detective in Brooklyn's decaying Bedford-Stuyvesant section and eventually as commander of detectives in the Brooklyn North Division. Named by Commissioner Stephen Kennedy to run the Narcotics Bureau in 1958, he had instilled renewed enthusiasm and purpose into the unit. Chief Carey was highly regarded by his men, whom he unhesitatingly backed in any dispute over 'regulations' so long as they were producing information, arrests and convictions.

He listened, hunched over his desk top, hands folded, expression blank, as Hawkes concisely described the two detectives' experience and their request to pursue the matter. Carey nodded at last. 'It's the first lead we've had on Tuminaro in six months.' He looked up at his second in command. 'Egan and Grosso – they're about the two best detectives we've got, aren't they?'

Hawkes allowed a small smile. 'They are.'

'Let them go. Give them what they need.'

Hawkes returned to his office and sat down. He eyed the

pair across his desk for a moment. 'Okay,' he said finally, 'what'll it take?'

'First a wire,' Sonny answered.

'*Two* wires,' Egan interjected – 'one on the store and one on his house.'

Hawkes scratched at his neck again. 'You know I have to get a court order for wiretaps. I don't know – a couple of Harlem cops wanting plants in Brooklyn, it won't be easy.'

'Try, okay?' Sonny asked.

'We know *you* can do it, Vinnie,' Eddie grinned.

Chapter Three

THE Narcotics Bureau of the New York Police Department is the largest counternarcotics unit in the world and widely regarded as the finest. It is also chronically short of almost everything it needs to function at top effectiveness: money, equipment, extent of jurisdiction, and of course, to those in its command, manpower. But one of the few material advantages the bureau has over the comparatively affluent Federal Bureau of Narcotics, with which it works closely, is the legal wiretap. Both agencies have courageous investigators with experience and ingenuity; both make good use of informers, or 'stools,' who are recruited for pay or other extrajudicial considerations to perform as undercover agents without portfolio; but one of the prime tools of gathering information pertinent to law enforcement and crime prevention, particularly in the murky world of illegal narcotics, is the monitored telephone. Federal law prohibits government agencies from employing this tool; not so New York State.

Still, it is not easy to get a warrant to tap a phone. There must be sufficient reason to believe, established by precedent and tangible evidence, that the telephones to be wired are used by suspected felons or conspirators and could lead police either to their apprehension or to prevention of additional felonies. It must also be shown that the telephones themselves are used to further illicit enterprises. This last point can be a bit tricky to substantiate, but, depending upon the circumstances and the applicants, most judges will issue the warrants.

Vince Hawkes took his facts to the department's Legal Bureau, where an affidavit was drawn and presented formally to a justice of the State Supreme Court. Within thirty-six hours, a court order was signed authorizing taps on Patsy Fuca's telephones.

Securing the legal authorization was only the first, if one of the biggest hurdles. Next the department contacted the New York Telephone Company to ascertain the coded 'pairs' for the Fuca phones – two key digit screws in the central panel box through which every telephone installation is fed, and which once hooked into, can put that instrument on monitor. With that knowledge, plus information as to where the feedboxes were located, the mechanics of installing the taps became the responsibility of the technicians of the C.I.B., the department's ingenious Criminal Intelligence Bureau. Their problems were twofold; they had to gain access to a telephone's central box which is usually on or close to the premises under surveillance; and they had to select the most convenient, undetectable site, preferably not too distant, in which to install the listening device with its automatic tape recording equipment. This sometimes required stringing telephone lines surreptitiously for many city blocks, over rooftops and through back alleys.

Wednesday afternoon, October 11, of that week, Eddie Egan and Sonny Grosso met a C.I.B. team on Bushwick Avenue in Brooklyn, a few blocks from Patsy's luncheonette at the corner of Maujer Street. The location chosen for that 'plant,' or listening post, was the basement of the modern apartment project across from the store. One of the C.I.B. men went to have a chat with the janitor of one of the buildings who was told only that the police were conducting a secret investigation and needed a quiet place at which to rendezvous. This janitor was nervous but cooperative, and he showed them an unused storage room in a remote corner of the basement.

Now they had to get to the feedbox of the two telephones in the luncheonette, which was situated on the exterior wall in an alley behind the store. This part was, as usual, less ticklish than it sounds. Two C.I.B. men merely walked into the luncheonette and identified themselves as telephone company checkers to the elderly man behind the counter. (He was checked out later and found to be Barbara Fuca's stepfather, Joe Desina, who frequently relieved the Fucas when neither could be in the store.) Going to the rear of the luncheonette, one 'repairman' examined the two public telephones while the other continued out into the alley behind the store. Quickly, the latter opened the narrow, three-foot-high panel box containing twin vertical rows of digital screws. From information gleaned from the telephone company, he located the two key 'pair' screws, and to these he hooked the bared ends of two wires. Then he rejoined his companion inside, and they walked back through the store and out the front entrance. Within moments, they had reentered the alley from behind the luncheonette and were camouflaging the wires now attached to Patsy Fuca's telephone call box.

Feeding their dual lines from one telephone pole to another across Maujer Street, the C.I.B. operatives strung them into the apartment house basement, where the narcotics detectives waited. The wires were attached to twin recorders – marked *Luncheonette One* and *Luncheonette Two* – and they waited to run a test. The automatic machines were activated only when a tapped telephone was in use and even then a human monitor did not have to be physically present. Whether anyone had the earphones or not, all incoming and outgoing calls were recorded on perforated tape, which also provided the advantage of enabling the police to decipher numbers dialed on the telephone in question. Finally, one machine began to whir. There were a series of clicks as tiny holes were punched unevenly in the moving tape. They played it back. It was a customer in the luncheonette calling his wife. The plant was operative.

The next morning, Eddie and Sonny again met a C.I.B. team, this time in southern Brooklyn, and much the same maneuvers were employed to effect the wiretap on Patsy and Barbara Fuca's home telephone at 1224 67th Street. The plant was set up in the basement of a building around the corner from the Fuca residence. Egan or Grosso would check it several times a day.

Thus began, officially, what was to become for Detectives Egan and Grosso, the New York Narcotics Bureau, and, eventually, law enforcement agencies on two continents, a long, tangled expedition into intrigue that in the end would shake the foundations of international crime. But within the first twenty-four hours, the investigation was almost 'burned' before it could get off the ground.

The police officers apparently had not been as inconspicuous as they had thought when moving lines and equipment into the apartment house basement across from Patsy's candy store. One of the handymen in the building might have noticed them or perhaps have spied the 'Luncheonette' labels. Or possibly the janitor was prone to gossip. In any event, Patsy got wind of the odd goings-on nearby, for on Friday morning Sonny was startled to overhear a call to Patsy in the luncheonette from a man named Louie. They seemed to know each other quite well. Patsy apparently had telephoned him from outside and left word to return the call.

'Patsy? What's new?'

'Fine . . . Listen, Louie, I need a favor.'

'Name it.'

'It's my phones here in the store. I want you to look them over.'

The other man was silent for a second. 'You mean a tap?'

'You know what I mean. When can you come around?'

'Hmmmmm . . . how about Monday?'

'C'mon,' Patsy protested. 'You can come faster than that!'

'Well, tomorrow's no good, Sunday?'

'Okay, Sunday. Thanks. Howsa family?'

'Oh, everybody's fine, they're—'

'Good. Okay, then I'll see you,' Patsy said and rang off.

Moments later, he was dialing again. This time it was to his home. Curtly, he told Barbara of his suspicion that something funny was going on around the luncheonette and warned her not to call him there again until Louie took a look.

Grosso hurried from the basement plant to the hospital, where Egan was stationed at the window of the vacant X-ray room. When he heard the gist of Patsy's two calls, Egan rasped, 'Shit!' and slapped the windowsill viciously with an open paw. 'How the hell could he have us made so goddamn quick? And who the hell's this Louie?'

'Probably some guy they use who knows phones.' Sonny was thoughtful a moment. 'You know, the way he talked, I wouldn't say Patsy is actually on to us yet. He's heard *something*, and I guess he figures who else could it be but him. But I don't think he knows yet what's happening.'

'Well, the main thing is,' Egan grumbled, 'we gotta bust this plant, get C.I.B. out here and get the taps off his phones.' He took another angry swipe at the windowsill. 'Not only do we lose our line, but now probably he'll be looking over his shoulders all the time even if his friend don't find nothing wrong with his phones.'

'That's what I mean,' Sonny said with emphasis. 'But suppose we could persuade Patsy that yeah, *somebody* around here is hot, but not *him*?' As he spoke he leaned on the sill, face close to the pane. Egan, watching his eyes, saw that Sonny was not looking toward Patsy's luncheonette but at the row of stores directly opposite the hospital.

'The *other* luncheonettel' Egan exclaimed, comprehending. 'Hey! All anybody knows is *some* luncheonette is wired. It could work. Let's check it out.'

Sonny borrowed a hospital telephone and first called a lieutenant he knew in the Brooklyn North Vice Squad who specialized in bookmakers and off-track betting in general. He asked for a rundown on the candy store on Bushwick Avenue across from St. Catherine's. Often such neighborhood shops in Brooklyn, as in most large cities, were busy exchanges for illegal 'policy' numbers or other betting enterprises. Usually, they were small-time, private operations, but the police continually harassed them in order to discourage the syndicate organizers from expanding. In a few minutes the lieutenant came back on the line and confirmed that this particular store had a number of marks against it, although it had not been hit as yet. Sonny then outlined his problem and his scheme. The lieutenant agreed to send some of his vice squad right away to stake out the place and cooperate with the narcotics detectives.

Next, Sonny telephoned his office in Manhattan and filled in both Vinnie Hawkes and Sergeant Jack Fleming, acting boss of the bureau's select Special Investigating Unit, which automatically had become interested in the Fuca case when Angelo Tuminaro's name came up. Finally, he called C.I.B. downtown and briefed them about Patsy's suspicions and the necessity of transferring the apartment-house plant in any event.

By Saturday noon, under the joint surveillance of vice squad detectives and Eddie and Sonny, a number of unsavory looking characters had been observed in more-or-less furtive comings and goings in the decoy luncheonette. And finally they spotted one known bookie with a long record of arrests who huddled with the proprietor, probably laying off bets. 'That should be good enough,' one of the vice cops said, and he and two comrades tumbled out of the hospital and, with intentionally overplayed dramatics, ran toward the luncheonette. As prearranged, two radio cars, sirens wailing, raced down Bushwick Avenue and squealed to a stop in front of the store. A knot of gaping spectators gathered quickly on the sidewalk, chattering and trying to manage a peek inside. Then, as the uniformed patrolmen made a show of holding back the onlookers, the detectives came out with their two unhappy prisoners, the bookie and the proprietor. As they led them to one of the waiting cars, one arresting officer, grinning to his companion, commented in a voice that carried to all in the vicinity: 'Someday these guys are gonna wise up about popping off on the telephone!' 'Yeah,' the other said, 'they won't have telephones where they're going!'

Within an hour, back at the basement plant, Sonny's recorder whirred again. It was Patsy, calling home. 'Relax, baby,' he told his wife cheerily. 'That thing I was worried about yesterday, about the phones? It's beautiful. It was the guy down the block, the other candy store. The fuzz just burned his book. We're clean. I better call Louie.'

The most important goal in the thinking of the detectives was some lead to the whereabouts of Little Angie Tuminaro, and in the days and weeks that followed Egan and Grosso grew bolder in their efforts to get close to Patsy. The detectives began visiting the luncheonette personally. Egan arranged with a hospital orderly to borrow two white jackets, and they dropped into the store daily along with other hospital personnel who frequented the place for cigarettes, a magazine, or to gossip during a coffee break.

The first time Eddie and Sonny went in, Patsy was behind the counter. The officers were nervous, and found it difficult to bring themselves to sit face to face with the man they had been observing clandestinely for two weeks. But Patsy was busy, and he didn't notice them any more than any other customers. The next day Patsy wasn't in his shop; the place was tended by the old man whom the C.I.B. agents had seen, Barbara Fuca's stepfather, and the short, stocky dark man who had been with Patsy and his wife that first Sunday when Eddie and Sonny started their surveillance. But the following day, a Sunday, their imagination began to be rewarded.

The detectives, in their white jackets, were hunched over the fountain about noontime, nibbling Danishes and sipping coffee. The youngish stocky man, who had proved to be Patsy's brother, Tony, was behind the counter. Patsy was just visible seated at a white porcelain-topped kitchen table in the back room, facing front, partially hidden by a rumpled green curtain separating the alcove from the rest of the store. There was only one other customer, a girl, browsing through the paperback book rack. Suddenly, Egan became aware that Sonny, seated nearer the street door, had tensed and half turned his body toward the rear. Two men were entering the luncheonette. 'Harlem connections!' Sonny murmured, lowering his head further.

Egan glanced idly at the newcomers and understood. They were hard-looking types, dark-haired and sallow-skinned, the sort a cop marks automatically as hood. And Sonny's terse exclamation added up to the warning that these were guys he knew from the old neighborhood, who would more than likely know him, too. But the men had eyes for no one but Patsy in the back room. They strode past the counter without hesitation and sat at the table behind the half-drawn curtain. Egan saw the one who sat alongside Patsy place a bulging brown paper sack on the table.

The three chatted for a few minutes. Then the man opposite Patsy stood, his back to the store, and seemed to half crouch over the table. Egan could see Patsy leaning forward, intent on whatever was being shown him. They're slicing bread – it's a payoff, Egan thought, and almost immediately his guess was verified when the one standing sat down and the detective caught a glimpse of Patsy stuffing a last handful of cash back into the sack.

Patsy rose then, holding the paper bag. He nodded coolly and said something to the two men before they turned and walked back through the luncheonette and out into the street. A minute later, Patsy donned a heavy gray overcoat and emerged from the alcove. 'Tony,' he said to the stocky one behind the counter, 'watch the store. I'll be back.' He went out. Egan and Grosso saw him turn the corner of Maujer Street.

Egan slipped off his stool. 'See you in the ward.'

As Egan left, Sonny called after him: 'You owe me a coffee and rolls.'

As Egan trotted across the street to his Corvair, parked in front of the hospital, Patsy was just starting his Oldsmobile, halfway up Maujer. Egan, still in the white doctor's jacket, tailed him to his house on 67th Street. He watched Patsy carry the brown sack filled with currency inside. Now we are starting to get someplace, the detective was thinking: Patsy is the guy the connections bring the bread to.

Having had the chance to survey Patsy's store, Eddie and Sonny now pondered how they could reasonably get a look inside his home. Two mornings later, Barbara Fuca offered the entrée. A check of the recorded tape in the 67th Street plant revealed that she had called Macy's and ordered a hundred and eighty-seven dollars' worth of draperies, to be delivered no later than the following afternoon. Egan telephoned the chief of security at the department store and elicited the information that the merchandise was to go out the next morning via United Parcel Service. He then contacted U.P.S. and learned the approximate time when the particular delivery truck would reach the vicinity of 67th Street and Twelfth Avenue and what route it was likely to take.

The following afternoon, Egan and Grosso intercepted the U.P.S. van a little less than three blocks from 1224 67th Street. Egan showed his shield and explained obliquely that they were on police business and wanted to borrow the truck for a half hour or so. He told the disturbed driver to call his security chief to verify. A few minutes later, he requisitioned the driver's brown jacket and peaked cap. Egan climbed into the van and drove off, while Sonny solicitously led the bewildered man to his own convertible parked on 65th Street near Tenth Avenue.

Egan arrived at the Fuca residence with the boxed drapes about 3 P.M. Barbara let him in. She wasn't bad-looking, but her hair wasn't bright blonde now, nor bouffant; it was short and unkempt and, Egan was surprised to note, really a dull mousy-brown. So she wears wigs! Good to keep in mind. Egan lugged the large package into the living room. The house appeared to be beautifully furnished, a professional job. There was a thick white rug, antique furniture with rich blue upholstery; they seemed to favor hanging chain lamps, and the brass or gold or whatever it was gleamed as though it were well cared for. Egan thought, in this kind of layout a woman would have to keep her own kids locked in the attic. But another woman was sitting on the sofa, and there were two small children on the floor, crayoning in coloring books. He remembered that the Fucas had only one baby, under two years, so these had to belong to the other woman. His practiced eyes also noticed something else: underneath the front window, barely noticeable behind white draperies, were wires leading to a burglar alarm terminal. Patsy *was* a cautious man.

It was a C.O.D. delivery, and Barbara went to the French provincial desk at the other end of the living room. She pulled open a drawer and then reaching inside – as Egan watched unobtrusively – she seemed to grope for a concealment of some kind; she found it, and a second hidden drawer slid out beneath the first one. Egan had to keep his hooded eyes from showing surprise because he had seen this kind of device before, a secret trap which was the specialty of a particular Italian carpenter who worked only for important members of the Mafia.

Barbara took a handful of bills from the hidden drawer, counted out a hundred and eighty-seven dollars and handed it to Egan. He asked her to sign a copy of the receipt and thanked her. She smiled, and he tipped his cap to the other woman. The children had never even looked up.

What Eddie and Sonny surmised from this episode was that whether or not Patsy knew it, his wife did know of his secret cache of money. The two detectives now assumed that not only was Patsy in the habit of keeping large amounts of cash in his house but that he himself might be delinquent in keeping up to date on how much he did have.

This in turn led logically to several further suppositions: If Patsy were involved in a heroin distributorship, he probably was acting as Little Angie's proxy in transactions with the big buyers; Patsy may have let his newly exalted position go to his head, and was becoming careless. Surely each 'connection' who laid out bread knew to the ounce how much junk to expect in return, yet apparently Patsy kept no records, just stuffed cash into his secret trap – which, considering that it was no secret to his wife, might be leaving him short. Patsy might not be exceedingly bright; Patsy was otherwise very cautious and should not be underestimated.

'Poor Patsy,' Egan clucked, 'if he don't have enough bread

to front the next shipment, some of those connections of his ain't gonna get their money's worth.'

'And when his friends get wise . . . ?'

One way or another, they were growing confident that Patsy Fuca would be the instrument to help them flush out Little Angie Tuminaro.

Chapter Four

By the middle of November, 1961, Patsy and Barbara Fuca had been under constant surveillance for six weeks. At various times and places connections delivered money to Patsy, either in view of the watching police or at clandestine meetings. On several occasions, the police felt, Patsy may have exchanged small amounts of heroin; they could have 'hit' him any one of these times. But a larger score was in prospect – specifically; the whereabouts of the big man, Little Angie – so they let Patsy operate at the end of a long leash.

Chief Carey by now had designated several other members of the department to work with Eddie Egan and Sonny Grosso. The Federal Bureau of Narcotics, under its New York Director, George Gaffney, also had taken sufficient interest to assign Special Agent Frank Waters to cooperate with the city police. Thus, during November there was hardly an hour of the day or night that every movement of the Fucas was not covered.

Egan and Grosso were still directing the overall surveillance, reporting regularly to their boss, Lieutenant Vinnie Hawkes, and to Sergeant Jack Fleming of S.I.U. The two detectives continued also to use their free time to delve more deeply into the Tuminaro-Fuca setup. Sonny took an occasional night off for bowling, or a Sunday at Yankee Stadium with his partner, watching the football Giants; and Egan managed to see Carol Galvin irregularly. But essentially they remained completely absorbed in the Fuca case and spent much of their free time dogging known pushers and dealers in Harlem as well as in Brooklyn, and pressing their most credible stoolies for further information about Patsy.

Egan's relationship with Carol Galvin was becoming a source of distraction to him. He felt a strong desire to be with her, and he was certain that she was strongly attracted to him. She was a genuinely beautiful girl. Never had he taken out such a lovely one. He had met her first at the Copa during a casual visit in September and when she responded fetchingly to the inevitable approach, he was soon coming around every night to escort her from the nightclub when it closed at 3:00 A.M. The late hour didn't bother him; he was rarely off assignment before then anyway. What rankled him was her request that he not wait for her in the club because among the Copa's customers were known mobsters and Carol feared that the management would resent the presence of a cop even though his only interest in the place was their hatcheck girl. So they met by Central Park, half a block away at the corner of 60th Street, and went somewhere for Chinese food or pizza. Soon they became very friendly.

Carol had the physical requisites to become a model or actress, but perhaps the necessary ambition or discipline were lacking in the nineteen-year-old girl. She had competed in the usual beauty contests, and had taken the Copa job to catch the eye of the 'right' people. But nothing exciting had turned up excluding, of course, the inevitable propositions form amorous patrons. Nothing, except that she had fallen for a redheaded cop.

Egan was most protective about her. He didn't like her working at the Copa precisely because of the well-heeled hoodlums who frequented the place. They both lived in Brooklyn, and he gave her a key to his flat. Carol had no family, and in the early hours of the morning when Eddie couldn't meet her, after the Copa closed she drove her own car to his place and waited for him to finally wend his way home after long hours of fighting the war against the heroin merchants. This arrangement was hardly satisfying to either of them, and Egan came up with a new plan, combining his constabulary instincts with his desire to have Carol more available. He learned of an opening for a barmaid at what he told her was a more 'respectable' restaurant downtown on Nassau Street in the financial district, not far from the Narcotics Bureau Headquarters. The Nassau Tavern's clientele switched dramatically from the luncheon crowd of brokers, bankers and lawyers to the nighttime covey of those who frequented the waterfront area. Even Patsy Fuca dropped in occasionally, and his brother Tony was a regular patron. Carol became a potentially valuable source of information.

At this new job Carol was finished with work at eleven each night, and more often than not Egan would arrange to meet her and take her with him on his surveillance of Patsy Fuca. This began to irritate his partner, Sonny Grosso, but Egan reasoned that he could sit outside of Patsy's store or house as easily, and certainly more happily, with Carol as with Sonny.

But Carol soon tired of this routine. She began to hint that this was no life for him, for either of them, that he should get out of police work, that they could make an exciting life together were he not so tied down. But Egan didn't really feel 'tied down': he was enthusiastic about his job, and felt a strong sense of purpose, in spite of his manipulation of regulations. He wanted her, but the job did come first. She countered that she had received several interesting proposals from well-to-do patrons of the restaurant and that maybe she ought to give them more serious thought. They quarreled more frequently.

Personal problems aside, Egan and Grosso were

everywhere. They had developed considerable intelligence on the pattern and background of the Fucas' lives. Barbara's stepfather had been a hijacker during Prohibition but had been 'retired' for many years and now helped out in the store. (It was his old Dodge that Patsy occasionally used.) Patsy's brother Tony was the dirty-looking, heavy-faced individual in the faded lumber jacket whom they had seen there several times. He was thirty-one, a year older than Patsy. Tony was a longshoreman who lived in a run-down section of the Bronx with his wife and two small daughters. Patsy's parents, in their sixties, had their own three-story house, the two upper floors of which they rented out, on 7th Street near the area of Brooklyn known as Gowanus. The elder Fuca, whose name was Giuseppe, or Joseph, had served time years ago on assault and robbery raps. The only friends Patsy and Barbara seemed to spend any time with were Nicky Travato, a longshoreman, and his wife, also named Barbara, who lived about four blocks from the Fucas on 66th Street, near Fifteenth Avenue. Although Nicky worked on the docks, and they lived in a shabby, sooty tenement practically beneath the New Utrecht Avenue elevated BMT subway tracks, the officers had noted with interest that the Travatos owned a five-year-old Cadillac. On several nights they had seen Nicky pick Patsy up and chauffeur him to various locations in Brooklyn, where one of them would get out and briefly visit some store or building and then resume their nocturnal tour. The detectives concluded that these were narcotics deliveries and perhaps payoffs; plainly, Nicky knew about them, so he too was added to the select but growing sheet on Patsy Fuca.

Patsy was not at home many nights. He was usually in his store until nearly midnight, and three or four nights a week he drove fifteen minutes into Manhattan to stop at a bar called the Pike Slip Inn. This was a dimly lit, sinister-looking bistro almost under the Manhattan Bridge, around the corner from the East River wharves and not far from the colorful Fulton Fish Market. It was run by a hoodlum named Mickey Blair, and had the reputation of being a haven for a variety of hijackers and bad actors.

Eddie and Sonny stirred with anticipation when they first tailed Patsy there, because in this squalid setting, it appeared that Patsy was received as royalty. Sonny followed him in the first time, and from the end of the bar near the door he could see that the dozen or so patrons knew of Patsy's important relationship with Little Angie and paid him due homage. But on subsequent visits, Sonny began to wonder if Blair's had any real significance, because Patsy's chief interest there seemed to be the barmaid, a petite, pretty Latin type named Inez. Patsy paid her a great deal of attention in a rough sensual way, flirting with her, kissing her or running his hands over her when she passed by, whispering into her ear, or laughing raucously at some private joke. Finally, he would drive up onto the Manhattan Bridge and cruise home to Brooklyn.

Because of these late hours, Barbara Fuca needed to find ways of amusing herself most evenings. Her favorite pastime was Bingo, and she must have become used to this mode of living over a long period, for she seemed to have a chart on every Bingo night in Brooklyn, and some in Queens. Three to four times a week, Barbara and Barbara Travato or another girl with striking red hair named Marilyn, went to some different church or social hall. At first, Egan and Grosso felt it wise to trail the girls to the community center chosen for an evening, because there could be no other way of telling whether or not these outings might be a cover and that actually Barbara was the medium through which Angelo Tuminaro communicated with his nephew. They kept close eyes on whomever Barbara talked to at these affairs, but there never was an indication that she attended for anything other than innocent diversion, and after a while the bored detectives stopped shadowing her at Bingo.

From time to time, Patsy did take his wife out for an evening, and at least once early in the surveillance their taste in entertainment leaned toward the bizarre. On a Friday night late in October, Eddie and Sonny followed Patsy and the two Barbaras out the Belt Parkway into Nassau County, to a gay costume ball at a country club in Lynbrook on Long Island's south shore.

The ball proved to be gay in more ways than one. It was crowded and noisy, and provided a glittering panoply of costume and hairdo and makeup. It also became quickly evident that many of the girls were boys and vice-versa. The two bewildered detectives soon learned that this affair was one in a series staged by some kind of homosexual society. Patsy and Barbara apparently were regular patrons, both getting their kicks from the squealing, bickering fairies and the competition of one bull dyke with another for the attentions of a lesbian queen. Eddie and Sonny giggled self-consciously to each other, simulating the manners of cavorting queers, and after an hour retired from the scene. Tomorrow, they would take up their surveillance again.

Early in November the police had begun to hear noises from stools that a 'panic' was developing in the streets; the available supplies of junk were rapidly diminishing. The rumor was that a major shipment was due in the city momentarily. The detectives doubled their vigilance, sure that if the break came Patsy Fuca would be in the middle of it.

Late on Saturday night, November 18, Eddie and Sonny were parked in Sonny's convertible across from Patsy's luncheonette. They had been on him since late afternoon, the night had turned chilly, and they were weary. Patsy was puttering about inside, making preparations to close the store, and the two officers almost prayed that he would go home and let them get some rest.

To amuse themselves, Eddie had donned a woman's floppy picture hat and a red wig, rolled up his trousers under his trench coat and nestled close to the hatless, black-haired Sonny in the driver's seat. A casual passerby would have received a touching, if perhaps somewhat ludicrous, impression of a thin swarthy young man and a decidedly hefty ruddy-faced girl in tender proximity.

Shortly after 11:30 P.M., a blue compact Buick with two girls in it stopped and honked in front of the luncheonette. The detectives were sure it was one of the Fucas' cars, but the driver didn't look like Barbara, and they couldn't identify the other girl either. In a moment, the lights went out inside the store and Patsy emerged, locked the door and climbed into the front seat with the girls, and the car pulled away.

It looked as though Patsy was going to a party. The detectives sighed because they had to stay with him; there was never any telling when or how he might try to contact Little Angie. They trailed the Buick onto the Brooklyn-Queens Expressway, southbound; at least Patsy wasn't going into Manhattan. The Buick followed the Expressway around the Brooklyn Navy Yard, down the shoreline across from the towers of lower Manhattan across the mouth of the East River, then swung over the Gowanus Canal, and exited near Fourth Avenue, whence it turned up to 7th Street. This was where Patsy's parents lived. The compact found a parking space midway in the block.

Egan and Grosso cruised slowly by on the one-way eastbound street. Patsy and the girls were entering his parents' house, No. 245, the middle one in a row of seven identical three-story structures. And now Sonny recognized one of the girls: 'That's Barbara, wearing one of her wigs!'

Egan agreed. 'And I make the other one now, too: her redheaded girl friend, Marilyn.' The office had checked out this Marilyn, and she was known only as a close friend of Barbara's.

'What's interesting,' Sonny commented, as they parked by a fire plug near the corner of Fourth Avenue, 'is that it seems kind of late to be calling on the old folks, and bringing a friend yet.'

The three came out after about twenty minutes and reentered the Buick, Marilyn driving. Now the detectives followed them west on 9th Street, where they drove up the ramp to the Gowanus Expressway. They ignored both the cut-offs to the Brooklyn-Battery Tunnel and to the Brooklyn Bridge, but at Flatbush Avenue the compact turned off toward the approach to the Manhattan Bridge. However, roadway construction made it difficult to get onto the bridge, and after some hesitation they drove back up on the Expressway and continued north to the exit for the Williamsburg Bridge.

From the moment of leaving the house of Patsy's parents, Egan had been on the portable two-way radiophone giving a running commentary on their itinerary to another car carrying bureau teammate Dick Auletta and Federal Agent Frank Waters, who together had remained behind in the Williamsburg area near Patsy's store; whichever way the subjects went, whether back toward the luncheonette or into Manhattan, Auletta and Waters were to be Egan's and Grosso's backstops. When the Buick finally indicated that it was turning onto the Williamsburg Bridge, Egan advised the other detectives to detach and head for the bridge too.

Traffic, though light at this late hour, moved slowly crossing the East River, slowing almost to a standstill near the Manhattan end of the span. Several cars were between the Fucas' and Sonny's now, and Egan, fussing with his woman's hat and wig, muttered a string of obscenities leaning out the right-hand window, craning to keep the blue Buick in view. A large green two truck with its red warning lights blinking was partially blocking the roadway off the bridge leading into Delancey Street. 'A goddamn police truck, must be an accident,' Egan yelled over his shoulder to his partner. 'Cops!' he spat. He could make out a patrolman from the truck, in faded blue work clothes, directing one vehicle at a time off the snarled bridge in the single lane still open. As he watched, the Buick was waved ahead into Delancey. Egan and Grosso remained motionless, three cars behind.

Egan threw open the car door. 'I'm gonna run for it, see which way they go. Keep an eye out for me . . .' and he jumped out and ran off the bridge after Patsy's compact.

It did not occur to him, nor would he have cared if it had, what an incongruous sight he presented galloping along Delancey Street at thirty minutes past midnight. This was an old, traditionally Jewish immigrant neighborhood, and, despite the hour, a number of places still blazed light because it was Saturday night following sundown of the Sabbath. It was Kosher delicatessens and Chinese restaurants for the most part that were still open. Quite a few pedestrians were milling about on the sidewalk, and they stared in surprise at the big florid-faced man, floppy hat in hand, red wig askew, trench coat flying, bare legs churning, only *one* bare now actually, for the other trouser leg had begun to unroll from beneath the coat.

Fortunately, Patsy's compact had been held up by two red lights, and Egan saw it take a left into Allen Street, heading down toward Pike Street and the river. Drenched with perspiration despite the November chill, his chest heaving for air, he waited agitatedly on the center island at the intersection of Delancey and Allen, searching for Sonny's Olds. When Sonny finally spotted him, Eddie was out in the middle of the crosswalk, dancing about dodging traffic, trying to keep one eye out for his partner and the other on Patsy's car, fast disappearing down Allen Street. Egan motioned to him to swing left, and as Sonny slowed he hopped back into the car. 'Allen . . . Pike Slip . . .' Eddie puffed as Sonny made the turn.

'Where are the other guys?' he wheezed after a moment.

'Still stuck back on the bridge.' Sonny glanced at his heavy-breathing partner, and a smile spread across his normally melancholy face.

'What's funny?' Egan demanded.

'I was just thinking: if Patsy's going in the Pike Slip Inn, you oughta go in. You look like an old hooker. They'll love you there.'

Egan inspected himself. 'Yeah, well next time *you* can go in drag, smart ass,' he snorted, removing the wig and rolling down his trouser leg.

Dick Auletta's voice cracked on the radiophone: 'Where are you guys?'

'You clear of the bridge?' Sonny asked back.

'What a mess! We're on Delancey.'

'Take your left on Allen. We're just coming up to East Broadway. We'll keep you informed, kay,' Sonny signed off in police fashion.

'Ten-four –' Auletta started to acknowledge.

'Wait, they're turning left on East Broadway . . .' Sonny interrupted.

The blue Buick had pulled over and double-parked midway to the next corner. Sonny drew his Olds to the corner of Allen and East Broadway just in time to see Patsy get out of the compact and stride alone across the avenue. Without a word, Egan hopped out and scooted across Allen and then started walking casually along East Broadway toward the point where Patsy had seemed to be headed. Meanwhile, Sonny made the turn and cruised down East Broadway, past the idling Buick, in which Barbara and Marilyn still sat. Near the next corner, Rutgers Street, he swung the Olds into a U-turn to come back up the opposite side of the avenue. But suddenly, ahead of Sonny, with a squeal of rubber, a big light-colored sedan swept out of the line of cars parked at the curb, made a sharp U-turn of its own and, after slowing in front of the compact, proceeded to gun uptown on East Broadway. The girls in the Buick compact followed.

Egan hustled to his partner's car. As Sonny swung around to start after the other two vehicles, Frank Water's voice greeted them: 'We're right behind you now. What's been happening?'

Sonny grabbed the mike. 'Did you guys see a big, light sedan just make a U and take off in this direction? Patsy's car looked like it was following.'

'Negative.'

'I saw it,' Egan exclaimed, still a little breathless, 'but I couldn't see who was driving. Was it Patsy?'

'I think it was. It happened fast. The car was like a tan color.'

'What about the plates?'

'Looked white to me.'

'Out of state.'

'Look!' Sonny exclaimed. Two blocks ahead, the Buick was turning right. The sedan was not in sight. As the detectives neared the corner, which proved to be Montgomery Street, Sonny slowed almost to a stop, and Egan jumped out and ran to peer around the corner of a loft building, raising his left arm in a cautioning signal. Down the dark street, toward the river, he could see two pairs of red taillights moving. About three blocks down, the car in the lead started to turn right again, the other still following. Egan dropped his arm and ran back to Sonny's car. They turned into Montgomery, Auletta and Waters now trailing close.

The third cross street was Cherry. Again Sonny braked the

Olds, and Egan once more crept to the corner of a large apartment building. Now the red pinpricks were about two blocks away . . . and now again they were turning, left this time. Egan dashed back to the car, signaling the detectives behind. The two cars turned onto Cherry and moved slowly past the sprawling LaGuardia high-rise apartment project. The street was poorly lit and, except for the empty automobiles along both curbs, it was deserted. Looming high before them was the Manhattan Bridge. They crossed Clinton and eased up approaching the next street, Jefferson. For the third time, Egan was out of the car before it stopped rolling and running across the sidewalk ahead on silent feet, like a burly toe dancer. At the corner of another loft building, he crouched low, right arm unstretched to keep his partners back. There were empty cars parked at the near curb, blocking his vision, but he thought he heard the low hum of an idling motor, and then he could make out the pale red glow of a taillight. His posture must have suggested impending action, for light footsteps came up behind him now. Egan glanced around, his fingers to his lips. It was Frank Waters. Egan looked back around the corner and, just as Waters reached his elbow, saw a flash of dull light across Jefferson and heard a car door slam.

'What is it? What was that?' the agent whispered urgently.

'Dome light. Somebody just got out of a car, I think. But I don't see nothing.'

Then there was another click, possibly of another car door being closed gently, and the sound of a motor accelerating. The red glow moved off.

Egan grabbed Waters's arm and started back toward their cars. 'They're going!' he said. 'Sonny and I will take them. You and Dick wait here until we call you. I don't know if Patsy switched cars again or not.' He piled into the seat next to his partner, barking: 'Let's go! They went down Jefferson!'

Sonny swerved around the corner. The taillights were just approaching South Street, underneath the elevated viaduct two blocks down. It was the only vehicle in sight now. Sonny stepped on the gas. The car in front of them turned right on South Street. It was Patsy's little Buick. The detectives could make out a blur of heads in the front seat – it could have been three, or perhaps only two.

As Sonny drew around onto South Street, Egan motioned him to pull into a darkened service station just off the corner. At the same time, he reached for the radio mike. 'Frank, Dick! It's his car all right. He may be in it, we can't be sure. You guys pick 'em up.'

'Ten-four.'

'– they're moving down South, going slow. Now they look like they're turning up Pike . . .'

Seconds later, Egan and Grosso saw Frank Water's white hardtop sweep out of Jefferson and disappear down South Street after the blue compact. 'We're gonna take a look around Jefferson where they stopped. He must've dumped the big car. Come back if nothing happens, kay?' Egan added into the mike.

'Ten-four.'

Sonny eased the Olds out of the back end of the service station, onto Water Street, and slid it around the corner facing Jefferson. Switching off the engine and lights, he and Egan got out and, one on each side of the street, started walking cautiously up Jefferson toward Cherry, inspecting each automobile along the curbs. About midway in the block, Egan hissed across the quiet street to Sonny: 'Tan-colored, you said?'

'I thought so,' his partner rasped back. 'White plates?'

'C'mere. I think I got it.'

Egan was standing behind a four-door Buick, tan or light brown, with whitewall tires. It was fairly new, about 1960 they guessed. Embossed on the right front fender was the designation Invicta. But what fascinated the detectives were the license plates: they were Canadian, from the Province of Quebec.

While Sonny jotted down the plate numbers and other items about the car on a match cover, Egan prowled further up the dark street, looking into each parked car. There was nobody about, not another vehicle moving in the vicinity. He glanced at his wristwatch: it was barely past 1 A.M. It had seemed like hours. What was the significance of all this, of Patsy driving into Manhattan so late with his wife and her girl friend, picking up a Canadian Buick, riding around and then leaving it in this small, obscure street? Had he been scared off, or had he dropped it for somebody else to pick up? And who would that be? His uncle, maybe? But why a *Canadian* car?

Egan returned to Grosso, and his partner greeted him: 'Did you know it was open?'

'I never tried it. Anything inside?'

'Nothing. It's clean.'

'Well, that don't mean anything,' Egan said. 'If there's anything valuable in it, they wouldn't leave it lying on the seat. How about the trunk?'

'Locked. Let's go back to the car and tell the other guys.'

They had hardly crawled into the Olds when the radio squawked: '. . . do you read me? Acknowledge, kay?'

'Popeye and Cloudy here, kay,' Sonny replied.

'We been trying to raise you guys,' Frank Waters exclaimed. 'What's up?'

'We found the car he dropped. Tan Buick, Invicta, about a sixty. Canadian plates . . .'

'Canadian! Hey, great!' The spunky little agent was excited. 'This is getting good! Canada—!'

'What about you guys?'

'We are now in the middle of the Manhattan Bridge, practically right over your heads. They're going back to good old Brooklyn – home, I hope.'

'So our boy *is* with them!'

'Correct. He was in the car, all right. They let the girl off around Canal Street, then he got out of the back and took the wheel, and he and the other one drove onto the bridge. The other broad, she got a taxi. Looked like she was headed uptown. We got the cab number; we can check his trip list later. I don't figure where the redhead fits, though.'

'Me neither. She could be just a cover. Well, we're gonna stick around here. Somebody might be around to pick up this Canadian car.'

'You better believe it!' Waters cried. 'You could be sitting on dynamite! Soon as we put this guy to bed, we'll be back. We'll signal when we get in radio range, kay?'

'Ten-four.'

Egan leaned over and pointed past Sonny, back toward Cherry Street. 'There's a parking lot up there in the housing project. It'll give us a good view down Jefferson.'

They drove up Jefferson, and Sonny positioned the Olds inside the parking lot near the exit. With the motor off and lights out, they stretched out in the blackness to wait and to ponder. Quietly, they reviewed the situation, and the more they talked the quicker rippled an undercurrent of enthusiasm that Waters probably was right, they had indeed stumbled upon Patsy in the middle of a big operation. For some time Canada and specifically Montreal had been a prime point of origin for narcotics smuggled into the States, so it was hardly stretching plausibility to deduce that *this* Buick could well be a medium of exchange, either having brought stuff down from the border or to carry back the payoff, possibly both. It that were the case, then surely somebody would come by to retrieve it. In any event, in their mounting anticipation it did not occur to them that this was the first time since they'd become interested in Patsy Fuca that their chief preoccupation was not solely the discovery of his uncle, Angelo Tuminaro.

'Waters here,' the portable radio interrupted thinly. 'Cloudy? Popeye? Do you read—?'

'Popeye here, kay,' Egan responded into the mike. He looked at his watch, surprised. It was almost ten minutes to two. They had been sitting for forty minutes.

'They went home all right. We turned right around and headed back. Look, we'll be with you in a few minutes.'

'Ten-four.'

Hardly, it seemed, had they settled back again than headlights, sweeping into Cherry Street to their left, illuminated the darkness around them. Eddie and Sonny slumped low in their seats. It was only the second vehicle to have entered the block since they had been there; the other was a panel truck, and it had continued down Cherry past Jefferson without any sign of loitering. Now the oncoming lights, approaching slowly along the perimeter of the housing project, eased to a stop abreast of the parking lot, and then the lights went out. It was an automobile, white. Peering over the ledge of his window, Sonny saw someone getting out, a man, husky, bareheaded. He was moving, gingerly, toward the entrance to the lot. Auletta.

Sonny sat up. 'It's them,' he breathed. 'Dick and Frank.'

He and Egan got out and silently directed the others into the lot, near their own car, then climbed into the back seat of Waters's car.

'Christ, you scared us!' Egan complained. 'We'd just finished talking with you and here comes a car down the block. Why didn't you say you were so close?'

'We just wanted to see if you were alert,' Waters chuckled. 'So what's new?'

Sonny and Eddie briefly summed up what they thought as Waters nodded vigorously. City police detectives and officers, who had mixed feelings about the effectiveness of many of their Federal counterparts, admittedly compounded by a combination of jealousy of the Feds' superior equipment, admired Frank Waters. Though short in stature (they had nicknamed him 'Mickey Rooney'), he was canny and tough, with unerring instincts and the courage of an astronaut. Him they liked and respected – he was 'a good cop,' the highest compliment they could pay any investigator.

'You know what we got here?' Waters exclaimed. 'You guys are sitting on promotions! – Sonny to first grade, Dick to second.' Egan already was a detective first grade; he could go higher only by civil service exam. 'We have lucked into a major score! Patsy Fuca, car down from Canada, dark streets, waterfront, two in the morning – it's gotta be a shipment, right? You watch, pretty soon there's going to be a truckload of Dons down here to unload this Buick. We're going to have us a little war. And man, you an' me, we's gonna be hee-roes!' he enthused, imitating the stereotyped Negro dialect.

The others looked at each other and then back at 'Mickey Rooney,' bubbling over in contemplation of the scenario spinning across his imagination. And as they thought about it, they began to get nervous.

Now it was almost 2:30 A.M., Sunday. The streets were still; no other vehicles had entered the area since Auletta and Waters arrived. Only a few windows remained lit in the tall apartments behind them. Other than sporadic bursts of new conjecture by the keyed-up Waters, the four were silent, each with his private thoughts. The only constant sounds were mournful groans of tugboats on the river, two short blocks east beyond the shuttered, gloomy piers; and they could hear the occasional clatter of an unseen truck on the cobblestones of South Street and the distant hum of tires skimming over the grated roadbed of the Manhattan Bridge high above them. The night was black and cold. They slouched there, daring neither to light cigarettes nor even to chance listening to the radio for fear of giving away their presence to any unknown persons preparing to retrieve the Buick. The silence grew more ominous.

Just before 3 A.M., headlights flashed again, coming toward them along Cherry Street. The four detectives hunched down out of sight, Egan and Grosso, in the back, curling onto the floor. Auletta, crouched in the right-hand seat, kept bobbing his head up to follow the progress of the car, now slowly passing abreast of their position in the parking lot. 'What's happening? Who is it?' Waters kept hissing, doubled over on the driver's side.

'It's an old sedan,' Auletta reported. 'Maybe a forty-nine or fifty Chevy. Beat up. It looks like a bunch of guys in it, four or five maybe.'

'It's them! See, I told you!' Waters exulted. 'It's the Dons. Oh, baby!'

Auletta whispered: 'They're turning on Jefferson . . . slowing down, near the Buick . . . No, they're still going, toward the river . . . I can't see them now.'

The air was taut inside the car for several minutes. Then Waters rasped: 'What d'ya see, for Chris—?'

'Hold it,' Auletta snapped, his eyes raised just over the top of the dashboard. 'A car's coming back on Cherry off the next block down – it could be them again . . . Coming up to Jefferson . . . turning, real slow . . . It's the same heap, all right. Looks like it's *filled* with guys . . . They're going past the Buick . . . slow . . . pulling into a space about three cars in front of the Buick . . .'

All four detectives had their hands on the butts of their service revolvers. They waited. Auletta's voice rose: 'Four of them. They're around the Buick . . . trying the doors. They're trying to bust into it!'

'Let's hit 'em!' Waters barked. He started the ignition. Crouched behind the wheel, the others still doubled out of sight, he swerved out of the lot onto Cherry without headlights, turned sharply into Jefferson and lurched to a halt abreast of the tan Buick. Before he'd even pulled the hand brake, the two right-hand doors were open and Auletta, Grosso and Egan burst from the car, .38's in their fists, Egan shouting, 'Police!'

It had happened so fast that the startled men around the Buick were unable to move more than a stride or two back toward their own car. All were short and swarthy. Within seconds, the detectives had them leaning, arms outstretched against the Buick Invicta, a pair on either side. A frisk produced three knives, one a switchblade, a length of tire chain and a set of jagged homemade brass knuckles. The men appeared to be Puerto Ricans. At least one spoke English. The detectives interrogated them harshly for several minutes. Both sullen and frightened, they answered little. And the cold realization settled upon the officers that these were *not* Dons.

'Nothing!' Egan finally exclaimed disgustedly.

'Just a bunch of punks out to boost a new car,' Sonny complained.

'They don't look like much,' muttered Waters. 'But you can't tell.'

'Shit!' Egan spat. 'Let's get'em booked.'

As Dick Auletta herded the suspects aside, Sonny got on the radio to alert the local precinct for assistance. Egan and Waters, dejected, strolled around the Buick. Egan gestured up toward the apartment towers. 'Well, if anybody was up there watching over this baby, we just blew the siren.' He knitted his brows at the little agent. 'Why don't we see what we got here, anyway?'

'You want to shake it down?'

'So let them sue us. Maybe this car is loaded, maybe not. It could have been unloaded already. Or maybe the whole bit was just a dry run. We might be sitting here for another week. So we find out at least.'

Waters agreed, 'Yeah, you're right. But let's wait until we dump these other punks first.'

In ten minutes, two patrol cars arrived and the four prisoners were hauled away, Auletta going along as arresting officer.

It was 4:10 A.M. before the remaining three detectives reluctantly conceded that their 'prize' did indeed seem to be a bust. They had examined the interior with minute care: glove compartment, dashboard, beneath the floor mats, ashtrays, under seats, upholstery on the door panels – finding only, as Sonny's cursory inspection previously had indicated, that the car was well cared for, clean. Waters removed the rear seat and backrest and, armed with a flashlight and what he called his 'burglar's tool,' a bent knife that could open almost any regular lock or latch, he crawled into the trunk compartment and unfastened the lock from the inside; but there, too, they discovered only the usual auto implements. Egan looked under the hood, Sonny even slid on his back underneath the chassis. Nothing. The Buick *was* clean.

Disillusioned, laden with weariness, the three went back in Waters's car to the parking lot. They sat there in the dark, and even Waters was out of words now. After about twenty more minutes, Auletta was seen walking up Cherry Street from the direction of Pike Street. Approaching the corner of Jefferson warily, Dick peeked toward the Buick, and, not seeing anybody, looked across toward the lot. Waters flicked his parking lights on and off.

When Auletta settled himself in the front seat, his face was grim. 'I had the patrol car drop me back at Pike, just in case. What's with the Buick?'

'Nothing,' Waters growled. 'We gave it a toss, and nothing.'

Auletta sighed. 'Same with the gloms we collared. They're nothing more than thieves. And now I got myself a little chore in the morning,' he scowled at his wristwatch, 'in a little over four hours, in fact. I gotta appear in court to make the complaint. Thanks a lot, *partners*,' he said with a touch of bitterness.

They were silent for a while longer. Then Waters asked no one in particular, 'Well, what'll we do?'

Egan thought of Carol for the first time in several hours and hoped she'd be waiting at his apartment.

'It's been a lovely evening,' Auletta grumbled, 'but *one* of us has to get to work bright and early.'

'Well, we can't just *leave!*' Sonny protested. 'What about the Buick?'

'It's going to be light soon,' Egan mused to himself.

Waters had been pensive. Then he said, 'Look, I think I'm going to bed down over at our office. Sonny, why don't you take the guys back to their own cars, and meanwhile I'll see who's around the office and send somebody out to sit on the Buick.'

'Well, okay,' Sonny acceded. 'Tell you what: after I drop them off, I'll ring you and see if you got anybody. If not, Christ, I'll come back and sit on it myself.'

It was agreed. Before they separated, Egan reminded Waters to put a trace on the Buick as soon as possible.

Egan and Auletta climbed into Sonny's Olds and they drove out to Brooklyn, near Patsy's luncheonette, where twelve hours earlier they had met. Egan and Auletta retrieved their own cars and started home.

Alone, Sonny prowled the Bushwick-Grand Avenue area

and found an all-night cafeteria near the BMT subway entrance. Feeling seedy and bleary-eyed, he took a few minutes to sit over a hot cup of tea. It seared his tongue, and was weak, but it was delicious; he hadn't eaten a thing since about ten Saturday night. At last he went to a telephone booth and dialed Frank Waters's number at 90 Church Street in Manhattan.

When Waters got on, his tone was funereal. 'We blew it,' he growled.

'What?'

'When I got back, Jack Ripa was here, and I hustled him over to Cherry Street. He just called in. The Buick is gone.'

'Oh, goddamn! You're sure he knew the right spot, he didn't—?'

'No, no. He went through the whole area. Pfftt. Lost.'

Sonny ground his teeth together, every muscle straining, then all at once he went limp as fatigue and despair finally overwhelmed him. 'Okay,' he sighed weakly.

They both were silent for a moment. 'Oh, that girl Marilyn?' Waters remembered. 'The cab took her to the Hotel Chelsea on Twenty-third. Mean anything to you?'

'No.'

'Me neither. Well, you might as well go home and get some sleep,' Waters suggested kindly.

'Yeah. You too. Hey, don't forget to get a make on that car anyway.'

Egan was only half awake when he reached his apartment in the Flatbush section of Brooklyn. It was a two-room third-floor walk-up which he called Popeye's Den. He was almost glad Carol wasn't there waiting for him, although her presence was always felt. She had decorated the place in tropical isle style, with grass carpets wall to wall and draperies which closed out the dingy street and presented a serene seascape of the sun setting over the ocean. Preserving this motif, Eddie had taken an old Central Park rowboat and, cutting out the seats and keel, made a bed from it. Driftwood decorations abounded.

In slow motion, he removed his coat, sports jacket and tie and emptied his pockets on the top of his dresser. He unclipped the holstered .38 from his belt and laid it amidst his wallet, keys, tie clip and small change. Then his eyes slowly widened. Off to the side on the dresser top were six bullets. He removed his revolver from its holster and flipped open the cylinder. All the chambers were empty. Good God! Suppose the Dons *had* showed up! His memory refocused on early Saturday afternoon, when his niece had visited him at the apartment for a couple of hours. He found her reaching for the gun on the dresser, and to be safe he unloaded it. He threw himself on his bed, slipping into restless unconsciousness.

Egan was jangled awake by the telephone at just past 9:30 A.M. Sonny was on the other end.

'You awake?' he asked.

'No,' croaked Egan.

'Well, wake up. The Canadian Buick, it's missing.'

Egan sat up. 'What?' he shouted. As his partner somberly related what had happened, Egan sank back against the head board.

'There's some good news, too,' Sonny added – 'and a laugh. Frank queried the Canadian Mounties, and they say the car is registered to a Louis Martin Maurice of Montreal, and this guy happens to be the biggest connection in Canada!'

Egan sat up again. 'So there *was* something there!'

'Wait, wait for the laugh. Now the Mounties go on to say they have this Maurice under constant surveillance in Montreal, and there's no way his tan 1960 Buick Invicta could have gotten to New York. How's that grab ya?'

Bristling, Egan snapped: 'Did Frank tell the Royal Canadian Police that he and three New York cops were sitting on that goddamn car all Saturday night and if they don't believe it, they oughta get their ass down here and find out?'

Sonny chuckled. 'You know Frank. He's like you – he told them. Doesn't make any difference now anyway, with the car gone.'

'Well,' Egan grumbled. 'I hope they make the trip for nothing, then.'

'You sound punchy, Popeye. Go back to sleep. I'll talk to you later.'

Neither Eddie Egan nor any of the detectives could have known of course that what they'd been sitting on, and let slip away, was more than a quarter of a million dollars in United States currency, ingeniously stashed within that 'clean' Buick – cash payment for some twenty kilograms of the highest-quality heroin which only Saturday afternoon had been removed from the same secret hiding place in the same automobile.

Chapter Five

ON the afternoon of November 29, 1961, a dapper Frenchman of forty-eight jauntily strode into a Paris agency for General Motors on Rue Guersant to take delivery of an automobile he had ordered earlier. He was immediately recognized by everyone in the showroom as Jacques Angelvin, an emcee on France's most popular television show, 'Paris-Club.' Throughout France, five days a week the program was broadcast at twelve noon, prime time because most Frenchmen went home for lunch.

The automobile to which Angelvin took title was a secondhand 1960 Buick Invicta. It had required a month for the General Motors agency to locate this particular model, and for a secondhand car it was remarkably new, only 1669 kilometers, or 1043 miles, on the speedometer. Until now, Angelvin had always driven one of the smallest and least expensive cars obtainable, a Renault Dauphine. Time payments on the Buick would cost Angelvin the equivalent of six thousand dollars, which was a thousand dollars less than his total income for the previous year. With great pride and a pleasurable feeling of luxury, which he so enjoyed, Angelvin accepted the keys to the virtually new Buick and drove away from the showrooms . . .

Jacques Angelvin had started with the television show as a casting agent, one who was familiar with the nightclubs. He was a part-time emcee at various boîtes in Paris and one of the three on-camera hosts of 'Paris-Club.'

Roger Feral, whose brother Pierre Lazaroff was the editor of the influential newspaper *France Soir*, interviewed personalities of general interest. Jacques Chabanner, a writer, talked with the literary celebrities. Jacques Angelvin took on the nightclub and show business people. Since he could 'plug' any restaurant or nightclub in Paris at will, he never paid for his evenings with the beautiful women with whom he occupied himself at every opportunity.

An associate of Angelvin's for several years before the purchase of the car was a youthful-looking thirty-four-year-old Corsican named François Scaglia, who sometimes used the aliases 'François Barbier' and 'Yves Systermans.' Scaglia was also known in the Paris underworld as 'the Executioner' because he was widely believed to be the most successful contractor for gangland liquidations in France. Scaglia was useful to Angelvin in securing emcee jobs because he was the owner of one nightclub, and had an interest in several others.

The records of the French Sûreté show that Scaglia was the prime suspect in three kidnappings from 1959 to 1962. In each case a rich man was abducted, taken to an obscure hideout near Paris and there tortured until he assigned all his valuables to his captors – jewelry, money and even his automobiles. However, the Corsican was never convicted of any of these crimes.

The police suspected Scaglia of another, perhaps even more unsavory enterprise, the white slave trade, and in this Jacques Angelvin unwittingly became involved. Pretty young girls from the provinces of France, and from Germany and other European countries as well, flocked to Paris hoping to get into the cinema and show business. Angelvin managed to meet most of them at the nightclubs he frequented. When a girl – blondes were preferred – expressed her interest in a career as a performer or actress, Angelvin would suggest that she try her act out of the country and then, with this experience behind her, she would be ready to take Paris by storm. Beirut in Lebanon was an excellent place to start out. And, as a matter of fact, he knew an individual who owned a nightclub there.

From here Scaglia took over. The pretty blonde did indeed have great talent, he would decide at an audition held in his apartment. He would give her a one-way ticket on Air Lebanon to Beirut, where his associate would meet her, get her a hotel room and start her working.

In a week, after she had run up bills, her employment was suddenly terminated and she found herself without a ticket home, and unable to pay her hotel bill. Now another associate appeared, a corrupt police official who would jail the girl for inability to pay her bills. The girl was grateful when yet another Scaglia associate bailed her out of her deep trouble. But now she was in his custody. Willing to do anything to get out of this whole Arab-world nightmare, she would consent to work for a few weeks for a wealthy Arab trader, and before she realized what was happening she had been sold for as much as $50,000, if she was a blonde, to some oil-rich sheik for his desert harem, from which sand-locked fastness she would never escape . . .

Largely through Scaglia, Jacques Angelvin was on intimate terms with much of the Paris demimonde – notorious homosexuals and lesbians and purveyors of exotic sexual experiences. His address book also contained, besides top theatrical names, a catalogue of helpful police and government officials, who were among his circle of acquaintances. Something of a hypochondriac, Angelvin was also the patient of six doctors, specialists in various maladies.

Angelvin had become a famous name in a short time, but Jacques himself was frustrated that financial reward constantly eluded him. He had been thoroughly spoiled as a youngster in a well-to-do professional family in Marseilles on the southern coast of France. By the time he was twenty, he had attended fifteen different schools without receiving a diploma. At the start of World War II, when he was twenty-five, he had escaped military service because of 'poor health.' Later, to protect him from the Germans, his family hid him away on an obscure farm.

When the war was over, Jacques moved to Paris, where he met a girl, Madov, and was married. A son, Daniel, shortly was born to them, and his family celebrated by giving them a posh apartment in the Invalides. Jacques's only responsibility remained to find himself a job.

He decided to try his hand at journalism, about which he knew nothing. For a while he did work on a paper, *Voici Paris*, collecting items for the cabaret columns. From there he moved into small-time radio as assistant producer of a French-American broadcast on which he, as emcee, introduced young entertainment hopefuls of the future.

He graduated from this to a bigger show, 'Paris by Night,' which originated from the Club Le Vernet. Angelvin had a certain style and he started to attract attention. It was at Le Vernet that he caught the eyes of the producers of a top-rated television show called 'Paris Cocktail.' They felt he had both the warmth and natural sex appeal to sustain the show that all of France looked upon as the 'journal of Paris.'

The money was not great on 'Paris-Club,' as the program was renamed. Angelvin made less than three hundred dollars a month, but he had learned how to turn his new popularity to good advantage in other areas. He became, as he was fond of boasting, 'the one man who can call everyone in Paris, *tu*.' Yet, fortune always hovered beyond his grasp. Two movies were flops. His wife left him, taking their two children, a girl, Veronique, having been born two years after the boy. Past forty, he had little but his superficial celebrity, his souvenirs and fan mail, and a bitter loneliness.

A 'dancer' whom he dated, named Jacqueline, once voted 'Queen of Strip-Tease' of Paris, suggested that Angelvin get into his own nightclub business. Jacqueline said she had well-placed connections who would finance such a venture. And, with the help of mysterious capital produced by Jacqueline, Angelvin took over an inn called the Ile d'Amour, which he made over into an indoor cabaret featuring swimming, tennis and miniature golf along with the dining and dancing.

Within a year, however, the character of the place had changed. It gradually became a meeting place for high-priced prostitutes and well-heeled underworld types straight from Pigalle, and legitimate customers began to stay away. When Angelvin protested to Jacqueline, she walked out on him. Like almost everything else he touched, Angelvin watched the Ile d'Amour go down the drain.

When his ex-wife Madov died early in 1961, leaving their son Daniel, sixteen, and daughter Veronique, fourteen, Angelvin brought them to live with his parents, and then he himself took a sabbatical. He stayed out of sight for weeks. It was rumored that he'd been to Rome, or to Beirut; others said he'd gone to his parents' country place near Saint-Tropez. Wherever he did go to try to recharge his battered life, it was when he returned to Paris and his television show that he began to associate regularly with François Scaglia.

Scaglia entertained him at nightclubs and introduced him to women including Scaglia's own sister, with whom Angelvin found himself in an affair. Scaglia helped the groping performer to land master-of-ceremonies jobs in some of the gaudier Paris clubs. Jacques's ego, so long deflated, stirred again. And, after having interviewed on his TV program a representative of the U.S. Travel Service, who suggested flatteringly that Angelvin should visit America and shoot film to be shown on 'Paris-Club,' just as the famous Ed Sullivan had done in France and other European countries, Jacques began to entertain sparkling notions of launching himself upon America. He thought of going to Canada as well, and perhaps doing some French broadcasting in Montreal or Quebec City. It could be the entry to a new avenue of life for him.

François Scaglia was watching 'Paris-Club' in early November when Angelvin ingenuously told his viewers of his bright plans, promising more information soon on his proposed trip to America.

Suddenly Scaglia was hit with an inspiration. Instinctively, he had always known that Angelvin could be of major use to him, far more than a mere scout for white flesh to be sold in the Middle East. Scaglia was very much involved in the heroin trade, both in Lebanon and Marseilles. He was a regular patron of a Paris bar, Trois Canards, on Rue de la Rochefoucauld, known to the Sûreté as a den for narcotics traffickers. He well knew the great hazard in transporting heroin manufactured in Marseilles to its most lucrative marketplace, New York. Who could be a more innocent-seeming courier than a French television star visiting the United States for the first time? And Angelvin was no stranger to drugs, either. In 1958, one of his own mistresses, a wealthy Paris matron, had died from an overdose of heroin.

The Corsican made immediate preparations to accept a transportation contract from the international heroin syndicate which he knew intimately. First, Angelvin would need the right kind of car in which to smuggle a large load of heroin. The New York end of the ring had discovered that the 1960 Buick Invicta had a peculiarity in body construction conducive to the installations of special traps.

Jacques Angelvin renewed his passport and secured a visa to enter the United States just one day after Scaglia made similar travel arrangements in mid-November – even before delivery of the car.

Chapter Six

THE day after it was discovered that the Canadian Buick had disappeared, Sonny Grosso contacted a close friend in the Federal Bureau of Investigation who maintained a widespread network of reliable informers. The FBI is not normally concerned with narcotics control, but they are adept at keeping their fingers on the pulse of most illegal operations current in the United States. Sonny asked the agent to find out whether a major shipment of heroin had hit the streets in the past twenty-four hours. The agent called back later in the day to report optimistic rumblings but nothing definite.

The next day he communicated with Sonny again. This time he said he had heard the 'panic' was off. The junk was in circulation.

The Canadian car had done its job.

By early December, however, the Narcotics Bureau perceived new indications that the November shipment had succeeded in alleviating the heroin shortage only temporarily. Apparently the well had been very dry, for police stools hinted that the city's addicted wretches already were beginning to whine about coming up tight again. The inference drawn was that another big load might have to be smuggled in soon.

Egan and Grosso, along with Dick Auletta and Federal Agent Frank Waters, continued their close surveillance of Patsy Fuca. Their original target, Angelo Tuminaro, remained in the background, as they focused on the interception of an important delivery of drugs, which they were now reasonably sure would pass through Patsy's hands. This second time, they were better prepared. If they kept on their toes, and were very lucky, they might drop the net over the whole gang, including maybe even Little Angie.

Patsy was rarely out of their sight. But, then, he didn't make it difficult during this period; he seemed relaxed, unhurried, living what appeared to be the predictable life of a workaday small businessman. He continued to spend most of his waking hours in the luncheonette, relieved by his father-in-law when he wanted to go anywhere, or, on weekends, by his brother Tony. He still hopped over to Manhattan some week-nights after closing up, to visit with his little friend Inez at the Pike Slip Inn, but he was not seen again on the street where he had dropped the Canadian Buick. And other times he repeated his familiar tours through several boroughs with Nicky Travato, presumably making collections or delivering goods. But he seemed to be absorbed by nothing out of the ordinary.

Egan had at least one memorable experience tailing Patsy, when one afternoon during the second week of December, he was with Patsy and Barbara as they went Christmas shopping in downtown Brooklyn. Egan followed the couple from bustling store to store, managing to keep them in view despite the milling crowds and turbulent preholiday traffic. After a couple of hours, they drove out Eastern Parkway to Kings Highway, where Barbara dropped her husband at a bank and went on elsewhere by herself. Patsy went into the bank, the Lafayette National, transacted some sort of business and left, taking a taxi back to his store in Williamsburg. There had been nothing unusual about the visit, with the possible exception, as Egan noted with wry speculation, of his seeming to have taken longer than perhaps was necessary to fill out his deposit slips while he glanced about with interest at the layout of the banking floor. Now he is going to be a bank robber too, Egan had smiled to himself.

Two days later, on December 15, two bandits with a machine gun did hold up the Lafayette National Bank on Kings Highway, killing a guard and critically wounding a police officer before escaping with $35,000.

Egan had not yet conceived of any reasonable connection between Patsy Fuca and that armed robbery, nor would he for weeks to come. On December 16, the day after the robbery, he and Sonny, wearing their white jackets from St. Catherine's Hospital, once more browsed through the magazines and the paperback book rack at the rear of Patsy's luncheonette. A natty, pin-striped, swarthy-complexioned individual entered the store and motioned Patsy toward the alcove in the back. 'There's a sharp piece of work,' Sonny muttered as the pair went behind the partially drawn curtain. They had never seen the newcomer before. Apparently oblivious to their surroundings, eyes intent upon the books in each of their hands, the detectives imperceptibly edged closer to the alcove, ears straining to overhear any snatches of conversation.

'Uncle Harry wants you to take another order of cigars, like before,' a hoarse voice said.

Patsy grunted. 'When they coming?'

'. . . due in next week.'

'Okay. Tell him I'll be ready,' Patsy mumbled.

The stranger came out in a moment, elbowing past Egan. At the front counter, he selected a cigar, then, with a nod toward Patsy, sauntered from the store.

Eddie and Sonny looked at each other. It wasn't much, but possibly meant that something would be happening soon.

On that very day, December 16, a shipment of 51.1 kilograms of nearly pure heroin, over 112 pounds, arrived in Montreal, by shipment from France. The potent white powder of living death, packaged in small quantities, was hidden in extraordinary, virtually detection-proof traps concealed within the fenders and undercarriage of a tan 1960 Buick Invicta.

The heroin was about to complete its evil life cycle, which in this case started in Turkey where the poppies are cultivated and the opium harvested. It had then gone to Lebanon where the oily, musk-scented brown paste is sold and chemically reduced to a powdery, white morphine base. It requires ten pounds of opium to produce one of morphine, which is then conveyed clandestinely to the sophisticated refineries in the south of France around Marseilles. Here it is chemically processed further into the drug known as heroin and makes its illicit passage throughout the world and to its primary market, the United States. When entering its market country, it goes first to the 'receiver,' then down to the big wholesalers or 'connections,' then along the line to the smallest street-corner pusher selling tiny glassine-enveloped 'pops' at three or five dollars a bag. (The greed of the middle men may have one beneficial effect. By the time pure heroin has been cut and recut with harmless mannite or lactose powders, the bags at the point of sale contain no more than a few grains of the actual narcotic, putting a minimal dose in the user's system, making it easier to kick the habit than were he getting the 'good stuff' which was sold in the twenties and thirties.) The load that arrived in Montreal could be expected to turn over as much as $32,000,000 on the street. Theoretically, it was enough to supply every addict in the United States for eight months. It was the largest single shipment ever attempted.*

* In December 1965 the Federal Bureau of Narcotics, in cooperation with U.S. customs agents and local police in Columbus, Georgia, seized more than 200 pounds of heroin shipped from France inside an electric freezer, and arrested four men. In April 1968 Federal agents, assisted by New York City police, again confiscated in excess of 200 pounds of heroin, secreted, interestingly enough, in a French automobile abandoned on a Manhattan pier. In the latter instance, however, there would seem to have been a 'leak' in security, for – unlike the present case, as will be seen – nobody claimed the shipment, and to date no principals have been apprehended.

The receiver in Montreal was to be one Louis Martin Maurice, who was in fact the number-one importer for the North American continent. Appropriately the large load was accompanied to Montreal by the French director of this, the world's biggest heroin network, Jean Jehan, who was known to the English speaking underworld as 'Giant.' (That was as close to pronouncing his name as the hoodlums could come.) To those few who saw and knew him, he was a figure out of melodrama. Giant was a tall dapper Frenchman in his mid-sixties who affected pearl-gray spats, a diplomat's striped trousers, a black cashmere blazer with matching velvet piping, a vest (sometimes lemon-colored), cravat and a gray homburg. This memorable sartorial picture was set off perfectly by the black malacca walking stick which he always carried.

Jehan had been a solicitous chaperone on this voyage from France, even more so than he had been back in November when he had accompanied the Buick which Grosso, Egan and Waters had spotted in New York. That operation had proved successful, but before it was culminated indications had reached Jean Jehan of some disquieting moments with the police. Possibly they had only stumbled upon something, but what disturbed him far more was the suspicion that a leak might have developed, or some sort of weak link, in the chain of operations. Of late he had become discomfited with the setup in New York, anyway. When Tuminaro was running his own organization, there had been order, security. But this nephew, Fuca, Jehan did not feel confidence in him. He had no savoir faire, no style, which was bad enough, the Frenchman reflected; but far worse, in this business at least, was the possibility that the man was not trustworthy.

His caution seemed justified when, upon arrival at Montreal, the Canadian police clamped an unexpected embargo on the ship and proceeded painstakingly to search the vessel.

The search was too thorough to be routine – the police kept at it for two days. Jehan and Maurice, who met him, guessed that there had been a tip that a shipment of narcotics was coming in.

Nonetheless, they considered brazening it through until news reached the Montreal conspirators of another alarming development. In Rochester, New York, an American mobster who had been a valuable associate in their smuggling operations was reported to have been shot to death.

Jehan and Maurice could not have known at the time that their contact had been gunned down in a simple gangland feud that was completely coincidental to the Canadian police having swooped aboard the French ship. For them, the timing of the two incidents was enough to sound a warning that the heat was on. They agreed that it was too dangerous now to try to move the merchandise across the U.S.-Canadian border in the Buick. The only alternative was to return it to France in the same condition in which it had come over, and find a way to transport it directly to New York.

Thus, on December 18, Jean Jehan flew back to Paris after the search was over and the tan Buick had been released by police and Customs inspectors. The car was reloaded aboard the ship and sailed for France, its cargo still intact.

In New York, the 'next week' which Patsy Fuca's informant had mentioned as arrival time of the 'cigars' came and went, and the heroin 'panic' was still spreading. The police were unable to determine whether the crisis had been self-induced by the Mafia, a cruel ploy frequently engineered for the purpose of causing prices of junk to soar, or whether the big importers were having problems getting the stuff into the country.

The narcotics detectives continued their rigorous surveillance of Patsy Fuca, his family and associates, and stayed with him many days now around the clock. There was some discontent about this, with the holidays so near, but Christmas notwithstanding, they knew they could not afford to let up on Patsy for a minute lest the break they had waited for so diligently be missed.

On top of this Eddie Egan had been having particular problems with Carol Galvin this holiday season. The beautiful girl continually tried wheedling him into spending more time with her, urging him more and more forcefully to give up his 'thankless' job and go into business with her. Egan was becoming distracted by their more frequent arguments on the subject, and he was further troubled by what he now detected to be a strong desire for material welfare above all else. Her most recent proposal had been especially annoying: it started one evening when Carol told him excitedly how an elderly patron of the Nassau Tavern, a gentleman of apparent means, had offered to buy her a nightclub in New Jersey! Egan rebuked her for giving a second thought to such a proposition, even from a seventy-year-old, and ordered her to forget it. But a few days later Carol again was bursting with the news that the ancient had sent his thirty-nine-year-old son to her with a gift of a new Thunderbird! She gloated over the possibilities: Eddie could quit the force and help her run the club full-time. As for her aged suitor, as she saw it, all she would have to do was have coffee with him occasionally and maybe let him kiss her once in a while. Egan, stunned at first, became furious. They fought again, and at last he walked out. But he couldn't stop remembering how good it had been when he and his nineteen-year-old blonde beauty had been together.

Jean Jehan wasted no time after his return to Paris from Montreal to contact the man who would take on some of the syndicate's most difficult and repugnant jobs for high fees. François Scaglia, pleased that his foresight should be rewarded so soon, listened smugly as Jehan discussed his dilemma – how to get the highly valuable and urgently needed heroin directly into New York, the tightest port of entry in the United States.

The demand for heroin was growing stronger, but there was heat being applied by the police, and reports reached Jehan that some of the biggest American receivers were complaining that the last shipment of heroin had not been of the high-grade quality promised. They wanted a good new supply, and soon. Jehan was even willing this time to send the ring's chief chemist personally to New York to verify the quality. But first, the major concern was to get the load there. Did the Corsican have any ideas? Scaglia told the Giant to be of good cheer and enjoy Christmas. The fifty-one kilos of heroin were as good as in New York City.

On Thursday, December 21, Jacques Angelvin announced on his television program that his plans to visit the United States where, as he put it, he would 'sound out America and its TV,' had been finalized. He told his vast and faithful audience that he would take his luxurious new car to America with him to 'see America like a perfect tourist.' Unstated, of course, was that his plans to visit America had been considerably hastened by Scaglia's importuning. The charge for transporting the car to America would come to about $475, more than his own tourist-class passage. He knew he was performing a dangerous 'errand' for Scaglia by taking the new car, and he had been promised $10,000, more than a year's salary, when the errand was completed in New York.

Scaglia told Angelvin that all he needed to do before departure was to make the Buick available for two days. He was to leave it, unlocked, at a spot on the Champs Elysées and retrieve it at approximately the same location within forty-eight hours. And once in New York, he was to lay up the car in the garage of his hotel, the Waldorf-Astoria, and not move it until so instructed. So simple. He himself, Scaglia confided, would be in New York at about the same time and would provide all guidance and moral support. And for so untaxing a task: 5,000,000 francs, 10,000 American dollars.

On January 2, 1962, Angelvin parked the Buick on the Champs Elysées and flew south for an uneasy two-day visit with his family. On January 4, returning to Paris, he picked up the car, packed, and drove toward the north coast, whence the ocean liner *United States* was to sail from Le Havre the next day. That night, he stopped over in Rouen at the Hotel de la Poste, where Scaglia met him and, over dinner, they reviewed the details of Jacques's 'errand.'

The next morning, the ingenuous Angelvin managed to throw a scare into the Corsican. Having experienced signs of difficulty with his Buick's generator the evening before, he rose early and drove to a General Motors garage on the other side of Rouen, to which he had been directed by the hotel concierge. When Scaglia arose to find his companion missing, he inquired of the concierge, and, learning of Jacques's destination, sped madly in a taxi the two miles to the garage to prevent any untoward discoveries by repairmen tinkering with the Buick.

That evening, January 5, Jacques Angelvin sailed from Le Havre aboard the S.S. *United States*, with his precious Invicta in a cargo hold. François Scaglia returned to Paris by train.

Thirty-six hours later, on January 7, Scaglia himself boarded an Air France jetliner at Orly and flew to Montreal, Canada. He checked in overnight at the Queen Elizabeth Hotel, and, later, in an apartment in the Rosemont section, he met with Louis Martin Maurice and Jean Jehan, who had arrived earlier on a different flight from Paris. The next night, Scaglia left for New York by train. Arriving the morning of Tuesday, January 9, he registered as François Barbier at the Victoria Hotel, on the corner of West 51st Street and Seventh Avenue.

Jehan departed Montreal by air later that day and, in New York, went to the Hotel Edison on West 46th Street between Broadway and Eighth Avenue. This hotel was less than six blocks from Pier 86 on the Hudson River, where the United States Lines' flagship was due to berth the following evening.

Aboard the *United States*, Jacques Angelvin found the crossing rather unpleasant from the beginning. The ship's departure from Le Havre had been delayed six hours, and passengers were unable even to board until well after midnight. He shared a tourist-class cabin with two other men, one a German to whom Jacques took an almost instant dislike. There were very few French people among the 1,800 passengers; most appeared to be Americans, and Jacques was dismayed at what he considered to be their indifference to elegance. The food he found undistinguished except for the hearty Anglo-Saxon breakfasts, although, with his mind frequently on his personal health, he did decide that the American custom of drinking water with meals might be good for his liver.

Angelvin fell victim to claustrophobia in the small, crowded cabin and had trouble sleeping. This growing annoyance was aggravated by his bombastic Prussian cabinmate, whose habit it was to arise every morning at 6 A.M., invariably waking Jacques just as he was finally dozing off. After the German and the diffident service, his greatest source of irritation was what he regarded as the excessive Jewish atmosphere on shipboard. There seemed to be Jewish religious services going on all the time.

Angelvin did meet a young French girl named Arlette who, though not especially pretty, was presentable enough to warrant his attention. But the crowded tourist class made it impractical to advance their relationship beyond the initial stages.

Angelvin thus found himself reduced to sitting in the

writing lounge, scratching out a diary of his comments about the frustrating voyage and his thoughts as to his plans in New York. He vowed that on the return trip he would travel first-class. He would be able to afford it then.

In New York that week, police informers began circulating word that no less than fifty kilos of heroin – '*good* stuff' – might hit the streets within days. At about the same time, the detectives around – and often inside – Patsy Fuca's store in Brooklyn began to notice more frequent visits by various hard types known to have interests in narcotics. Several were observed passing money to Patsy. It looked certain that something big was building up.

Late in the afternoon of January 9, Detective Sonny Grosso, clad in his white jacket, entered Patsy's luncheonette. Egan was across Bushwick Avenue at their familiar post in St. Catherine's Hospital. Sonny stopped at the fountain and said to the old man behind the counter, Patsy's father-in-law: 'Coffee, a cruller, and a Pepsi to go.' Patsy himself was seated at the table in the back room, with his elbows on the table, spooning soup. Sonny and Eddie, in their roles of 'doctors,' had been in the store so often during the past three months that they had come even to exchange greetings with Patsy, and now, as Sonny walked toward the telephones in the rear, he waved a casual hand and Patsy nodded back.

Just as Sonny was reaching for one of the phones, it rang. Automatically, he lifted it off the hook. 'Hello?'

'Bongiorno, Pasquale?' It was a resonant Italian accent.

'Who?'

'Pasq—Patsy, please?' The English was heavily accented.

'Oh, yeah. Just a minute.' Sonny leaned around the curtain into the cubicle where Patsy sat, absorbed in his soup. 'Telephone.'

Patsy came out and took the phone, as Sonny wandered

over to the magazine rack. Patsy's conversation was short, and he did most of the listening, responding mainly with grunts. Then Sonny heard him say in rough Italian, 'Okay, I'll see you then,' and he hung up.

As Sonny started back to make his own call, Patsy was saying to his father-in-law: 'Make sure you're here tomorrow, Pop. I'm going to be busy most of the day.'

Chapter Seven

THE Narcotics Bureau of the New York Police Department was on the third and fourth floors of the ancient 1st Precinct building on a short, narrow street called Old Slip near the southeastern tip of Manhattan, several blocks away from the financial district. Old Slip was actually two parallel east-west streets, each barely two blocks long, connecting Water and South streets along the East River, and divided in the middle by even narrower Front Street. The 1st Precinct station house filled a small square block on the river end of the street. It was a dreary graystone structure dating back to the turn of the century, if not earlier. Every room was paneled with dark wood, had high ceilings and faded green plaster, and with the big sparsely furnished assembly room with scarred wooden floors, gave the immediate impression of a police station in the movies of the thirties. On the street level was a waist-high wooden rail fence facing the main doors in front of a tall, massive desk, behind which loomed the head and shoulders of a blue-uniformed sergeant who scanned each entrant with sad eyes as though he had seen everything twice and wished that he didn't have to again. The rest of the main floor, out of view, was subdivided into patrolmen's lockers, supply rooms, offices, interrogation cubicles and prisoners' cages. A creaky wooden staircase with heavy mahogany banisters led to the precinct detectives' squad rooms and pistol range on the second floor. At the second-floor landing, the finger on a crude black-and-white poster pointed up the stairs: NARCOTICS BUREAU.

The third-floor landing was almost a twin of the one below. A washroom faced the staircase, flanked by a relatively modern water cooler and cork bulletin boards covered with Wanted sheets, mug shots and artists' sketches of sour-faced fugitives, mimeographed procedural bulletins and, tacked in a corner, handwritten notices of Police Benevolent Association activities or upcoming Communion breakfasts. To the right of this central corridor was a large room – an area, really – partitioned at eye level into rows of small cubicles large enough for one or maybe two desks; half of these were occupied at any one time by trim-looking men mostly in their twenties and thirties. They talked quietly into telephones, or pored over sheafs of typewritten pages, or transcribed handwritten notes into legible reports. Their main traits in common were the stubby .38 revolver each had holstered on his hip and the expressionless face. Otherwise, one felt that if they got up and left the building en masse, they would present all the variety of a crowd in a city street.

Some dressed in dungarees and leather jackets, some in causal but neat sports outfits, others in jacket-and-tie business suits; several wore the exaggerated costumes of modish 'swingers.' Some were fair and Anglo-Saxon-looking, some swarthy Latins, a few were Negroes. Haircuts ranged from close-cropped to shaggy and flowing; they were tall, short, lean, husky and portly. Few looked like cops. Many of these men were the Narcotics Bureau's strategic undercover operatives, assigned to move surely along the web of narcotics traffic by passing for spiders themselves. Others were 'field' detectives, who stalked the city's pushers and users openly. Some were headquarters personnel.

Deputy Chief Inspector Carey's office in the far corner was

entirely enclosed. It contained a large, worn desk, a bookcase, two windows, one high in the wall, the other looking out over the elevated South Street Viaduct and the piers pointing across the East River to downtown Brooklyn. On one wall just inside the door, where the chief could see it from behind his desk, was a large blackboard charting the current roster of the bureau. And framed four-feet-square against the left-hand wall there was a hand-lettered genealogy of a subculture which no cop publicly admits exists: THE MAFIA (U.S.). Heading one of the subordinate 'families' was the name Angelo Tuminaro.

When the new Police Commissioner, Stephen Kennedy, had brought Ed Carey in to head up the Narcotics Bureau in 1958, the unit appeared to be suffering from a letdown of interest on the part of entrenched department brass. Narcotics did not become a major factor in crime until after World War II; before the war it had been under the jurisdiction of the so-called Vice Squad, along with gambling, prostitution, pornography and similar 'social' offenses. A special Narcotics Squad had come into being in the late forties when it became obvious that the international Mafia had turned full-scale attention to traffic in drugs as an enormously profitable means of financing not only its myriad illicit enterprises but also its entry into 'legitimate' commerce. The original Narcotics Squad, later to be renamed Narcotics Bureau, consisted of a couple-of-dozen hand-picked police officers who knew little about the wily intricacies of narcotics smuggling and had to learn by experience.

The squad grew rapidly in a vain effort to keep pace with the tremendous buildup in the narcotics traffic through New York. The city had become the narcotics center of the Western Hemisphere: one half or more of all users in the United States were clustered in the Metropolitan area, and perhaps seventy-five to eighty percent of all illicit shipments entered the country through the port and airports of New York.

By the mid-fifties, the Narcotics Bureau had over two hundred men in the streets, about one percent of the total police force; but theirs was an increasingly discouraging assignment. Appetites of addicts for drugs, and of the underworld for the huge profits, had expanded the traffic beyond effective control by law enforcement agencies. The preventative struggle was bogged down in the time-consuming, often fruitless harassment of street-corner 'pushers' and low-level gang 'connections' with only a rare windfall that might provide a glimmer of the vital but always elusive *sources* of supply.

During the same period, there seemed to be less than general agreement within high police circles as to the extent to which the fearsome rising incidence of crime of all types could be linked significantly with the surge of narcotics traffic. Different commanders held varying theories, with some of the more traditional minded tending to play down specialization in narcotics investigation in favor of tried-and-true tactics of a broad frontal assault on crime. When Carey took charge in 1958 the bureau had been depleted to 164 men. Morale was not high: he found many officers who were discouraged by the seeming futility of their objective. They had lapsed into contenting themselves with a self-limiting 'quota' system of arrests; few were exerting any effort or ingenuity beyond minimum performance.

But Carey had several things going for him in reshaping his new command. For one, he was a favorite of the commissioner, Kennedy, an intellectual but steel-hard administrator who *did* subscribe to the probability that much new crime, organized and otherwise, was feeding upon narcotics. Kennedy gave Carey complete freedom in the matter of reorganizing his personnel, and in dramatizing to the public the peril with which they were faced.

The new chief took almost a year to learn his subject and his assignment. He learned to know his men intimately, transferring some out and bringing in others. He began to form and nurture a small cadre of his most purposeful and energetic detectives into an 'elite' squad called the Special Investigating Unit, whose unilateral objective henceforth was no longer the routine drug traffic in the streets but the 'big' scores, the tracking and smashing of the 'higher-ups' – the higher the better.

Finally, Carey strengthened the local bureau's relations with the Federal Bureau of Narcotics. The Federals had resources, manpower and equipment that the locals could use to advantage. The New York police had information, contacts and certain legal leeway – such as court-authorized wiretapping – that the government agents found useful. At least weekly, Chief Carey met with the Federal Regional Director, George Gaffney, to trade reports and strategy.

With this new vigor and esprit, the drive against narcotics had begun to show strength, both in the arrests of important distributors and renewed public awareness of the frightening dimensions of the problem. The police began to receive indications, in fact, that the older-generation Mafia were becoming discouraged with the future of the narcotics business, as the law probed closer to the core of leadership. Word was seeping out that the veteran Dons, many of whom had long since turned substantial outlaw profits into the establishment of their now equally profitable legitimate 'cover' businesses, had grown to feel that their ill-gotten respectability was increasingly facing unnecessary jeopardy. Many either were 'retiring' their narcotics franchises, turning them over to younger, more reckless 'family' members, or liquidating their interests altogether, thus opening their preserves to new management by a new pirate breed of Puerto Ricans and expatriate Cubans.

Because of this continuing changeover, the operation that Detectives Egan and Grosso; along with Agent Waters, had stumbled upon assumed perhaps even greater significance: the key figure, Patsy Fuca, was related to the old boss, Little Angie. If the thing proved to be as big as the police had come to suspect, any major arrests and convictions could possibly enable them to pull the aging, worldwide syndicate fabric apart. Accordingly, for the past four months Chief Carey had granted Egan and Grosso and the S.I.U. team wide latitude, as George Gaffney had also done with his force of Federal agents.

During this time, Egan and Grosso had maintained tight rein over the investigation with respect to keeping manpower to a minimum, for fear of betraying surveillance prematurely; but now, following the telephone call to Patsy at his store, which indicated strongly that something important was about to happen, they decided to go to Lieutenant Hawkes and request all additional aid possible, starting at once. At eight-thirty on Wednesday morning, January 10, they met at Narcotics Bureau headquarters with Chief Carey, Hawkes, Sergeant Fleming of S.I.U., and Director Gaffney, Frank Waters and Special Agent Ben Fitzgerald of the Federal Bureau, to plan new strategy and the personnel assignments. Carey ordered that every member of his 200-man squad, unless critically committed to other key investigations, stand by to assist on the Fuca case at any hour anywhere in the city. Gaffney also detached all available agents in the New York area. In all, a force of some three hundred detectives was thus organized.

Individual radio cars were to be fitted with taping equipment to record all communications between units working on the case. The Federal offices at 90 Church Street were chosen as the central command and communications post because of the superior facilities there; a base radio system was set up, through which all reports and advices were to be transmitted by police and agents alike to the three pivotal officers, Egan, Grosso and Waters.

Shortly after noon that Wednesday, the tenth, Grosso and Waters, having tailed Patsy Fuca from his home in Brooklyn, were parked near a construction site on East 45th Street in Manhattan, just east of Vanderbilt Avenue. The area, at the rear of Grand Central Station, was busy with trucks and barricades, as workmen banged away on the finishing touches to the new Pan-Am Building. Grosso and Waters were growing anxious as they watched the main entrance of the Hotel Roosevelt, half a block west between Vanderbilt and Madison Avenue. They had staked out Patsy's house early that morning, and finally followed him to midtown. Patsy had parked his compact Buick illegally in a No Standing zone opposite the Roosevelt and entered the hotel. Ten minutes had passed, and he had not reappeared.

Sonny opened the door of the car. 'I'm going to take a look,' he said edgily. He walked along the south side of 45th Street until he was directly across from the hotel entrance. Patsy was not in view, but it was about lunchtime, and office workers were beginning to fill the sidewalks. Sonny decided he had better chance a look inside the lobby. He crossed 45th Street, pushed through the revolving door, started up the broad carpeted stairs to the main level . . . and stopped dead still.

What halted him was the imposing figure descending the stairs – a tall and awesomely distinguished-looking man with luxuriant gray hair under a black homburg, a black cashmere overcoat with velvet collar, striped gray trousers, a black walking stick swinging jauntily from one hand, and pearl-gray spats. Sonny stood immobile on the steps, watching the man, who might have been sixty, pass him. He was smiling now at someone below, one of those polite drawing-room smiles that could impart warmth or frostiness with the slightest variance at the corners of the mouth. Sonny glanced down the steps. Patsy was standing at the foot of the stairs, also smiling, only on his face it could just as easily have been a leer.

The two shook hands and turned to go out into 45th Street. Sonny retreated down to a side door, reaching the sidewalk just as Patsy emerged from the revolving door behind the tall man, and strode quickly back toward Waters's car, glancing over his shoulder a couple of times to keep them in sight. They were strolling toward Madison Avenue. Sonny tumbled into the seat beside Waters. 'Did you see *that*?'

'Yeah. What is it?' the agent grinned.

Patsy and his companion now had sauntered back in front of the Roosevelt and stood to one side of the entrance in the sub-freezing cold, deep in conversation. The stranger certainly seemed to be well above the class of acquaintance with which the detectives had associated Patsy. 'I'll bet that's the guy who called yesterday,' Sonny mused. He wished somebody had invented a way to read puffs of winter breath, in the same way one could interpret sign language or Indian smoke signals.

'Looks like the first team is coming into the game,' commented Waters.

A few minutes past twelve-thirty, Patsy and the man in black turned and walked briskly across the street to Patsy's blue compact. In a moment, they had joined the strangle of traffic inching its way west across midtown Manhattan. Waters and Sonny followed, several car lengths behind.

It took more than twenty minutes before the Buick drew up on West 46th Street between Eighth Avenue and Broadway, near the rear entrance to the Edison Hotel. The dapper stranger stepped out, went around the car, leaned into Patsy's window for some parting word, then grandly entered the hotel. Patsy drove off, now headed east. Farther back on 46th Street, nearer Eighth Avenue, Sonny sprang from Waters's car and hurried toward the Edison. Waters headed out after Patsy.

Sonny reached the hotel lobby just in time to spot the tall man going out the main door on 47th Street. By the time the detective had hustled through the lobby and emerged on 47th, the man had walked almost to Broadway. Now the old boulevardier was meandering, taking in the sights and sounds of gaudy, brassy Times Square, which by day always had struck Sonny as blowsy, like a prostitute with too much mileage on her and a hangover to boot. He appeared oblivious to the attention of passersby, many of whom eyed him with a mixture of admiration and curiosity. At least he shouldn't be tough to tail, Sonny thought. He traversed the Times Square–Duffy Square area, where Broadway cuts across Seventh Avenue, and paused at shop windows or by billboards in front of movie theaters. The guy's killing time, Sonny judged, staying a block or so behind. The man strolled back to the west side of Broadway and made his casual way uptown. At the corner of 48th Street, he stopped a moment to gaze into McGinnis's Restaurant, then went on. At 51st Street, he recrossed Broadway, going east again, keeping the same easy pace. Finally, after almost an hour, at one fifty-five Sonny watched him enter the Victoria Hotel at 51st and Seventh Avenue.

The detective waited on the corner a few discreet moments, then followed inside. Up a flight of stairs, in the main lobby, the tall man had seated himself on a settee facing the elevators. Sonny wandered to the newsstand. Within a few minutes, the man rose to greet another individual advancing across the lobby.

This was a considerably shorter man, about five-seven, Sonny estimated, and much younger, perhaps in his early thirties. Hatless, he was clean-cut, except that he wore his dark brown hair somewhat fuller than did most Americans of his age, more in the European style; his clothes were also black and well cut. The tall one seemed to show more genuine pleasure in seeing this individual than he had in meeting Patsy. They embraced each other's shoulders lightly, then, after chatting for several seconds, they walked out of the hotel together.

Sonny now followed the two back to Broadway and down to 48th Street, where, to his mild surprise, they entered McGinnis's Restaurant. This was a big, informal place that featured strictly American food, hamburgers and hot barbecue sandwiches. Having thought the pair were foreigners, quite possibly French or Italian, Sonny thought they would have chosen an eating place more of the continental type. They went downstairs to McGinnis's small, quieter dining room and were given a table by themselves against a wall. Once they appeared to be settled, Sonny went to a telephone on the main level and called in to base, requesting that they send somebody to help him cover the restaurant. Then he himself went downstairs, where he claimed a small table only two removed from the subjects and to their left. They were talking animatedly in what, from the occasional words he could hear, Sonny identified as French, although some of the inflections struck him as less nasal and more guttural than the polite French he remembered having heard before.

When a waiter came, the tall one ordered a sherry for himself in accented English and a bottle of imported beer for the other. Sonny studied the menu, waiting to see if they were going to order food. In a little while they did: two luncheon plates. Sonny then decided on a beefburger and cup of tea.

He ate slowly, timing his lunch to the leisurely pace of his subjects. He refrained from studying them closely, but when he did let his eyes stray toward the two, Sonny could see that they had unfolded a large sheet of paper, roughly legal size, and were tracing their fingers over it this way and that, as though it were a map or a plan or a sketch of some kind.

It was almost 4:30 P.M. when the older man called for their check. Sonny immediately rose, left a couple of dollar bills on his table, and went upstairs and out into the street. Lounging against a lamppost facing the door of the restaurant, with an open newspaper in his hands, was a familiar burly figure – Eddie Egan. Sonny walked over and stood alongside him, his back to the restaurant, as though waiting for the traffic light to change. Without giving any sign of recognition, Sonny murmured: 'In a minute two guys in black are coming out, an old one, tall and classy, and another guy, short, younger. You take the little one. I'm sure they're foreigners. Mine was with Patsy earlier.'

'Mm-hmm – here they come,' Egan warned, not seeming to have taken his eyes from the newspaper before him.

The subjects paused at the corner, conversing quietly, then shook hands and separated. The tall one ambled down Broadway, and Sonny stepped out behind him. The other headed east across Broadway, with Egan in his wake.

Sonny's man returned to the Edison Hotel. He stopped at the front desk for his key and walked toward an open elevator. The detective stepped aboard before him. At the ninth floor, the man got off. Sonny went up to eleven, then caught another elevator back to the lobby. He found the house telephone and asked for the hotel security officer, a former city policeman whom he knew. In a few minutes, off in a quiet corner of the lobby, Sonny was asking the security man to check the hotel register. He wanted the names and points of origin of recent foreign check-ins who had rooms on the ninth floor.

Sonny wandered around the Edison lobby while he waited, pausing by the newsstand, examining window displays, but always remaining within view of the elevator bank. Within twenty-five minutes, the house officer caught his eye from near the main entrance. There, shielded by a billboard on an easel advertising the hotel's Green Room, Sonny was told that the individual he was interested in was the single gentleman from Canada. He had come in the previous day and was registered in room 909, a Mr. Jean Jehan of Montreal.

Sonny didn't know the name, but he was going to get to know Mr. Jehan very well. He called in to report his location and to get additional men sent to the Edison. Then, through the security officer, he borrowed an off-duty bellman's jacket and posted himself at the bell captain's desk to wait.

Egan, meanwhile, had tailed the younger man to the Victoria Hotel at 51st and Seventh. Following their standard technique, he got into the elevator with his subject and watched him get off at the eleventh floor. Downstairs, twenty minutes later, Egan learned that his quarry had arrived early the previous day from Montreal; he was in room 1128, and his registered name was François Barbier.

Egan telephoned base and was told that his partner was staked out at the Edison Hotel on an individual named Jean Jehan. He bought a magazine, looked about for a comfortable chair, and made himself at home.

A little over three hours later, at 6:45 P.M., François Barbier emerged from an elevator, bundled warmly in a heavy black overcoat with a furry collar, and walked through the lobby, downstairs and out into icy winds on Seventh Avenue. A big electric sign a few blocks away in Times Square put the temperature at ten above zero. Egan following, Barbier hurried over to Broadway and down to 47th Street, where he turned off and entered the Edison Hotel. Jean Jehan was waiting for him in the lobby, wrapped in greatcoat and muffler, the ever-present black walking stick in hand. Stationed at the bell captain's desk, his sad brown eyes taking in everything, was Sonny Grosso. Sitting casually in an easy chair on the far side of the lobby, reading a newspaper, was Federal Agent Frank Waters. Without the flicker of an eye, Eddie Egan strolled in and stopped by the newsstand to scan the magazine rack and final editions of the newspapers. After a brief conference, Jehan and Barbier went out into 46th Street together and began walking west toward the Hudson River. Sonny doffed his bellman's jacket and put on his overcoat, and the three detectives followed, one by one. It was a little after 7 P.M..

The foreigners were in no hurry passing through the graying, scarred area of midtown Manhattan's west side once notorious as Hell's Kitchen – now reduced to stark clusters of crumbling tenements, warehouses, parking lots, service stations and garages. It took them fifteen minutes to negotiate the five long blocks from the Edison to Twelfth Avenue, a wide, dreary thoroughfare running alongside the river underneath the elevated West Side Highway. The avenue is the outlet for the piers of most of the major shipping lines. At the corner of Twelfth and 46th, Jehan and Barbier stopped to gaze up at the mighty prow of the S.S. *United States*, which had docked but a short time earlier.

The two Canadians, or Frenchmen or whatever they were, stood huddled on that corner, in a cutting wind off the river, hands buried in their pockets, dancing little steps against the cold, for more than an hour and a half. Across Twelfth Avenue, the pier at first had been a minor bedlam of passengers flocking from the ship, porters manipulating bulky luggage, honking taxis and private autos trying to maneuver closer to the exit gate. But as eight o'clock wore on toward eight-thirty, the pedestrian and vehicular traffic thinned out, and still the two men waited on the opposite corner.

To the frozen detectives – Sonny in a doorway on Twelfth Avenue between 46th and 47th streets, Egan and Waters on either side of 46th, midway in the block behind the subjects – their wait was puzzling. If the two had come to meet someone disembarking, surely they had missed connections; all but a few stragglers and the ship's crew seemed to have departed the pier. The detectives' fingers and toes were numb and actually beginning to ache. Their ears were burning, and each in his own way cursed the 'goddamn Frogs,' as Egan had taken to referring to the pair.

Once, Sonny had additional cause for indignation. As he shivered on Twelfth Avenue, a car rolled by him, and he saw a man's face pressed against the right front window, grinning at him. Sonny started as he recognized Jack Fleming of S.I.U. and Federal Agents Jack Ripa and Bill Carrazzo. Ripa had the middle finger of his right hand pointed skyward in the harsh unmistakable masculine gesture. As they passed, from his frozen doorway Sonny threw a sign back, his left hand clapped into the crook of an upraised right arm.

One of the Frenchmen finally made a move about eight-fifty. Barbier left his companion and walked across Twelfth Avenue toward the pier. He stood a few minutes, gazing on tiptoe into the unloading area. Then, he turned and came back, striding rapidly and, the watching detectives felt, with just a hint of jauntiness. Whatever he reported, Jehan patted his shoulder, and they started walking back along 46th Street.

This time they passed by the Edison and crossed glaring Broadway, just beginning to accelerate its blurred pace, assimilating the streams of nightly theater-goers and fun-seekers. They continued west all the way to Fifth Avenue, where they turned left and walked north, still meandering like two old friends out on an evening's constitutional.

Comparing notes along the way, the officers were convinced that these two foreigners were the *big* heroin connections whom Patsy Fuca had been waiting for. Either they were the suppliers themselves or represented the principals directly. It was also evident that the big shipment being buzzed about by local pushers and junkies either was already in, and it remained only for the conspirators to accomplish distribution, or it was due at any moment. For the first time, Eddie and Sonny were particularly buoyed by visions not of finally zeroing in on Angelo Tuminaro, who had been the unwitting target originally, but perhaps of lucking into a bigger score than they had ever imagined. Thus, despite the cold, they were almost exuberant as they tailed the mysterious Frenchmen – whom Egan had whimsically dubbed 'Frog One' for Jehan and 'Frog Two' for the man Barbier.

The three officers deployed into the classic on-foot surveillance pattern known to intelligence agents the world over as 'A-B-C' or 'parallel' pursuit. Two of them, one behind the other – in this instance, Egan (A) trailed by Grosso (B) – followed the subjects at a respectable distance on the same side of the avenue; the third, Waters (C), walked on the other side of the avenue approximately abreast of the Frenchmen. Waters kept his eye on the subjects; Egan watched both them and Waters across the way; Grosso followed the leads of his two fellow officers. Every few blocks, the three would switch positions. It is a near foolproof method of maintaining visual contact with the pursued, because C can always keep the subjects in view regardless of what corners they turn or evasions they attempt. And shortly the effectiveness of the pattern was demonstrated.

Near St. Patrick's Cathedral at 50th Street, the Frenchmen crossed over to the east side of Fifth Avenue, and continued their casual trek north. But then, turning the corner of East 55th Street, they ducked quickly through the revolving doors of the elegant Hotel St. Regis, only a few yards from Fifth. They might have eluded their trackers right there but for Agent Waters on the far side of the avenue who caught a glimpse of their sudden move.

The pair lingered in the St. Regis lobby for several moments, probably to watch for anybody coming in behind them who might look like a cop, and just long enough to give the pursuing officers a chance to regroup outside. When apparently satisfied that they had been unobserved, Jehan and Barbier walked the length of the lobby and down the carpeted stairs to the luxurious Maisonette supper club one flight below.

Egan and Sonny decided not to follow them into the Maisonette, on the off-chance that either might be recognized from earlier proximity to the Frenchmen, so Waters went down. Sonny said he would wait around the main lobby, and Egan volunteered to post himself out on 55th Street within view of the canopied separate entrance to the Maisonette. When Egan bundled up and went outside, it was nearly 9:30 P.M., and the temperature had fallen to eight degrees.

Jehan and Barbier sat in the softly lit Maisonette for an hour. Unmindful of the lilting music of the hotel orchestra or of the dozen or so smartly dressed couples dancing, they sipped cocktails, picked at light salads and talked, as Agent Waters watched from across the room. At about ten-thirty, Jehan rose and went upstairs, and his companion remained at the table.

Sonny, slouched in a chair near the entrance to the St. Regis's King Cole Bar, started as Jehan passed him and stopped at one of a row of partly enclosed public telephones just off the lobby. Sonny stepped into an adjoining cubicle, keeping his face averted, and tried to eavesdrop. Jehan's conversation, which lasted some ten minutes, was entirely in French; all Sonny was able to distinguish was a tone of urgency in the man's speech. When he had finished, Jehan returned downstairs to the Maisonette and, after a few more minutes of discussion, the two Frenchmen called for the check.

Waters waited until they had ascended the stairs before leaving his table. Above, Sonny watched them exit into 55th Street; and outside, a frostbitten Egan, hat pulled down over his red mop, saw them come out and walk toward Fifth Avenue again. All three detectives trailed the Frenchmen back down Fifth to 50th Street, then east two blocks to the Waldorf-Astoria Hotel on Park Avenue. It was approaching 11 P.M.

The subjects went to the 50th Street side of the Waldorf and down the ramp into the hotel garage. Feeling it wiser not to follow them into such close quarters, Egan and Sonny waited on the street, watching the garage entrance, while Waters hurried to the elevator bank in the lobby of the hotel. In about ten minutes, Jehan and Barbier came out of the garage and entered the front door of the hotel. Barbier found a house telephone and, as Jehan stood by, held a lengthy conversation with somebody, probably – judging by his frequent gesticulation – in French. The officers could only speculate whether Barbier was conversing with the same party Jehan had called from the St. Regis. They could not understand the implication of the brief visit to the Waldorf garage.

Barbier rejoined Jehan and, without pausing, the two men strode to the elevators, entered one and disappeared behind the sliding doors. It happened too fast for the surprised officers to follow. There was nothing they could do now but wait. The 'Frogs' might be anywhere in the huge Waldorf.

Nearly an hour passed, but there was no further sign of the subjects. It was past midnight now, and the detectives had been tailing these people for more than half a day with barely a chance to eat or even relieve themselves. Their enthusiasm of only a few hours before had waned considerably, and they were growing irritable, at themselves, mostly, because now they seemed to have lost their men. They knew the hotels where each was staying, but their experience had taught them never to take anything for granted.

Still keeping an eye on the main elevators, the officers half-heartedly prowled the great lobby of the Waldorf. Sonny and Waters were becoming resigned to having lost the Frenchmen for the night, but Egan, with his stiff-necked Irish temperament, was nettled. An inexplicable intuition persuaded him that their Frogs had *not* left the hotel and that there might be a lot more to do yet that night. Drifting off from the others, he wandered downstairs at the Lexington Avenue end of the Waldorf and looked into the Bull and Bear Bar. The neo-English pub atmosphere still was lively with nightcapping banquet refugees and convention guests, all male, some in black tie.

There, relaxing at a corner table, two fresh drinks before them, were Jehan and Barbier. Egan ducked out and raced upstairs to inform Sonny and Waters. Either the Frogs had visited somebody up in one of the rooms and then slipped down to the bar in the lower lobby by the rear elevators, or they had taken a circuitous route there in the first place. Either way, they had them again. They could only hope that nothing significant had occurred in the interim.

The S.S. *United States* had docked about seven P.M. that evening. For Jacques Angelvin, the tortuous edging of the great ship into the pier had seemed almost interminable. The trip had been a terrible bore, even though he and the girl Arlette, who would continue on to Chicago the following day, had made plans to meet later at her hotel, the Summit. He could barely wait to disembark and get his car to the Waldorf-Astoria as instructed by Scaglia. He was curious, also, to meet the young lady who he had been told would meet him ashore. He envisioned a youthful beauty, charming and agreeable.

Lilli DeBeque *was* lovely, and charming. Before Angelvin went through the lineup for Customs, he waited to watch his precious Buick unloaded and set down on the pier. At almost nine P.M. he was still waiting for Customs clearance when the girl approached him. She was tall, with long, shiny black hair, shapely, her clothes chic. And a woman, not a girl – twenty-five, perhaps older, he guessed. With his meager English he was having difficulty explaining to the inspectors who he was and why he had brought his American-made auto to America from France.

Lilli came to his rescue. Introducing herself in French, she told him how pleased she was to meet the television personality known throughout all of France. Then she turned to the inspectors and, in what sounded to Jacques like charming English, described him as 'the Jack Paar of France . . .'

They waited together, chatting easily, as the Buick was brought off the pier. Lilli was French, but she had been in the States for several years, and was a secretary in a law firm. Jacques, always sensitive to women, felt a spark between them.

Following her directions, he drove through the midtown traffic to the Waldorf on Park Avenue. The broad boulevard, its rich glass towers aglow with night lighting, thrilled him. Angelvin deposited the car in the hotel garage, then invited Lilli up to his room. She declined, suggesting that she wait for him in the lobby. Disappointed, but realizing that he would have at least a week to pursue Lilli and that Arlette undoubtedly was waiting, and presumably willing, at the Summit Hotel, he in turn pleaded fatigue and arranged to telephone Lilli the following day.

Also, he remembered that he should be hearing from François Scaglia.

Jacques had not long to wait. Near ten-thirty P.M., a Monsieur Jehan called to make sure he was comfortable and that his car was in the garage. The man said that he was with Scaglia and that they wished to visit Jacques in his room. Angelvin asked if it couldn't wait until tomorrow because he was very tired. Actually, he wanted to pursue his affair with Arlette as soon as possible. Jehan was insistent on a meeting that evening, and finally Angelvin reluctantly agreed after the five-million-franc fee was mentioned.

The meeting in his room lasted about twenty minutes. Jehan and Scaglia were satisfied, having seen the Buick in the Waldorf garage with their own eyes. Petulantly, Angelvin asked to be able to use his car tomorrow, but Scaglia was adamant. They arranged a meeting for noon the next day, the place to be determined by Scaglia in the morning. Then, to Angelvin's relief, the two left him alone. He had tried not to think about his part in this unsavory affair, and now he was determined to find diversion.

He left his room, going out of the Waldorf at the Lexington Avenue entrance, across the street and down a block to the Summit Hotel. He called Arlette from the lobby and she soon joined him, and they went back to the Waldorf for a drink at Peacock Alley. After the drink Angelvin invited the girl up to his room and she readily accepted. By now, it was after midnight and the hotel security system was operating in full force. Angelvin threw dark looks at the house officers and hotel servants, and Arlette became nervous when on Angelvin's floor a security man followed them to his room. They decided to go back to the Summit and found the situation the same. They were obliged to sleep in their separate rooms in separate hotels that night.

About 12:30 A.M. of January 11, Sonny Grosso was at the Waldorf's Bull and Bear Bar, a foot on the rail, apparently staring moodily into a sweet vermouth. Egan and Waters were out on East 49th Street, clapping hands and jigging to ward off the biting cold. Egan's feet were pinched and stinging again. At first he'd had the sudden fear that he might literally be suffering the first stage of frostbite; but then he remembered the new pair of brown shoes he had bought too hurriedly that morning. Egan was cursing the ill-fitting shoes, the cold, his feet, himself, the job, the whole lousy world, when at 1:00 A.M. Jehan and Barbier emerged from the side door of the Bull and Bear and walked east on 49th Street.

Egan and Waters stayed with them, well to the rear and on the south side of the street. Grosso left the bar and took up the chase, far behind the Frenchmen on the north side. Jehan and Barbier turned downtown at Third Avenue. They walked past 42nd Street . . . and 34th. The detectives changed places with each other, alternating back and forth to either side of the avenue, even switching hats occasionally to minimize any chance of the subjects perceiving a pattern of men following them. And they grew more puzzled; surely any minute something would have to happen. The Frogs would make some significant move; who just *walks* on such a night, with the mercury sinking toward zero, and the wind whipping at a man's body? But Jehan and Barbier went on down Third Avenue, hardly looking about them, past 23rd Street, to 14th Street. There, finally, without hesitation, they turned right. It was 1:45 and they had strolled thirty-five blocks, almost two icy miles. The chilled, weary officers perked up: this might be it.

The Frenchmen walked west on 14th two blocks to Union Square and there, by Klein's department store, with the frigid wind gusting mercilessly across the broad, deserted square, they turned right on Park Avenue South (Fourth Avenue), and started back uptown.

Wracked by the cold and fatigue and mounting despair, the three detectives maintained pursuit. Egan was hobbling now, on feet sodden with pain. They trudged all the way back up Park to 46th Street, thence west again, past Madison

Avenue and Fifth and Sixth, until at last, at twenty minutes before three in the morning, on the corner of 46th Street and Seventh Avenue, with no more than curt nods and a small handshake the Frenchmen bade each other good night after nearly eight hours.

Jehan continued west on foot, apparently heading back to the Edison, Sonny and Frank Waters staying on him. Egan dragged himself along after Barbier, who walked north on Seventh five more blocks to the Victoria Hotel. Inside, he went to the front desk and retrieved his room key, then made straight for an elevator and was gone. Egan watched the elevator indicator stop at eleven before he went to the public telephone to call in. He requested relief at the earliest possible time.

It was 3 A.M., Thursday, when with a weary groan, he plopped himself on a couch in the lobby and wrestled with his senses to stay awake. It was a tough fight. His eyes, stinging with fatigue, kept drooping shut, and when he felt that warm blanket of relaxation begin to creep over him, he shook himself back to alertness.

About three-thirty, he decided to walk around the lobby, despite the acute soreness of his feet. He strolled back and forth for fifteen minutes, feeling like a house detective, then, hoping that enough adrenalin had been stirred up, sat down to rest his feet. But minutes later he caught himself drifting off again, and he jumped up. The lobby was empty now, except for a clerk behind the front desk, a porter shuffling cigarette butts from the floor into a silent butler at the end of a stick, and the night bell captain slouched behind a waist-high desk near the elevator bank. The bellman had been watching him, sympathetically Egan thought; he wondered if the fellow had guessed he was a cop. He decided to see if he could enlist some free help.

'Say, pal,' Egan smiled, approaching the desk, 'maybe you could do me a big favor.'

The slight, sallow bell captain studied the big red-eyed man with indecision.

'Such as?' he asked.

'You probably seen me around here,' the detective said. 'I've been waiting for a friend to come down from upstairs' – he winked – 'you know . . . and I can hardly keep my eyes open. I was wondering, maybe you'd keep an eye on the elevator for me, and if it starts to come down from eleven, you could let me know, in case I doze off?' He patted his back pocket as a hint that he had a ready wallet there.

The bell captain shrugged. 'Sure, why not? The eleventh floor?'

'Right,' Egan smiled. He turned away, about to return to a comfortable chair, when the bellman hissed behind him: 'It's coming down from eleven right now, mister!'

Caught virtually in the middle of the deserted lobby, Egan tried to hustle around the corner of the elevator bank before the doors slid open. He didn't quite make it. A haggard-looking young man stepped from the elevator in a rumpled suit, and when he glanced over and spied Egan, half hidden behind a pillar, he simply stopped and stared.

The detective blushed, hoping it was not noticeable. Who is this character? What the hell is he staring at? Does he make me as fuzz? The man had come from the eleventh floor; could he be somehow connected with Barbier? These thoughts sped through Egan's mind in a split second, and in the next he was walking toward the man, determined to bluff.

'Can I help you, sir? I'm the house officer,' he announced quietly.

'No – no, I guess not,' the young man stammered, obviously ill at ease. 'I thought you looked familiar . . . but I guess . . .'

'Is anything wrong?' Egan persisted. 'It's kind of late to be roaming around.'

The other's eyes widened. 'Aren't you Egan of Narcotics?'

Now it was Egan's turn to stare. 'Who are you?' he demanded.

'Johnson. Federal Bureau.' He seemed to sag, both in relief and weariness. 'I wasn't sure you'd be down here.'

'I didn't know *you* were up *there*!' Egan declared, leading him to a corner of the lobby. 'What were you doing on eleven? We don't want to burn these guys, you know.'

Agent Johnson sighed. 'I'm in the room next to Barbier, trying to bug him. There's this ventilator between the bathrooms . . . I've been sitting in the *bathtub* all day, getting practically nothing. And, well, I just about had it, you know, I had to get out of there, get some air, something to eat.'

Egan started to laugh. 'Okay, go ahead and grab a bite some place. I'll be here. But don't stay out all night.'

'Thanks a lot,' the young agent responded brightly. 'I'll come back right away.' As he turned to go, Egan called after him:

'Hey, Johnson, how long you been with the bureau?'

Johnson blushed, and on him it *was* noticeable. 'Just a couple of days. They needed someone who could understand French.'

'Okay, I'll see you later.' He won't stick, Egan thought, watching him go.

It was past four now. Egan wandered around the lobby, sat down, got up, sat again in another chair, stood again, then slumped down on a divan. He was becoming depressed at his inability to ward off the urge to sleep. His head was nodding once more when a hand on his shoulders roused him. It was the bell captain.

'That wasn't your friend a while ago, eh?'

Egan struggled to an upright position. 'No,' he yawned, 'that was another friend.'

'Look' – the man glanced about with practiced caution – 'I

got something that'll perk you up. It'll cost you a coupla bucks, but it's worth it.'

This woke the detective up. The sucker was trying to sell him a goofball! He managed to mask his renewed interest with another yawn. 'Two bucks, huh? What is this stuff?'

The bellman grinned, 'Come with me.' Egan hauled himself up and followed him over to the desk. The bellman reached into a pocket of his trousers and withdrew a small green metal box, which he opened carefully beneath the desk top. Egan glimpsed an assortment of tablets of various sizes, shapes and colors, as the other extracted a familiar pink, heart-shaped pill and dropped it into Egan's palm. It was a 'benny' – Benzedrine. 'Swallow that down,' the man said, 'and in a few minutes you'll be doing a jig.'

'Thanks a million,' Egan said, mustering great sincerity. He passed two dollar bills across the counter and walked away. He was thinking to himself: Easiest 'score' I ever made. When this Fuca business is over, first thing I'll do is come back here and bag *this* monkey.

Chapter Eight

IT WAS 8 A.M. on Thursday, the eleventh, before a young Federal agent named Luis Gonzalez arrived to take up the vigil with the bleary-eyed Egan. Joints stiff, muscles aching, his stomach contracting with hunger, unshaven, feeling seedier than he ever had as a Marine after a week's bivouac, the detective hauled himself off the couch in the hotel lobby and stumbled downstairs to the coffee shop. Testily, Egan realized that even now he could not leave, because the relief agent couldn't pick up Barbier until Egan could point the man out to him.

He and Gonzalez waited miserably in the Victoria lobby for four more hours. By noon, Egan's frustration had about reached the point where he was ready to barge up to Barbier's room, with Agent Gonzalez in tow, kick down the door, and shout, 'There, that's him!' and then go fall into the nearest bed. Finally, shortly after twelve the elevator doors glided open for what seemed the thousandth time, and out walked Barbier. He looked crisp and well-rested – lousy bastard, Egan damned him, nudging the agent. The Frenchman in his heavy overcoat went down the front steps of the hotel and out. Then, lightheaded, Egan walked over to the desk and asked for a room.

At 4:30 that afternoon, Egan returned to the lobby, refreshed after a sound three-hour nap, a shower and a shave. Luis Gonzalez had been replaced by Jack Ripa. The agent looked sour. 'I hope you had a good rest,' he greeted the detective. 'You may be up all night. Barbier's lost.'

Ripa explained that when the Frenchman had left the Victoria around noontime Gonzalez followed him on foot down to the Edison. Barbier had entered through the main entrance on 47th Street and lingered in the hotel lobby only a few seconds, where he was seen by other detectives staked out on Jehan there. Then he ducked out the 46th Street exit, jumped into a taxi and disappeared before anybody could react.

Egan's eyes rolled in exasperation. 'Great!' he croaked. 'Well, we'll just have to stick here. What about the other Frog, and Patsy?'

'Quiet. Patsy's covered in his store. Nothing with Jehan at the Edison. Sonny is there with some of our people. We got a guy who speaks French next door with a bug on his room. The same as here.'

'Okay. Look, I'm gonna go out for a few minutes. I'll be back.' Egan went out onto Seventh Avenue. The frigid air braced him. Before he did anything else, he was going to his car and get a change of shoes; it could well be a long night again. He walked across Broadway toward the garage where he'd left his Corvair the previous afternoon, and there put on a well-worn, soft-soled pair of shoes kept in the trunk among assorted changes of clothes. Then he walked back toward the Victoria, stopping first at a corner lunch stand for two hot dogs and a Pepsi. It was about 5:05 P.M. when he returned to the hotel lobby. Ripa was stationed off in a corner, and when he saw Egan the agent shook his head. Egan nodded and sat in an armchair facing the stairs from the street.

A few minutes after seven, he saw Ripa summoned to the telephone at the assistant manager's desk. The agent conversed briefly, his eyes shifting to Egan. When he put down the phone, he strolled over to the detective.

'They just spotted Barbier again over at the Edison. He came back in the lobby from the same door he went out, looked around a minute, and went out on Forty-seventh. Jim Gildea's on him.'

'Probably coming back here.'

'We'll soon find out.'

At 7:25, Detective Gildea walked up the lobby stairs and came over to Egan. 'Barbier's downstairs in the bar having a drink.'

'Right. You stick up here with Jack Ripa, he's over by the desk. Watch the elevators. I'll go down and keep the Frenchman company.'

Egan went out the front entrance, bypassing the door to the bar off the lower lobby, and walked into the dimly lit Parasol Lounge from 51st Street. The place had a long curved bar which was about half filled, with booths along the 51st Street wall and tables in the back, most of which were occupied by couples or groups of men. He spotted Barbier alone at a small table next to the outside entrance. Egan went straight to the end of the bar, where he could follow any movement of the Frenchman's without looking directly at him. After ordering a shot of Seagram's 7 with ginger ale on the side; Egan sipped the ginger ale, tipping only a few drops of the whiskey into it. After about fifteen minutes, he was aware of a waiter at Barbier's table, and then Frog Two rose and walked toward the front of the lounge with his overcoat on his arm. In the lower lobby he turned up the steps to the main lobby. Egan paid his check and followed. When he got upstairs, Gildea was alone by the elevator bank.

'Ripa took him up,' he said, his eyes on the floor indicator over the closed elevator doors. 'Eleven – okay. Looks like he's in for a while.' Egan and, soon, Agent Ripa settled down in the Victoria lobby.

* * *

That morning, Patsy Fuca, who had been quiet all the previous day after dropping Jehan, had left his home on 67th Street in Brooklyn, driving his compact Buick. Agent Frank Waters, keeping a light tail, had followed him east on 65th Street all the way to Coney Island Avenue and then lost him in traffic.

Two and a half hours later, Patsy was observed by Detective Jimmy O'Brien entering Blair's Pike Slip Inn in lower Manhattan. At 3 P.M., Patsy left the bar, and the officer tailed him back to his store in Brooklyn. When he arrived, Detective Dick Auletta, sipping a Coke at the counter, heard Patsy's father-in-law tell Patsy in Italian that 'you-know-who' had telephoned to confirm that 'the meeting is on.'

But afternoon wore into night without Patsy making any move to leave the luncheonette. About 11 P.M., his brother Tony was seen arriving in his old, dusty Chevrolet station wagon. The two were in the store together for thirty minutes. At eleven-thirty, Patsy doused the lights and, coming out, locked up. Tony got back into his Chevy and drove off, followed by Agent Artie Fluhr, who later reported him safe at home in the Bronx.

Patsy, meanwhile, in his blue Buick, had headed into Manhattan, with Dick Auletta not far behind giving other unmarked radio cars at various points in Brooklyn and Manhattan a running report on the subject's itinerary. He drove across the Williamsburg Bridge ('He's going to the Lower East Side, maybe back to Blair's,' Auletta speculated); but at the Manhattan end Patsy turned north off Delancey Street instead of south toward Pike Slip; and at Houston Street he turned right again and, after a few blocks, swung onto the East River Drive. ('Everybody look alive. He's going uptown. Maybe the meet's at the Roosevelt again?')

This time, the trailing detective was proved correct. Patsy got off the Drive at 42nd Street, continued up to 45th, then went left and proceeded west as far as the Roosevelt, where, passing by the hotel entrance, he turned the corner and parked the Buick on Madison Avenue. Auletta turned the other way on Madison and parked across the avenue. He watched Patsy glance about with nervous caution and walk back around the corner to the Roosevelt's main entrance, where he joined two men standing under the marquee. One, of medium height, wearing a gray hat and a dark overcoat, was a stranger to Auletta. The other was about the same size, hatless, with a healthy shock of brown hair, and he *was* familiar to the detective: it was François Barbier, 'Frog Two.' Remembering that the last information he had heard was that Eddie Egan was on Barbier, Auletta radioed his observation to all cars.

At that moment, a car bearing Sonny Grosso and Frank Waters was also turning onto Madison Avenue, one block north and to the rear of Auletta. When Sonny heard the report that Patsy was now in front of the Roosevelt with two men, one of them Barbier, he chortled with anticipation. For he and Waters had just tailed Frog One, Jean Jehan, to the same location. Less than ten minutes earlier, at about 11:45 P.M., Jehan, inactive all day, had rushed from the Edison Hotel, carrying a blue valise, and hailed a cab. Sonny doffed his bellman's jacket, changed back into a jacket and overcoat, and ran outside to be picked up by Waters. The taxi had gone straight east on 46th Street and turned south on Madison, depositing Jehan at the corner of 45th opposite the Roosevelt. The tall Frenchman was now crossing the avenue toward the hotel.

'This could be it,' Sonny said to Waters, 'Patsy's got his French connection.'

'I don't know,' the agent mused, 'that doesn't look like any fifty kilos he's carrying in that bag.'

'Unless the tip was wrong. Or it could be just a sample.' Sonny threw open the car door. 'I'm gonna walk down to the corner and take a look.'

'Keep an eye out for Auletta,' Waters reminded him as Sonny strode away.

Coming within view of the Roosevelt entrance, he could see the four of them there, Jehan still holding the valise. Sonny tried to make out the fourth man, but the distance and the night shadows intensified by the bright lighting under the hotel marquee made identification difficult. He didn't think that he had seen the man before. The four, standing close together amid the trickle of people moving in and out of the hotel and the bustle of late commuters hurrying toward last trains at Grand Central Terminal, might have been a group of business associates separating after a night on the town. They were conversing animatedly now, and Patsy seemed to be doing much of the talking.

Then the sidewalk conclave broke, and they started walking abreast toward the corner. Sonny's wristwatch read 12:05 A.M. He turned and strolled back to Waters's car. The quartet had entered Patsy's little Buick, and it was pulling away from the curb, going uptown on Madison. Sonny grabbed the radiophone and alerted all cars. Waters moved out and at 45th Street began a screeching U-turn, only to jerk to a halt in the middle of the avenue to avoid colliding with a taxi. (Dick Auletta, who followed the same procedure between 45th and 44th, came back northbound to find himself blocked by a red light and crosstown traffic streaming west on 45th.) In those few seconds, Patsy's blue Buick was out of sight.

Sonny and Waters prowled the east midtown area, as did Auletta in his car as well as half a dozen others, hoping that one of them would regain contact with the fugitive Buick. Radios squawked with frantic exchanges among the searching officers: 'He was going up Madison.' 'Did anybody see him turn off?' 'Who's on Fifth Avenue?' 'Who's on Park?' 'Didn't ANYBODY see him?' Then, at just past 12:15 A.M., base reported: François Barbier had reentered the Victoria Hotel minutes before and was in his room.

'That's funny,' Waters commented as he cut off Madison on 53rd Street, toward the West Side.

'What?'

'We never did hear from Egan. Wasn't he supposed to be with Frog Two?'

'Yeah . . .' Sonny mused.

There was no trace of the blue Buick in the vicinity of 51st Street and Seventh Avenue, and the two were driving westbound again on 51st, listening glumly to the discouraged commentary from the various radio cars, when an authoritative voice broke in: 'This is Gaffney. I make Patsy's Buick at Fifty-seventh and Fifth. Somebody get up here!' Following the Federal regional director's terse directions, Waters raced up Fifth Avenue and east on 57th Street, and, back at Madison Avenue; going south, they overtook Gaffney's car, still behind Patsy.

There were only two others with Patsy in the blue compact now, Jehan and the unknown man, and for another half hour they continued to drive unpredictably through the elegant east midtown rectangle, crisscrossing streets, cutting corners haphazardly, moving uptown and down, east and west. But now other police vehicles had converged on the area, and they initiated their own complex in-and-out surveillance pattern, practiced many times before. This contrived to place at least one observing automobile waiting to pick up the subject car at the end of any block it chose to enter. Thus Patsy was not able to shake his stalkers again that night, if that was what he meant to do. To Grosso and Waters, who maintained the closest tail, it seemed that the three men were having a lively, even heated, discussion as they drove around. They had to be talking about the transaction, the detectives surmised: perhaps Patsy *didn't* have all the bread yet, and was trying to buy more time; or maybe they were arguing about the sample Jehan had 'fronted,' or put on display, if that was what was in the valise he'd brought. Maybe Jehan was short of the quantity Patsy needed right away. Or maybe it was true, as police stoolies had been suggesting, that there was some question about quality.

Finally, about 1 A.M., Patsy drove straight across 49th Street, turned south on Broadway, still garish and crowded, and stopped at the corner of 47th Street. Jean Jehan stepped from the Buick, *without* the blue valise, and picked his way among pedestrians toward the Edison, leaving only Patsy and the unidentified individual in the Buick. Sonny hopped out of Waters's car back near 48th Street and hustled after Frog One. Dick Auletta advised that he would park somewhere and meet Sonny in the hotel lobby.

Patsy, meanwhile, at the change of traffic signals, cut adroitly across the confluence of Broadway and Seventh Avenue, east on 46th, followed by Waters, now alone. But by the time the agent reached Avenue of the Americas (Sixth Avenue, always, to New Yorkers), two other cars were backing him up, Jimmy O'Brien in one and Sergeant Dan Leonard and Jim Hurley in another. Patsy drove uptown on Sixth, then, at 51st Street, west again. Waters and the other trailing officers speculated via radio that the trio was heading for the Hotel Victoria at the next corner. But a few hundred feet shy of Seventh Avenue, the little Buick slowed and drew up before the Abbey Hotel, situated on 51st adjacent to the Victoria. There, the other man got out and went directly inside, and Patsy accelerated away. Waters directed Leonard and Hurley to cover the Abbey, while he and O'Brien continued on after Patsy.

The blue valise was still in the car. Had they made the exchange?

Jim Hurley scrambled to the sidewalk and into the Abbey.

The man in the gray hat was waiting for an elevator. Hurley got on with him. The man was neatly dressed in a business suit and a striped tie. He was shorter than he had appeared from afar; wiry, dark, with a tan cast to his skin; late thirties or fortyish, the detective guessed. They rode in silence to the fourteenth floor, where the man stepped off. Hurley went up to fifteen, found an Exit staircase, and slipped down to fourteen. At the end of a corridor, the subject was just putting his key to a door. When the door closed behind him, Hurley sauntered down the corridor until he could see the room number, 1437. Hurley returned downstairs to the front desk, spoke with the night manager and learned that the newcomer was registered as J. Mouren, from Paris, France. Frog Number Three. He had checked in with a reservation just that previous afternoon of the eleventh. Hurley went out to Sergeant Leonard's car and radioed base that they were sitting on another Frenchman at the Hotel Abbey.

What had happened to Egan? If he was on Barbier, why hadn't he advised which way Patsy had headed during those demoralizing ten minutes when everybody lost the Buick and, it turned out, Barbier was being dropped off back at the Victoria? These questions had plagued Waters and particularly Sonny during their hectic chase after Patsy and the Frenchmen. It wasn't until later, when they had a chance to piece together events of the night, that they understood what really had happened.

Egan had spent the entire evening in the Victoria lobby. He had been composed enough for the first hour or so after Barbier had gone to his room around eight. But as nine o'clock became 9:30 and then 10 P.M., and the night continued to crawl on, he had grown increasingly edgy. He prowled the lobby, repeatedly checking the front desk to see if Barbier's key was still out, understanding it to be the custom of Europeans, unlike most Americans, to deposit their room keys whenever leaving a hotel. Barbier still had his key. Egan couldn't understand it; nobody was making any kind of move. His calls in to base radio every hour brought the same report each time – all suspects accounted for and quiet. He didn't like it.

His last call had been about 11:30 P.M. Shortly after midnight, the morning of Friday, January 12, as, unknown to him, his comrades were frantically trying to relocate the blue Buick bearing Patsy Fuca and the Frenchmen, Egan sprawled irritably on a plastic-covered divan in the lobby of the Victoria, trying to force himself to relax. Then, his eyes popped: coming up the stairs from the street, fully dressed in suit and heavy overcoat, his hair mussed by the wind outside, was François Barbier – who was supposed to be upstairs in his room all this time. Fascinated, Egan watched Frog Two cross the lobby and board an elevator without a glance about him.

Oh, God! Egan flayed himself, how long has *he* been out? Have I blown it? He sprang from the couch to the elevator bank, his eyes on the floor indicator. It stopped at eleven. Well, he's up there now at least. Glancing around, he saw the two young Federal agents who had relieved Jack Ripa staring at him anxiously.

Chapter Nine

NONE of the suspects stirred until after noon of Friday, January 12. Egan had finally gone home for a few hours to get some rest in his own bed and a change of clothes. But before leaving the Victoria he satisfied himself by figuring out how Barbier had eluded him the night before. One elevator, he discovered, in the hotel's bank of four went down below the lobby level to the Parasol Lounge at street level. Barbier obviously had taken this one and simply walked out through the bar.

At 12:30 P.M., Agent Jack Ripa and Detective Jim Gildea saw Frog Two leave the Victoria's front entrance and within seconds join a man who had sauntered out of the Abbey Hotel next door, Frog Three, J. Mouren. Trailed by both Ripa and Gildea, the two strolled east, across Sixth Avenue, and turned into Rockefeller Plaza. It was a clear, bright winter's day, the air brisk but not biting as it had been. The pair stopped by one of the stone and marble abutments encasing the sunken ice rink and gazed down at the colorfully dressed skaters circling and whirling to the festive amplified music.

After about ten minutes, Barbier and Mouren eased out of the group of cheery lunchtime spectators and made their way across the narrow street to the RCA building. Ripa and Gildea moved quickly to keep the Frogs in view in the milling concourses inside. The Frenchmen seemed in no hurry, just two more tourists – until suddenly they darted into an elevator corridor. The officers sprinted toward the corner turned by the subjects, but they were too late. Barbier and Mouren already were ascending into the massive RCA building's complex maze of floors, corridors, offices, stairways, elevators and, to be sure, exits.

At about that same moment, out near 67th Street in Brooklyn, Eddie Egan, looking and feeling chipper once again, sat in his Corvair with Agent Artie Fluhr, waiting for Patsy Fuca to do something. Patsy had not left his house all morning, since his return about 2 A.M. from the running meeting with the Frenchmen.

Just before 1 P.M., both Patsy and Barbara appeared on the white iron-railed porch of their house, he wearing a suburban coat and she a short furry car coat. They got into their blue and white Oldsmobile parked outside.

'Patsy must love blue,' Egan said. 'This car is blue, his other one is blue, inside the house they have blue. So what's with blue?'

They followed the Oldsmobile onto the Gowanus Expressway and up to the Williamsburg section, where Patsy and his wife went to their luncheonette, which was being tended by Barbara's father. Egan checked with base radio and learned that his friend Barbier had managed to fade again, taking the newcomer, Mouren, with him this time. Otherwise, nothing was doing.

'That Barbier is something else,' Egan remarked to Fluhr. 'Here we got two, three hundred cops all over the place, and he still loses us three times in twenty-four hours. Now *there's* a guy who's been around the track!'

'You think he feels heat?' the agent asked.

'He might. They all might. They might not, too. Guys like these bums, they're so used to looking over their shoulders, lots of times they see things that aren't even there. They'd duck behind a tree if they were alone on a desert island. But as long as we don't push them too hard, chances are they'll go right ahead with their plans as though nobody *is* watching them.'

'So what we have to do is not lose them and just wait until we see which way they jump.'

After about a half hour, Patsy and Barbara came out of the store and reentered their Olds. They drove back busy Grand Avenue and up onto the Williamsburg Bridge toward New York. As he had the night before, Patsy cut off Delancey to Houston Street and swung into the uptown lanes of the East River Drive. But this time he ignored the 42nd Street exit and continued up the East River Drive to 61st Street, where he turned off. He made a right on York Avenue, going north. At the near corner of 79th Street, the Oldsmobile stopped, and Patsy backed into a parking space on the east side of York. Egan drove past and pulled into a space just beyond 79th. As he watched in the rearview mirror, Patsy stepped out of his car and crossed 79th, walking up York toward them; Barbara remained in the Olds.

Fluhr unfolded a newspaper and held it up to read, hiding his face, while Egan, porkpie hat low on his forehead, studied the storefronts along York Avenue. It was an old, established neighborhood of apartments and small shops.

Patsy went by them, striding along at an easy pace. When he reached 80th Street, Egan slid out of the Corvair. 'I'll see you,' he said. Then he thrust his head back into the window: 'Tell the people where we are.'

Patsy went another block to 81st, where he turned right and walked the block to a modern apartment house on the northeast corner of 81st and East End. It was difficult for Egan to place a thug like Patsy in this fashionable neighborhood of tall luxury apartments, many of them exclusive cooperatives – the sort of area where the high-rise buildings had their own private underground garages, where personal chauffeurs wore black and maids in tiny white hats actually walked miniature poodles. Only a few blocks north on the avenue was Carl Shurz Park, a strip of woodland overlooking the East River, the setting for Gracie Mansion, long the home of New York's mayors.

Patsy entered the corner building, No. 45 East End Avenue. Egan waited a minute or two, then he entered the richly furnished lobby. There was no one there, but the elevator was in operation. He watched the floor indicator halt at fifteen, and went out to check the resident directory, just inside the front door. He recognized none of the names listed on the fifteenth floor, but then, Patsy could just as easily have stepped off there and walked up or down to another floor. Why Patsy's sudden visit to such a place, which he hadn't been near in the months the police had had him under surveillance? The detective ambled back across the avenue and waited on the far corner of 81st Street.

After about fifteen minutes, Patsy emerged from No. 45 and walked back to his car three blocks away. He chatted with his wife for a moment before starting the motor and heading downtown on the drive, back to Brooklyn.

While Egan and Fluhr were heading back downtown on the East River Drive behind Patsy Fuca, Frog One, Jean Jehan, was stirring for the first time that day. At 2:45 P.M. he appeared in the lobby of the Edison, dressed for the outdoors. In the lobby, or in the immediate vicinity, were Detectives Sonny Grosso and Dick Auletta and Agent Frank Waters.

Jehan left the hotel on 47th Street, walked up Broadway to 51st Street, and thence east. He moved gracefully, apparently savoring the crisp January air, looking every inch like an accomplished man of the world. He crossed Seventh Avenue, but instead of going to the Victoria Hotel or the Abbey, as the officers expected, he entered the Hotel Taft, on the corner of 51st Street directly opposite those hotels where his compatriots had rooms.

Jehan went to the barbershop in the lobby and had his shoes shined. Then he bought a newspaper at the hotel newsstand and settled himself on a circular red-leather banquette in the center of the lobby. The three officers who had followed him from the Edison roamed about, one stopping at a telephone to report to headquarters on the current whereabouts of Frog One. The police had trained their primary attention upon Jehan, who exuded the importance of being the key figure in the conspiracy, whatever that conspiracy might prove to be. They were convinced that when the break came it would evolve out of action originated by Jehan.

Frog One sat calmly reading the New York *Journal-American*. He was absorbed in a front page story, one in a series by ace crime reporter Jim Horan, exposing the spread of narcotics addiction in the metropolitan area. Over the next half hour a dozen more detectives and Federal agents drifted into the Taft lobby, all believing that action was imminent. Some were dressed rather oddly. A winter track and field meet was beginning that afternoon at Madison Square Garden, and midtown hotels were crowded with amateur athletes representing colleges and athletic clubs from throughout the country. To observers, then, it might not have appeared strange that a number of agile-looking young men wearing sneakers and baggy gray sweatsuits, with shirt fronts bearing the names of various amateur athletic organizations, were gathered in the lobby of this particular hotel, which long had been popular with tourist groups.

The 'athletes' milled about, as did the other officers in normal street attire, all trying to keep Jehan under observation without daring to look directly at him. Then, at 3:30

P.M., there was a sudden sensation that something was wrong. Incredibly, Frog One had vanished from within their midst! No one had seen him make a move. The hotel lobby became a buzz of confused excitement, with shouts of 'Where the hell did he go?' and 'He was right here a minute ago!' Even more embarrassing, perhaps, than the fact that the suave Jehan had slipped away from under their very noses was the likelihood that he'd seen through their disguises, which now seemed a little silly, and was aware of the massive surveillance being directed at him.

Actually, however, the situation was not as bad as it appeared in those first moments. Jehan had in fact managed somehow to walk through the front door of the hotel without detection, but outside he was spotted by Jimmy O'Brien and Jack Ripa. They followed him as he window-shopped casually on Broadway; then, about 4 P.M., he bought a ticket to the Trans-Lux newsreel theater at 49th Street and Broadway. When he went inside, O'Brien hurried back to the Taft to advise Sonny and the others of Frog One's whereabouts, while Ripa waited outside the theater, dividing his attention between the entrance and the fire exit.

A small mob of narcotics agents soon gathered outside the Trans-Lux. Sonny, O'Brien and Ripa went in. Taking pains not to appear obvious in the half-full theater, they tried to single out Jehan – but they could not spot him. Back outside on Broadway, they were trying to decide what to do next, when the chief of the Federal agents, George Gaffney, arrived.

Gaffney was a diminutive, wiry veteran investigator who rarely allowed himself to be derailed by momentary setbacks. When Ripa and Sonny outlined the predicament, Gaffney said, 'Let's go back in.' Positioning the others in the rear, Gaffney doffed his hat and coat, padded briskly down the center aisle as far as the front row, then, like any theater manager, turned and walked back up the aisle, glancing right and left as though counting the house.

When he rejoined the waiting detectives, Gaffney whispered: 'He's in the sixth row, seventh seat on the right.' And he put on his hat and coat and left.

Soon, half a dozen agents were seated all around Jean Jehan, watching the Trans-Lux newsreels.

By the time Frog One came out of the Trans-Lux at 6:30 P.M., Eddie Egan had rejoined the dozen detectives and agents strung around the theater. Earlier, Egan had followed Patsy and Barbara Fuca back to their home neighborhood in Brooklyn, where Patsy went shopping for sports clothes at a men's shop while his wife was in the beauty parlor. When Agent Jim Bailey showed up to assist, Egan left the Fucas to him and Artie Fluhr and headed back to midtown. He prowled around the Victoria and Abbey hotels, but agents staked out at those hotels reported no trace yet of either Barbier or Mouren. Other teams of detectives had the Edison and Taft hotels covered, as well as the Roosevelt. In addition, not only were Patsy's home, the luncheonette and his parents' house on 7th Street on twenty-four-hour watch, but also the tenement where the Travatos lived, four blocks from Patsy and Barbara; Tony Fuca's apartment in the Bronx; and the area downtown around the Pike Slip Inn. It was hard to imagine any of the principals making a move without the police being aware of it and reacting instantly. And as far as all were concerned, the 'principals' were Patsy and Jehan.

Emerging from the Trans-Lux, Jehan appeared perfectly cast for the neon-splatted make-believe of nighttime Broadway. He was a stage figure almost larger than life, a supremely confident supporting player out for a breath of air after dress rehearsal. Egan and Sonny almost admired the man, he was so cool and assured.

They wondered what he was thinking as he paused at the corner of 49th Street, glancing about so diffidently, and then walked through the crowds down Broadway, with his cane swinging. Had he in fact recognized the surveillance, or was he merely taking normal precautions by diverting to a newsreel theater for two and a half hours? Or had he purposely withdrawn himself from circulation while the two missing Frenchmen culminated the deal? The fact that Patsy had been covered all day seemed to remove the latter possibility, but then Patsy had escaped observation for at least fifteen minutes in that apartment building up at East End Avenue. Barbier and Mouren might have met him there and made the exchange. And what about that blue valise last night? What was in it, and what had happened to it? Full of questions and doubts, Eddie and Sonny, with the unseen agents around them, followed Frog One back to the Edison Hotel.

There, Jehan checked the mail desk for messages, but there were none for him. He looked at his watch; it was 6:45 P.M. He walked to the 46th Street exit and, outside, waved down a taxi. While Sonny stayed behind at the Edison, Egan and Frank Waters, who had been in the lobby when they arrived with Jehan, ran out to Waters's car and went after the Frenchman.

The cab led them straight across midtown to Third Avenue, where it turned north, then, at 52nd Street, made a right, stopping midway toward Second Avenue in front of a restaurant called La Cloche d'Or. Egan and Waters, having watched Jehan enter the restaurant from the corner of Third Avenue, walked along the opposite side of 52nd Street until they came abreast of the place. There was a fairly good view into the small, cozy-looking, French-rustic style café. Jehan was being seated alone at a table for two, and the host, with a slight bow, was handing him a menu.

'Could be a meet,' Waters said.

'Maybe. Anyway, it looks like he'll be here for a while. Have you eaten, Frank?'

'Not lately.'

'Why don't you grab a bite?' Egan suggested. 'I had a sandwich before. I can stay here.'

'I think I'll do that. See you later,' the agent said as he returned to his car.

Egan strolled to Second Avenue, then came back past La Cloche d'Or to Third Avenue, and finally he folded himself into the shadows of a brownstone structure across from the restaurant and lit a cigarette, shielding the flame of his Zippo with his hand.

At the Edison, Sonny Grosso also had taken time for some nourishment at the coffee shop. His stomach had started acting up again as it always did as tension built in a case. Intestinal rumblings and a little queasiness had warned him of an impending case of the diarrhea that had embarrassed and almost incapacitated him on several previous occasions. So he indulged himself in a cheeseburger, tossed green salad and two large glasses of milk. He remembered his mother often saying that milk 'bound up a loose stomach.'

By 7:30 Sonny was back in the Edison lobby. Agents covering the hotel reported no further word on Jehan since Frank Waters's signal that Eddie Egan had the Frenchman at the restaurant on East 52nd Street. Sonny decided to go over and keep his partner company. He left the hotel and walked to his white Oldsmobile convertible, which he had left parked on 47th Street near Eighth Avenue. Warming up the engine, he flicked on the portable radiophone. Somebody was reporting on Patsy Fuca.

'—in his blue Buick on Grand Avenue. Traffic is heavy, a lot of shoppers out. Now he looks like he's heading for the

Williamsburg Bridge.' There was a staticky pause . . . 'That's it, the bridge. He's going into Manhattan again. Anybody around Pike Slip?' A brief gaggle of voices confirmed that Patsy's favorite hangout was under wraps. Sonny reached for the mike. 'Cloudy here. Who's on him, kay?'

'Fluhr and Bailey.'

'Artie: he's by himself, right?'

'He's alone.'

Sonny listened as the agents crossed the East River behind Patsy. 'Coming off the bridge now, on Delancey Street. Oh-oh, he's going right, uptown. Turning on Houston, approaching the Drive, yeah, he's going uptown on the Drive.'

Back to the Roosevelt? Sonny asked himself. Why not? That was where he had met the Frenchmen each of the past two days.

'Cloudy again. I'm on the west side by the Edison. I'm going to start moving east. I think he may be going to the Roosevelt again. Give a yell the minute he gets off the Drive.'

Sonny turned the corner of Eighth Avenue, went north one block, then east on 48th Street. As he negotiated the stream of crosstown traffic, the metallic radio voice of Artie Fluhr continued to relate Patsy's progress: 'Past Fourteenth, past Twenty-third . . .' Sonny wished Egan and Waters were with him. 'Passing Thirty-fourth now. He's moving along pretty good, traffic's light here. He's getting over in the left lane, looks like he's going to get off at Forty-second.' Sonny had reached Fifth Avenue on 48th. He waited for confirmation. 'That's it: Forty-second Street!' Fluhr cried. 'All cars in the vicinity,' Sonny broadcast, 'get in position around the Roosevelt.'

He raced across Fifth Avenue over to Madison and, cutting downtown to 45th, opposite the Roosevelt, drew over to the curb just short of the corner and doused his lights. The streets were busy with pedestrians, but there was nobody familiar to him outside the Roosevelt. '. . . continuing west on forty-fifth,' Fluhr reported. Sonny peered beyond the hotel into darkened 45th Street, trying to wish Patsy into view. It was eight o'clock. A bus stopped at the corner of the Roosevelt and left its rear sticking out into the crosswalk, blocking his view of the hotel entrance.

At the other corner, on the south side of 45th, a man in hat and overcoat paced outside a public telephone booth occupied by another man. Sonny marked the nervous one as a home-bound commuter anxious to reach his wife.

Then Sonny rolled down the left window and stared. *Sonofabitch!* Frog Three! And Barbier was the one in the booth! He snatched the radio mike: 'Cloudy here, at Forty-fifth and Madison. Guess who I found? The two missing Frogs! They must be waiting for our boy.'

'. . . approaching the Hotel Roosevelt,' Artie Fluhr signaled. Sonny glanced away from the telephone booth. A car was nearing the front of the Roosevelt. As it came into the bright glow from the marquee, he recognized Patsy's blue Buick. A couple of other sets of headlights followed half a block behind, one of which had to be Fluhr and Bailey. Patsy swerved to a stop by a fire hydrant next to the telephone booth near the corner. Mouren tapped on the glass pane, alerting Barbier, then walked around the front of the compact and climbed into the rear seat. Patsy's head swiveled in every direction. He doesn't like sitting there any longer than necessary, Sonny thought. In a moment, the booth went dark as Barbier emerged and got into the car beside Patsy. The signal light had just changed to green, and the Buick spurted across Madison, westbound on 45th Street.

Sonny quickly looked for the car carrying the two agents who had trailed Patsy from Brooklyn. He spotted it almost at the intersection of Madison. Sonny snapped, 'Artie!' and simultaneously flashed his headlights, 'you guys hang back while I take them. Pull into that space they just left. I'll flash you whichever way they go. Everybody else stand by.'

Sonny turned right into 45th. Patsy's Buick ahead was waiting for a light at Fifth Avenue. The signal changed, and the compact made a left, heading downtown. Sonny just beat the light and came up behind them as Patsy, left directional blinking, waited out opposing traffic before turning into 44th Street. 'They're going into Forty-fourth back toward Madison,' Sonny radioed the other police cars in the area. He could picture Fluhr and Bailey leaving their spot opposite the Roosevelt and pulling around to the corner of 44th and Madison.

The Buick, however, maneuvered into a space midway between Fifth and Madison. Sonny also edged in to the curb well to their rear. The three men got out and Patsy locked the car doors. They walked across the street to a bar-restaurant called the Game Cock, a beamed English pub-style bar that Sonny knew to be a favorite of advertising and publishing people in the Grand Central district. At eight-fifteen on a Friday evening, the place was crowded with junior executive types. A few were flirting with pretty, fashionable young editorial assistants or secretaries. Patsy and the Frenchmen found a booth and were ordering drinks, while Sonny managed to wriggle some elbowroom at the end of the bar. He asked for a sweet vermouth on the rocks.

The subjects were seated around a semicircular table, bent forward over their cocktails, heads together, talking earnestly. Sonny, sipping his sweet wine sparingly, cast only an occasional glance in their direction. He thought more about the deployment of police vehicles that he hoped was taking place outside. After about fifteen minutes, Patsy stood, looked around and made his way to the rear of the bar, where he entered a telephone booth. He was on the phone for about ten minutes; Sonny saw him deposit at least one additional coin. Then he returned to the table and resumed the intent discussion with the two Frogs. It must have been growing heated, for Sonny could see Patsy gesticulating as he made a point and Barbier and Mouren responding in kind. They paused to order another round, Patsy a highball and the Frenchmen brandy in snifters. Ten minutes or more later, Patsy again rose and went back to the telephone. They seem to have problems, Sonny thought. So they couldn't have set the deal yet.

On 52nd Street, between Third and Second avenues, Eddie Egan's conviction that Jean Jehan was waiting for someone in La Cloche d'Or had waned considerably. The detective, first standing next to the stairs of the brownstone across the street, then pacing the block, had been sure that Frog One must be keeping a prearranged appointment at the little French restaurant. But he had just sat there, alone, apparently savoring the various courses served him, a small bottle of wine at his hand. Nobody had approached him other than the maître d'hôtel and a waitress. Once, about eight o'clock, he had arisen and moved out of Eddie's view, returning, still alone, after several minutes; it could have been a trip to the men's room, or perhaps a telephone call. Since then, he had not stirred, concentrating with leisurely care on the food and drink before him. A little after eight, Frank Waters had come back and informed Egan about the new tail on Patsy, who had picked up the missing Frogs. They waited together out of sight across from La Cloche d'Or.

Now it was eight fifty-five, and Egan had gone through almost an entire package of Camels, when Jehan appeared about to leave. Smiling and nodding graciously, he paid his check, gathered himself together and stepped out into 52nd

Street. Drawing a deep and apparently satisfied breath, he strolled west, toward Third Avenue. Egan and Waters followed separately, glad at last to be going *some place.*

The question of *what* place, however, remained unanswered. For Jehan wandered slowly and without apparent aim toward the West Side. He paused here and there to glance into windows of luxury auto showrooms on Park Avenue and the elegant shops along 57th Street. At Fifth Avenue he turned up toward the Park and strolled diagonally through Grand Army Plaza, its great fountain and pale statuary softly lit, a courtyard in front of the majestic Hotel Plaza.

Here it is, thought Egan, watching from the corner of Bonwit Teller's at 58th Street: he's meeting somebody right here in the open. He gestured to Waters, across Fifth Avenue. But then Jehan started walking again. No, Egan guessed, he's going into the Plaza. But Frog One went by the hotel's entrance, its broad steps crowded with smartly dressed people awaiting transportation, and turned the corner onto Central Park South.

Egan grew irritable. How much do these creeps like to walk? How far are they going to make *me* walk? When the hell is the breakout? Jehan led them to the next intersection, where he stood a moment outside the Hotel St. Moritz before continuing south on Avenue of the Americas. When Egan came around the corner, waving Waters on, Jehan was almost across 58th Street. On the far sidewalk he hesitated, then detoured toward a brightly lit bar on 58th, a few steps off the Avenue. He looked in the window a few seconds and then went inside.

The place was called the Thunderbird. From a vantage point across the street, Egan, joined now by Waters, could see that the bar was practically empty, although it was ten o'clock. Frog One had seated himself at the bar and ordered a drink. The only other customer Egan could see was a flashily dressed blonde with a gaudy bouffant hairdo a few seats along the bar. Jehan had spotted her too, and was eying her, smiling and raising his glass.

'Now who's *this* broad?' Egan pondered.

'She looks like a hooker,' said Waters.

They waited in the street until several more customers had entered and the place didn't look so barren, then pushed through the door themselves. Jehan by this time was perched next to the blonde. They were engrossed in what appeared to be amused repartee. Egan and Waters took a tiny table at the rear of the lounge, where the lighting was dimmer, and ordered two ryes and gingers and some pretzels. Egan went to the telephone and advised base as to Frog One's current location. He was told that for the past hour, since 9 P.M., Patsy Fuca, with the other two Frenchmen, had led some twenty cars full of police and Federal agents an exasperating chase throughout midtown.

Egan returned to the table and had scarcely finished bringing Waters up to date, when a familiar face popped through the door from the street, Dick Auletta. He picked them out at once and advanced through the bar, passing behind the Frenchman and the woman. Auletta leaned over the two at the rear table.

'Sit down,' Egan offered.

'I can't. I just wanted to see if anybody else came in here, Patsy or the other two Frogs.'

Waters stiffened. 'Don't tell me they're completely lost?'

'Naw. My partner and I just lost them around here somewhere, and I heard you guys were in here. We got about eighteen or twenty cars on them. Somebody will pick 'em up.'

'What the hell are they up to?' Egan asked.

'Damned if I know,' Auletta shook his head. 'Well, I'm

gonna go back to the hounds.' He glanced guardedly toward the bar. 'I see the old fox is making out. Need any help?' he asked Egan.

'No, I don't figure what he's up to either, but he's been easy so far. Me and Frank will handle him.'

But Waters stood up. 'Eddie, if you don't mind, I think I'll tag along with Dick a while. I'll be back later.'

Auletta and Waters went out, leaving Egan alone to watch Jean Jehan.

Sonny Grosso was perplexed and upset. Since leaving the Game Cock on 44th Street about 9 P.M., Patsy and his friends had run everybody ragged. As soon as Patsy had finished his second telephone call, they paid their check and went out to the Buick. In a minute, Sonny followed. Waiting for him in the doorway of a shoe store next door was Special Agent Ben Fitzgerald, and together they walked rapidly to Sonny's car up the block. Fitz, florid-faced, his eyes bright behind his glasses, told him that the area was saturated with detectives, some on foot, most in automobiles.

As he had the night before, when he had succeeded temporarily in throwing off pursuit, Patsy wheeled his compact around onto Madison Avenue and sped northward. But this time there were too many trackers for even as skillful a driver as Patsy to outsmart. Radiophones churned out rapid-fire bursts: 'There he is!' . . . 'I got him . . . Pick him up at Fifth' . . . 'Somebody take him off Fifty-fourth . . . We're on him . . . Who's at Park and Forty-ninth?'

The radio frequency used by police officers in surveillance situations was a well-kept secret. A Mafia Don did once steal a police portable radio transmitter, but the organization lacked the electronic expertise needed to modify the set to pick up the new frequency to which the police quickly changed when the theft was discovered. Thus the narcotics officers could broadcast in the clear, although they never used subjects' names.

'He's headed west on Forty-seventh . . .' came over the air; and the combined force of police and government agents built a complex structure of surveillance. One car would follow the Buick a block, then turn off, and another car, approaching at right angles to the direction of flight, would swing after Patsy; or the Buick would make a turn, and the trailing police car would continue on, but yet another would already be in the block Patsy had just entered, waiting to take up pursuit. It was tricky, but given experience, instinct and daring, it worked. Nevertheless, Patsy made it exciting, and at times perilous. He drove like a Hollywood stunt man, in and out of streets, up and down avenues, twice around whole city blocks. Surveillance cars were all but running into one another at intersections, maneuvering to get out of Patsy's way as well as that of other police cars.

The chase had been going on at a frantic pace for nearly two hours. In all that time, Patsy never left the area of midtown Manhattan circumscribed by 42nd Street to the south, Broadway to the west, 57th Street to the north and Third Avenue to the east, roughly a hundred square blocks. By ten forty-five, Sonny felt he would go out of his mind if the chase continued. He and Fitzgerald must have been through every one of those hundred blocks. Together with Waters, who had joined the chase with Dick Auletta, Sonny masterminded the mobile surveillance. They hadn't lost the Buick, but what disturbed Sonny more and more as the night grew later was the question of Patsy's intentions: Was he actually trying to shake the tail? Or were he and his companions running through an incredible elaborate 'rehearsal,' a dry run? Or were they playing games, enjoying themselves at the cops' expense? And there was the recurring doubt: while they played the decoys, was the deal being made somewhere else, perhaps by persons not even suspected by the police as yet?

Sonny's speculations ground slowly to a halt, as, just before 11 P.M., for the first time in an hour the blue Buick continued in one direction for more than a few blocks. From Sixth Avenue, Patsy turned east on 46th Street, and now he had crossed Fifth, Madison, Park and Lexington avenues and was still going east. Oddly, the straight path was the one weakness in the sophisticated police logistics; it eliminated the effectiveness of a number of cars going in different directions and critically reduced the number able to adjust to follow directly in Patsy's wake.

At Second Avenue, the blue compact made a sharp right and raced downtown. Patsy lucked through several changing lights and cheated on some others, and as he passed 34th Street, still on Second Avenue, from what Sonny and Fitz could make out from garbled, conflicting radio transmissions only they and another car bearing Jimmy O'Brien and Jack Ripa had managed to stay close to Patsy and the Frenchmen. But the others were coming now.

At 24th Street, Sonny saw Patsy swerve left toward the East River. This was an area of old, sooty-gray brick tenements – it was in fact the street where Sonny's parents had lived when he was born. But Sonny had little opportunity to entertain nostalgia. Patsy halted the Buick down at the corner of 24th and First Avenue, facing the Veterans Hospital and the downtown perimeter of the big Bellevue medical complex. His passengers stepped out, and even as the door slammed shut, the Buick was hurtling around the corner and up First Avenue. 'Who's got Patsy?' Fitz yelled into the radiophone. Sonny had stopped the Olds on the dimly lit street about two thirds of the way toward First Avenue, watching the Frenchmen. 'He's off Twenty-fourth and going back uptown on First!'

'We'll take him,' Jimmy O'Brien responded as he and Ripa whisked past in their car.

Sonny got out. Barbier and Mouren had walked a couple of dozen yards back along 24th Street and gone into a dingy bar on the north side of the street. The detective walked down the opposite sidewalk. He stopped by a ramshackled old grocery store, still open, across from the bar whose only identification was a red neon BAR over the entrance. The windows of the place were opaque, so he couldn't tell what the Frogs were doing – having a drink after their prolonged excursion in Patsy's hands, relieving themselves or telephoning someone. Wondering suddenly what his partner Egan was doing with the other Frog, Jehan, Sonny went into the grocery. The smell was Italian, like home. He picked out a vanilla cupcake and asked for a Coke. Then he went to the store window and, tearing the cellophane wrapping off the cake, focused upon the door under BAR.

He'd had only one bite out of the cupcake and a gulp of Coke when the two Frenchmen came out. They walked to the corner of First Avenue. Sonny withdrew further into the store. The men seemed to be looking down First. Barbier raised an arm, and presently a taxi stopped alongside them. Sonny put the soda and cake down and dashed outside. Waving to Fitz to pick him up, he ran down to the corner to watch the cab as it continued north on First Avenue.

Barking directions into the radio mike as Fitz drove, Sonny traced the route of the Frogs' cab, across town to the West Side, up Eighth Avenue to the interstate Port Authority Bus Terminal at 41st Street. As they went, Fitz told him that O'Brien was tailing Patsy downtown toward his Lower East Side haunts.

Barbier and Mouren scrambled from their taxi into the bus terminal. Grimly aware that the huge, bustling pavilion, a full block square with countless exits, had often been exploited as an escape hatch by individuals fleeing detection, Sonny and Fitz jolted to a stop at a hack stand and dashed after the Frenchmen. They could only pray that other cars were now arriving in the vicinity. The main concourse of the terminal was crowded by orderly turmoil of Friday night stay-outs herding this way and that for late buses to New Jersey. Sonny spied Barbier and Mouren groping and dodging toward an exit on 40th Street. Swiveling to Fitz, he pointed to them and shouted, 'Get the car!' and without a break in his stride he pushed his way through the flow of commuters after the two Frogs. But before Sonny burst onto the sidewalk on 40th Street, Barbier and Mouren had clambered into another taxi and shot off east.

Swearing breathlessly, Sonny ran to the corner of Eighth Avenue, where Fitz was having trouble backing the car down the one-way avenue against traffic. Trembling with anger and excitement, Sonny jumped out onto the street, waving his arms, trying to stay oncoming vehicles so that Fitz would have a chance to swing around on 40th.

What Sonny didn't know at that instant was that the tail *was* still intact. In response to Sonny's urgent radio directions, Lieutenant Vinnie Hawkes had arrived at the scene at almost the same time as Sonny and Fitz and had driven around the terminal, checking the exits. As he came back east on 40th along the south side of the building, he had seen Barbier and Mouren dash out and pull away in the cab. Hawkes shouted the news into his radio and took out after them. Sonny learned this as he finally rejoined Fitz and was wheeling his Oldsmobile across 40th Street. All they could do now was follow Hawkes's continuing reports.

The Frenchmen's cab took them to Grand Central Terminal. Hawkes had stayed close all the way. Now, as the subjects crossed 42nd and entered the giant railroad terminal at the corner of Vanderbilt Avenue, the lieutenant parked outside the New York Convention & Visitors Bureau under the Park Avenue viaduct spanning 42nd Street and dodged traffic across to the entrance.

Barbier and Mouren behaved now as if they were unobserved. At the bottom of the ramp into the main terminal, they stopped at a cigar stand to buy early editions of the *Daily News* and the *Herald Tribune*, then ambled down another ramp toward the lower level. They could have been a couple of old friends on their way to a train for the suburbs. They're feeling cool, Hawkes thought, a respectable distance behind – maybe we're getting lucky for a change. By now, he imagined, cars would be coming from all over, blanketing Grand Central. It occurred to Hawkes that the load of junk might well be in a locker in the terminal. All this driving and running around tonight could have been to pass a locker key.

However, the subjects didn't go to a storage locker, or to a train. They went into the Oyster Bar, a large counter-type restaurant midway between the main and lower levels that is popular with commuters and late-nighters. Hawkes lingered outside for a few minutes, window-browsing at a locked bookstall. The Frenchmen sat down at one of the counters and ordered. At the entrance to the station's lower level a young man had materialized, lounging near a flower stall, reading a newspaper – a Fed. Okay. Hawkes ambled into the Oyster Bar.

The Frogs weren't there.

Hawkes was startled only a moment. At the rear of the Oyster Bar was a glass door leading to a cocktail lounge, and from there, he remembered another exit into the terminal. That's where they went – the bastards, he swore to himself. He went into the almost empty cocktail lounge and then walked to the men's room outside. They were not in there, either.

After some time the word spread among the officers now strung throughout and around Grand Central that the Frogs had managed to slip through the net, and gloom descended. The lieutenant tried to console Sonny. 'So they're lost for a while. They've ducked before. Their hotels are covered. Both of them will probably turn up there soon.'

'I wonder,' Sonny murmured.

'Well, we've still got the other Frenchman, and Patsy, and they're the big fish, right?'

'I hope so.' Egan apparently was still sitting on Jehan at that bar on 58th Street; *that* was a consolation. When Popeye wrapped himself around anybody, he was like a sticky snake. Patsy seemed to be under control, too. Ripa and O'Brien had reported that he had driven all the way downtown to his old neighborhood, parked the Buick near his grandmother's house on squalid Henry Street and entered a supposedly vacant storefront where, the police knew, high-stake poker games frequently went on all night behind darkened windows curtained with burlap. Six more cars of men, including Frank Waters, had reinforced Ripa and O'Brien in the area. Patsy still was inside, or so they assumed.

'I think I'll take a run downtown and see what's happening with Patsy,' he said at last to his boss.

'Okay. But keep in touch,' replied Hawkes, giving his arm a friendly squeeze.

As he drove southward on the East River Drive, the only ray of hope Sonny could think of was that his partner was still on Jehan.

Eddie Egan heard about the loss of Frogs Two and Three when he made one of his periodic calls to base radio about 1 A.M., Saturday, January 13. Up to that point, the detective had been growing progressively more impatient with the assignment he had chosen. It had begun to appear that Jean Jehan had no other significant purpose that night than to try to secure a bed companion for himself, drink, and spend money. By Egan's calculations, in about three hours Frog One must have laid out seventy-five dollars on the Thunderbird bar in support of the continental charm which he was lavishing upon the hard-looking blonde. He was engaged in a persistent campaign of persuasion that she either accompany him back to his hotel or else take him to her own place. She kept playing it coy – probably figuring she had a live one in the old Frenchman, Egan had concluded early. If anything passed between the two this night, Jehan was going to pay heavily for it.

Egan had grown progressively more bored and fatigued, until he learned from base the stunning news about the escape of the other Frenchmen. His immediate reaction was that Barbier and Mouren might be headed to the Thunderbird to meet Jehan, and all at once his flagging interest in the subject at the bar heightened considerably.

Several times during the evening, the detective had switched his location in the place, alternating from his rear table to a corner of the bar, on the fringe of a small cluster of male customers who had come in; later, he moved to another table up front, then went back to a different spot at the bar. This was all to minimize chances of Frog One happening to notice a red-haired, beefy stranger fixed in one position all the while he'd been in the Thunderbird.

Not that Jehan was paying much attention to his surroundings. Gradually, over the next hour and a half, he seemed to become lost in a fog of intoxication blended of both alcohol and desire, while the blonde played him out beautifully. During this time, Egan himself dallied with a buxom brunette of about thirty-five who had come in and sat at the bar near him, obviously trying to be picked up. His new companion, who said her name was Sonya, tried to entice him to her 'place,' a third-rate hotel on West 58th Street, but he put her off by insisting he couldn't leave right now, there was some guy he had to meet. How about later? By then, it was nearly three.

Sonya said she had an 'appointment' herself about three, but she ought to be free in a half hour or so. They could get together again then, and maybe think up something to do? Her mouth and eyes showed well-rehearsed hunger as she dictated her address, which he scrawled on a cocktail napkin. And then to be sure he remembered the message, she stood and leaned against him, soft belly urging his arm, fingers caressing the inside of his thigh, and her tongue fluttered quickly in his mouth.

Egan was relieved when she had gone. As detached as he thought he was, he had been aroused. He went to the telephone again. Base reported that nothing had changed: the two Frenchmen still were missing, Patsy was still staked out down at Henry Street. They did advise him that Dick Auletta now was in his car outside the Thunderbird, which Egan was glad to hear. If Jehan and the blonde happened to leave separately, he wanted Auletta to check her out.

Time crawled toward three-thirty. Egan's hopes about Barbier and Mouren dissipated. Jehan was getting too sloppy for business. Only one other couple remained in the Thunderbird aside from Egan and Jehan and his friend, and the detective was thinking he had better leave. Frog One was heavy-eyed and almost incoherent as he alternated between fumbling with his cognac and his change at the bar. Egan guessed that by now Jehan had blown close to a hundred and forty dollars in five and a half hours, and he now was seriously trying to paw the floozy next to him.

Abruptly, the blonde gathered her personal items and dumped them into her black bag, which she snapped shut with a gesture of finality. In practically one motion, in a few seconds she had shouldered her imitation leopard coat, patted the old reprobate's knee and breezed to the door and out into 58th Street. Jehan had neither the time, nor the reflexes, to utter a protest. He just sat there, stupefied.

Unable to stifle a malicious grin, Egan called for his own check. Now it *was* time to cut out of there, before the Frenchman could patch his senses together and get a good look at him. Putting on his coat busily as he passed Jehan, Egan stepped outside. The rush of cold air felt good. He looked around, but the blonde was gone, nor was there any sign of Auletta, which probably meant that Dick had followed her. He walked across the street and went up a few steps into the vestibule of an old apartment building. In a few moments Jehan lurched out of the Thunderbird. He stared around, getting his bearings, then walked slowly toward 57th Street and Sixth Avenue. At the intersection he waved for a taxi, and Egan had to hustle to hail another before Frog One got out of sight.

Jehan's cab deposited him at 47th Street and Broadway at 3:50 A.M., whence he shambled to the Edison Hotel. In the hotel, Jehan picked up his room key, boarded an elevator and disappeared. The lobby was not quite deserted, for the last-ditch stayouts were beginning to straggle in now that the bars all over the city were closing. Behind the front desk, 'assisting' the regular night clerk, was a Federal agent. Egan motioned him aside and asked for the latest information. No Frenchmen, was the word, and the guys still were on Patsy downtown.

Now that Jehan had been put to bed, and the long, confusing night was over, Egan felt numb all at once, his eyes sandy and hollow. But, dammit, he had to *do something!*

In his pocket, his fingers closed on the crumpled paper napkin from the Thunderbird. Sonya? He toyed with the thought for a moment, before balling the napkin and tossing it onto a sand-filled receptacle for cigarette butts. No, he'd better get in his car and go help the others down at Henry Street. With a heavy sigh, he started for the exit.

Then he returned and retrieved the discarded paper napkin. You never knew: her kind of talent could prove useful one day.

Chapter Ten

SONNY GROSSO and Frank Waters were among the dozen or so bleary-eyed officers staked out around 137 Henry Street. It was a dreary street, crowded on both sides by three-, four- and five-story tenements, weathered storefront shops and auto repair garages. Detectives slouched in unmarked cars at either end of the block in which Patsy had last been seen entering the store where the gambling was going on; other cars were scattered on side streets through the area, which, Egan was reminded, was but a few blocks from Blair's Pike Slip Inn and the section where, back in November, he and his comrades had futilely chased Patsy in the Canadian Buick.

Sonny and Waters had parked on Pike Street, around the corner from Henry Street and within view of Blair's, six blocks east toward the river. Egan climbed in with them and fell on the rear seat with a grunt. 'So what else is new?' he asked hoarsely.

His partner eyed Egan. 'You look terrible.'

'What the hell, I been sitting in a gin mill all night, while you guys were out getting the air.'

'They gave us the air, all right,' Waters cracked.

'Frog One is safe and sound, huh?' asked Sonny.

'With the amount of booze he put away tonight, he oughta sleep for a week. He's probably got a good case of blue balls, too.'

'Yeah, what happened with the blonde?' Waters grinned.

'Nothing. A big zero. Poor Jehan. *I* came closer to getting laid than he did.'

'With his blonde?' Sonny exclaimed.

'No. Some chippie tried to pick me up at the bar. A big leaguer all the way. We fooled around awhile, then she had to go take care of a customer. I was supposed to meet her at four o'clock.'

Waters glanced at his wristwatch, eyes twinkling. 'Well, it's almost five now. Where you been for the last hour?'

'Christ, I couldn't get it up now with a jack. Man, I'm whipped. So, is Patsy still playing cards with his *paisans*?'

'We *hope* he is,' Sonny said. 'He went in there, and nobody seen him come out yet.'

'He could've gone out the back way, huh?'

'Who knows? All we can do is wait and see. But as long as Jehan is on ice . . .'

Egan yawned loudly.

'Why don't you go log some sack time?' Sonny suggested. 'You've been out like three nights in a row.'

'I oughta stick around here with you guys.'

'Popeye, the area is covered,' Waters said. 'Sonny and me, we've had a chance to relax. Go on, grab a couple of hours. You may have to relieve *us* by then.'

Egan thought it over sluggishly. Finally he muttered, 'Okay,' and heaved himself from the car. Even the click of the door as he closed it behind him gently seemed to echo in the deserted street. 'I'll catch up with you guys later,' he said.

In a fog, Egan drove his car not up onto either the Manhattan or Williamsburg Bridges which would have taken him home to Brooklyn but, by some reflex, back uptown on the East River Drive.

The black rim of the sky far to the east was being smudged with gray as he realized that he'd driven almost to midtown. He swerved off the three-lane drive at 42nd Street, thinking he'd have to go back downtown half a dozen blocks to the Midtown Tunnel in order to get back to Queens and Brooklyn. But then he thought of what a drag it would be hauling out of his own bed only a few hours hence and driving into Manhattan again. Why not stay at a hotel? He turned up First Avenue, broad and almost desolate at five-thirty on a Saturday morning, past the towering United Nations. He turned left at 49th Street and, three blocks west, found himself at the corner of Lexington Avenue waiting for a light, facing the Waldorf-Astoria. Why *not* the Waldorf? Could the city begrudge him a little indulgence for once? Screw the city, anyway. He knew security officers at the Waldorf.

When Detectective Eddie Egan finally crawled into a soft, crisply fresh bed in the Waldorf-Astoria about 5:45 A.M., Saturday, January 13, it is debatable whether he would have roused even had he been aware of the identity of the handsome visitor from Paris, France, sleeping somewhat fitfully in a large bed-sitting room upstairs in the same hotel. Egan had never heard of the French television star Jacques Angelvin. But they would meet four days hence, and that introduction would transform despair into sunshine for the New York Narcotics Bureau.

Egan awoke after only four hours, and he couldn't get back to sleep. His wristwatch on the night table said it was nine-forty. Slowly Egan hauled himself upright, and sat on the edge of the bed in his underwear, staring morosely at the green carpet. He reached over and called in to base. On the phone they told him the force still was zeroed in on Jehan at the Edison. Frogs Two and Three still had not returned to their hotels, and as for Patsy, he'd finally left 137 Henry Street around 7 A.M. without incident and gone to his home in Brooklyn. Sonny Grosso and Frank Waters had also gone home and would be in later.

What now? Egan went into the bathroom for a glass of water and decided to take a shower. All we can do is stick to Frog One. They've got to contact him. He shaved with the toiletry kit he had brought from his car, then dressed in his rumpled, slightly soiled shirt and suit, and left the Waldorf without checking out. He drove across 49th Street, parked in a lot near Seventh Avenue and stopped at a drugstore for orange juice and coffee. Then he walked to the Edison Hotel.

It was 12:30 P.M., and, because it was early Saturday afternoon, the theater district was quiet and unhurried as Egan approached the main entrance of the Edison on 47th Street. He saw no one he recognized on either side of the street. Egan paused a moment at the revolving door as a man started to push through from the interior. Then he stepped into the moving glass entranceway and was just emerging into the lobby when he froze. The man who had spun past him out into the street, an elderly, distinguished-looking man in black, was Jehan: *Jehan?* Nerves suddenly taut, Egan looked quickly about the quiet lobby to see only a few old people reading newspapers or just daydreaming. A couple of women were getting into an elevator, and he saw two bellmen chattering near the empty front desk.

Holy Mother! The sonofabitch just walked out the door, and there must be twenty of our guys around here somewhere, and nobody's on him! Egan whirled and slammed out through the revolving door, to find that Jehan had almost reached the corner of Broadway. Egan desperately searched 47th Street for some sign of police awareness that Frog One was calmly strolling out of the picture, but he spotted no one. Taking a deep breath, Egan started after the man.

Jehan appeared little the worse for wear after his long Friday night. He was walking easily south on Broadway toward Times Square. Egan was confused and angry. How could so many supposedly professional police officers blow one old bastard who stands out like a giraffe in a field full of cows?

Jehan continued to amble without apparent purpose along the 'Great White Way,' which by daylight was dingy and pallid. Pedestrian traffic was minimal, so Egan was able to keep a clear view of the tall gray-haired figure in black. When Jehan paused at a shop window near 46th Street, Egan, at the corner of 47th, took another moment to look around him once more for assistance. A man and a woman were entering a cab in front of the Edison, but still he saw none of *his* people – until he recognized two hatless, overcoated men lounging at a soft-drink stand on the opposite corner of 47th Street: Detectives Frank Meehan and Roy Cahill.

Egan whistled sharply, and as the two officers looked up he jerked his thumb viciously in the direction Jehan was going. The Frenchman was just moving away from the shop window that had caught his attention and had resumed his leisurely pace. The two detectives, looking very surprised, downed their drinks and stepped out behind Egan.

At 43rd Street, in Times Square, Frog One strolled to the BMT subway kiosk and descended the stairs. Not once in the four blocks, so far as Egan could make out, had the Frenchman so much as glanced back nor otherwise indicated any suspicion of being observed; and now he had gone straight down into the subway as though he knew exactly where he was going. Egan enjoyed a flush of elation: the Frog must be making a meet; maybe our luck *is* changing. But then, he thought, surely this guy, this cool one, must know by now that the operation had been burned, that the other Frogs had faded? And he must have guessed that he himself was carrying a tail? So why the subway bit all of a sudden on a Saturday afternoon?

Underground, Jehan did not go to the BMT trains. He headed for the crosstown shuttle, the short subway line that plies back and forth between Times Square and Grand Central Terminal. With Meehan and Cahill right behind him now, Egan bought a token and cautiously followed the subject through the brightly marked passageway from the main subway station to the shuttle platform. Unlike the streets above, the underground complex was crowded. Tourists goggled at the dreary, noisy, impersonal efficiency of New York's vaunted transportation system. New Yorkers from outlying sections of the vast city, many with children, streamed glumly to and from Manhattan weekend excursions. Egan had to press forward to keep Jehan in view.

Both tracks of the shuttle run were unoccupied, and the platform on one side was filled with citizens waiting for the next train in from Grand Central. Egan figured he had three or four minutes to call in and alert base radio. Catching the eyes of the other detectives he threw a nod toward Jehan, who was standing easily behind a cluster of people, appearing as unconcerned as a headwaiter on his way to work. Meehan and Cahill moved separately to an edge of the crowd at either end of the platform, keeping their undivided attention on the tall Frenchman.

Egan found a public telephone cubicle, also within sight of Jehan, and dialed base. 'I'm sitting on Frog One,' he began. The voice at the other end droned, 'Yeah, we know, we got the Edison covered like a tent.' It was Agent Ben Fitzgerald.

'The Edison? Balls! I got him down in the subway at Times Square. He's about to take the shuttle to Grand Central. You got any men over there? Send some more over. What the hell's going on? I make him coming right out of the hotel, free as a bird. Not a soul around. If I hadn't run into a couple of cops at a snack bar, it'd be a real sweat.' The two-car shuttle train clanked into the station and began to unload its packed cargo. 'The train's in. I gotta go. Have those guys stake out Grand Central!'

Jehan had boarded the second car as Egan came up behind the last knot of passengers edging through the doors. Meehan and Cahill had seated themselves at each end of the car. Jehan sat near the middle, close by the center door. Egan waited until all passengers were in, then quickly pushed into the now crowded car. Taking pains not to look toward Frog One, he shouldered his way toward the front end of the train, where he stood with his red-haired fingers grasping a chin-high hand grip, staring at the advertising in front of him.

His mind's eye, however, was scanning what could happen when they reached the Grand Central end of the half-mile trip. Base had advised that several detectives were already in the terminal keeping close watch on the banks of storage lockers. Frogs Two and Three had loitered in Grand Central the previous night before losing their tail, so there was still some suspicion that the load might be stashed there after all. And now, presumably, other officers in cars would be speeding to the terminal area to help Egan.

Egan's only possible plan was to get off the train first and let the Frog catch up and pass *him*. From there, he and the other detectives would just have to play it carefully, with Meehan and Cahill keeping a sharp eye out for fellow cops. When the train lurched to a stop, Egan made his way to the forward door and, on the crowded platform, proceeded slowly toward the tunnel corridor connecting the shuttle with the main station.

Several minutes passed, and the crowd streaming past Egan from behind him became a trickle, but Jehan had not appeared. Egan chanced a glance back. No one else was coming from the train now – no Jehan, not even Meehan and Cahill! Shucking caution, Egan bolted toward the two-car train he'd just left, now almost filled with return passengers. He marched grimly through both cars, checking every occupant. Nothing. Oh, good Christ Almighty! He jogged back along the passageway to the main 42nd Street subway station. Neither Jehan nor the officers were in sight on the various platforms. How could he have missed them? He raced up the long flight of stairs into the terminal, and saw Detective Dick Auletta standing by the entrance to the lower level, peering over a folded newspaper. When he spied Egan, Auletta lowered his eyes without recognition, obviously awaiting some signal. But Egan, breathing hard, went straight to him.

'Dick, have you seen Frog One?'

Auletta looked quickly up at the other's flushed face and shook his head. 'What's happened?'

'I lost him,' Egan groaned, rapidly surveying the ramps leading from 42nd Street down into the terminal. 'I can't figure it, but I did . . . Let's check some of the other guys.'

They hurried about Grand Central, seeking out other officers now posted by various exits, but no one had seen either Jehan or Detectives Meehan and Cahill. Egan felt clumsy and powerless. He and Auletta slumped against the marble counter outside a shuttered New York Central ticket window in the cavernous main terminal.

'What are you gonna do?' Auletta asked.

'Christ, I don't know. If we've blown him, I guess that's the ball game. I better call in. Maybe somebody else has got a lead.'

'Why don't we check out the Roosevelt first?' Auletta asked. 'That seemed to be their favorite meeting place.'

'Yeah, that's a thought,' Egan acknowledged, without much genuine enthusiasm. He and Auletta trudged up the stairway to Vanderbilt Avenue and walked two blocks north to the hotel. It was scarcely more than an hour since Egan had happened upon Jehan at the Edison, but the afternoon seemed endless.

After circling the block-square Roosevelt together, the two

separated and searched the lobby and lower-level arcades inside. It was fruitless.

They met outside the hotel's Rough Rider Room on the 45th Street side, and Egan decided to call base from the lounge. After a few minutes, Egan rejoined Auletta at the bar, and they ordered two Pepsis. Egan appeared thoughtful.

'So?' Auletta probed.

Egan swallowed a mouthful of cola, set the glass down deliberately, leaned one elbow on the polished wood bar and turned to his companion. 'So,' he said softly, 'Mr. Frog One is back in his room at the Edison Hotel.'

On the way crosstown to the Edison in Auletta's car, Egan related what he had been told. When he had boarded the shuttle at Times Square and pushed to the head of the car, consciously avoiding looking at Jehan, the Frenchman had left his seat and seconds before the train departed nimbly slipped through the closing doors. Fortunately, Meehan and Cahill had detected this sudden move and managed to scramble to the platform themselves just as the doors closed. Of course, they had had no chance to alert Egan, who continued on to Grand Central rapt in his plans for maintaining surveillance when he got there. Meanwhile, the perplexed officers had followed Jehan up to the street and back to his hotel, where he took an elevator and returned to his room on the ninth floor.

After the return of Jehan, there was considerable agitation among the dozen or so narcotics officers posted in and around the Edison as to how their subject had succeeded in breezing out of the hotel. The next hour was an uneasy jumble of fierce speculation and recrimination, with the New York police and Federal agents generally taking sides against one another.

Shortly, the men staked out in the lobby received word from the French-speaking agent in the room next to Jehan's that Frog One had just had a telephone call from Frog Two. The listening device, which was not attached to the telephone, could pick up only Jehan's end of the conversation. But he had referred to his caller as 'mon petit François' – surely the missing Barbier – and had said in French: 'You were right, I think. It is best to leave it where it is . . .'

This set off a new round of heated speculation downstairs. 'What did he mean by "you are right"?' It means we burned the tail good, stupid.' '*Who* burned it? *I* wasn't sitting on the lobby!' And, as they snapped at each other thus in anger and frustration, Jean Jehan put on his black coat and hat, picked up his cane, and calmly went out for another stroll . . .

Auletta dropped Egan at the corner of 47th and Broadway and drove off. Sapped of enthusiasm, Eddie was struggling to revive his spirits as he again approached the main entrance of the Edison. Suddenly, Jean Jehan came out of the revolving door and walked past him.

Egan took two full steps before stopping short. He whirled, startled to see, as he had earlier, the same tall, dark ethereal figure striding up the street toward Broadway. Jesus, Mary and Joseph – is this a dream? Am I going nuts? Shaking his head, he looked toward the hotel entrance and saw Detectives Meehan and Cahill emerging cautiously behind the Frenchman. Spotting Egan, one nodded in the direction of Jehan up the block. Egan acknowledged with a curt nod of his own and turned after Frog One, with the others trailing.

Jehan again went down the subway stairs at 43rd Street. Egan, half a block behind, couldn't shake the eerie feeling that he was somehow reliving a portion of his life. But Jehan proceeded this time not to the shuttle but to the BMT main line, descending another flight of stairs to the downtown platform. Egan and the others followed separately. Jehan stood on the Local side, apart from a handful of other passengers scattered along the platform. Egan guessed that a train must have just gone through and, because of curtailed Saturday service, he estimated that he would have several minutes to report the situation to base.

The two other detectives drifted apart to opposite ends of the platform, while Egan looked for a telephone. The only booth he could use without losing sight of Jehan was within a dozen feet of the man. Egan swallowed and with outward brazenness walked in front of Frog One and settled in the booth.

'Send all your available cars to the west side,' he told base. 'Find out where each BMT local station is and spot a man up at every street exit all the way downtown. If we don't show up with the Frog at one stop, have the guys rotate, keeping a couple of stations ahead. We'll stay with this guy. Got that? Hold it. A train's coming in. Let's see what he does this time. I might hang up fast . . .'

The noisy gray-green subway train squealed to a stop. The doors rattled open, and the passengers got off and those on the platform stepped aboard; all except Jehan who stood quietly, hands clasped gently around the grip of his black walking stick in front of him. When the doors closed again and the train left the station, Jehan and one overcoated man at each end of the platform were the only people visible. Egan said into the telephone: 'He didn't get on. Stay with me. I don't want to be wandering around the station.'

Another train arrived and departed without Jehan, and now Egan, still in the telephone booth, began to grow restive. 'I don't like this,' he reported. 'He's waiting for something, or somebody . . . Christ, maybe he wants to use this telephone.' Egan swung open the folding glass door and raised his voice into the receiver. 'I've worked in plenty of joints, bartender, waiter, even a bouncer. All I'm asking is a chance to show you what I can do. Can I come see you today? I'm telling you, I want this job bad.' He prayed that his urgent tone had carried over the constant rumble of the subway and that his expression reflected the concern of a man struggling for livelihood.

Several more people had walked onto the platform, one a middle-aged woman in a Kelly green coat with a yellow kerchief around her head who stopped just outside Egan's telephone booth. Jehan came over to her, not six feet from where the detective sat. The elegant Frenchman doffed his Hamburg and spoke to the woman. He must have been asking directions, Egan thought, for the woman nodded, and with a curt bow Jehan turned to wait for another train. Egan gave the woman in the green coat a hard look, before deciding that she was no more than a passerby.

Another Local clattered into the station, and Frog One seemed to edge toward it. 'Here we go, I think,' Egan muttered into the telephone mouthpiece. Jehan stepped aboard the train. 'See ya,' Egan said, jamming the phone into its cradle. He left the booth and hurried to the same car as Jehan. Meehan and Cahill boarded the train at either end.

Jehan sat in the forward corner of the car, gazing blankly up at the advertising placards opposite. There were only five or six other passengers besides Egan. The detective took a seat midway along the car, across the aisle from the Frog, averting his face but keeping the dark figure firmly in the corner of an eye. As the train pulled out of the Times Square station, glancing to his right Egan could see Meehan in the car immediately behind, weaving into position; presumably Cahill was doing the same in the car ahead.

The train pulled into the next stop, 33rd Street. Jehan arose casually and stood studying the subway map next to the door. Egan smiled grimly to himself: he's beautiful; the doors will open, and he'll wait till the last second, and wham! then he'll jump off the train – and I guess I'm supposed to just sit here like a dummy. He hoped the other officers were ready to move.

The doors opened. A man got on, passing Jehan, who had not moved. Action hung suspended for a long second. Then, with a hiss the doors began to come together. Jehan shoved his cane against the rubber edging; all the doors reopened. Jehan quickly stepped out. Egan leaped across the car and out another exit just as the doors were closing again. Egan was grinning.

But not for long. Where was Jehan? He was nowhere in sight. Meehan and Cahill had made it to the platform, and now they were approaching Egan. The train started to move out of the station. The three were alone. And then a familiar figure appeared in a window of the car he had supposedly just left. Frog One, bent slightly toward them, was smiling at the police officers and daintily waving a gloved hand. In a moment, the train had rattled into the black subway tunnel, Jean Jehan with it. There was no way all the exits on the long subway line could be covered this soon.

Chapter Eleven

By nightfall of Saturday, January 13, it appeared certain that Jean Jehan would not return to the Edison Hotel. François Barbier and J. Mouren also remained at large. The narcotics officers covering the hotels in which the Frenchmen had stayed now suspected that the three had regrouped and perhaps were even on their way out of the country.

Others were still watching Patsy Fuca, but he had not left his home in Brooklyn all day Saturday. Detectives had observed his wife go shopping, and Barbara's father and Patsy's brother Tony together tended the luncheonette on Bushwick Avenue. It was not until nearly 6:00 P.M. that Patsy finally made an appearance, after his day-long rest from the arduous night before. He left his house on 67th Street and entered a gray 1956 Cadillac, his friend Nicky Travato's car. Late Friday night, while Patsy had been diverting the police in the 'Keystone Kops' chase around mid-Manhattan, officers watching Travato had observed him drive his Cadillac the four blocks from his house to 67th Street and leave it parked there.

The mystery of this move was increased when Patsy, with his own Oldsmobile and Buick both standing in front of his house, proceeded to drive Nicky's Cadillac to a point on Graham Street, three blocks away from his luncheonette. He spent the rest of the evening in his store. At about 11:00 P.M., Nicky Travato drove up in Patsy's blue and white Olds. Patsy emerged and climbed in behind the wheel, leaving Tony to close up shop.

Detective Jimmy O'Brien and Agent Jack Ripa, watching the store from the hospital across the Avenue, climbed into their own car and fastened onto Patsy as he turned the corner of Maujer Street and drove over to Graham, where he let Nicky out next to his own Cadillac.

It didn't take O'Brien and Ripa long to realize what Patsy and Nicky were up to. After dropping his friend, Patsy drove south on Graham Street. The detectives hung back, expecting Nicky to follow the Olds. But Nicky didn't even switch on his headlights. So O'Brien decided to stay with Patsy, who by then was turning a corner several blocks down Graham.

Hardly had they passed by Nicky, however, than headlights flashed behind them as a car pulled away from the curb. The officers made the same turn Patsy had, and moments later Nicky's Caddy came around the corner.

'Why, the sonsabitches!' O'Brien swore. 'Patsy's got his buddy riding shotgun for him!'

'Let's fix that,' Ripa commented cooly.

They stayed with the Oldsmobile until it turned again, into a one-way street. Instead of following, O'Brien continued on through the intersection. The detective studied the rearview mirror. Nicky's car, after hesitating at the last corner, made the turn and went after Patsy. O'Brien jammed to a stop and U-turned, cornering into the street taken by Patsy and then Nicky.

They followed the Cadillac for a while. The procession moved slowly, Nicky keeping pace with the Olds ahead, staying two to three blocks to its rear. There was no doubt: Patsy was experimenting, trying to determine if there *was* surveillance on him by using Nicky to watch for any tails. This suggested either that, one, Patsy had cause to suspect heat; or, two, he didn't really know whether the cops were watching him, but he was feeling out the situation preparatory to taking some kind of action. Maybe the case *wasn't* dead yet, as the increasingly gloomy voices on base radio seemed to imply.

The officers accordingly played the game with a certain relish. Patsy, trailed by Nicky, drove in and out of streets throughout the Williamsburg section, up around Greenpoint, east to the Queens line near Maspeth, finally back along Grand Avenue toward Bushwick. Part of the way, O'Brien and Ripa stayed behind the Caddy, other times they eased ahead and followed the Olds, and then, just when Nicky might be wondering about the car between himself and Patsy, they'd turn off and let the Caddy go by, only to whip around and again wind up tagging after Patsy's 'shotgun.'

It was after midnight when Patsy and Nicky returned to the luncheonette. Tony was still there. The three talked a few more minutes before the lights went out and they all got into their cars and started home, Patsy and Nicky in their own vehicles, Tony in his beat-up Chevy station wagon.

On Sunday, January 14, the pattern of the investigation continued to vex the anxious police. Patsy went to his store at mid-morning and stayed there, joined shortly after noon by his wife Barbara.

At 3:00 P.M., the investigators got a further salvo of discouraging news which seemed to intensify their growing hopelessness. First, the Edison Hotel received a telephone call from Mr. Jean Jehan, who said he wished to be checked out of Room 909 and he would send payment by mail within a day or so. He asked that the hotel hold his bags and clothing until he advised where they should be forwarded. The switchboard operator could offer no clue as to the origin of the call, but the assistant manager who actually spoke with the Frenchman thought he had heard an operator's voice interrupt at one point, indicating that Jehan had telephoned from somewhere outside the city. Detectives then searched Room

909 – having thus far refrained from doing so on the off-chance that Frog One might return after all – but they found nothing other than a suitcase and briefcase containing personal items of apparel and toiletries. Disappointed, they left Jehan's belongings intact.

They had scarcely reported to base when, as if on cue, there were successive reports from the Victoria and Abbey hotels that each had received a Western Union money order – the Victoria from François Barbier, the Abbey from J. Mouren – in the exact amounts due on their respective rooms. Each had requested that the hotel store their belongings until called for. Both money orders had been placed in Yonkers, a suburban city just north of New York. The Yonkers police were alerted, but a check of the Western Union office there turned up nothing more than confirmation that a lone man with what might have been a foreign accent had paid for both telegrams; there was no way of telling where he might have gone after leaving the office. Meanwhile, agents examined the bags and clothes that Frogs Two and Three had left behind. Results again were negative.

The taps on the telephones at Patsy's luncheonette and his home had remained in operation throughout the investigation, but hardly anything of use was ever detected. The automatic tape monitors, played back several times daily, recorded mostly conversations that were either irrelevant to the case or that consisted of unintelligible monosyllables. This Sunday evening, however, with the Frenchmen all having left the scene, an interesting exchange did take place.

The call came in to one of the telephones in Patsy's store. The caller obviously was Giant. The suave gentleman was extremely concerned about what had seemed to be undue police attention upon Patsy's operations. Nervously, Patsy tried to alleviate the Frenchman's fears; if the heat *were* on, Patsy certainly knew that his uncle, Angelo Tuminaro, would not hesitate to cut him out of this deal and the whole 'family' business as well, and advise him to go out and get a job – like sweeping subways. Frog One suggested that it might be wise to postpone negotiations.

Patsy's greed, on top of his dread of jeopardizing his newly promising position of eminence in the narcotics trade, thus led him to a decision that in the end proved to be a major factor in compromising Tuminaro's junk trade and the international syndicate feeding it: feverishly, Patsy assured Jean Jehan that the police were only interested in certain paperback books he was selling which had been judged pornographic. At first the Frenchman was incredulous that the American police would waste their time tracking down purveyors of dirty books. But this book, Patsy hastened to argue, was disgusting even to him. It was called *Tropic of Cancer*.

Somehow, the sophisticated French narcotics czar, Jean Jehan, was convinced, and he agreed to pursue negotiations with the youthful manager of the Tuminaro narcotics ring.

On Monday morning, January 15, a meeting was held at Narcotics Bureau headquarters in the 1st Precinct station house. Present in Lieutenant Vinnie Hawkes's office was essentially the same group of detectives and Federal agents who had met there five days earlier to map out strategy that would destroy Patsy Fuca and his associates. In grim, quiet voices, they discussed what ways and means were left them to salvage the long investigation.

That Patsy was now a major dealer in narcotics was not questioned. That Patsy had been on the verge of concluding a major transaction with the French connections was also beyond doubt. The pivotal question was whether the Frogs' abrupt departure signified that the deal had been culminated, the junk having been delivered and paid for in part. But perhaps they had been scared off before the exchange could be made. The only other alternative was that they had been disturbed by police surveillance but had *not* aborted their plans as yet and were regrouping for a final exchange of smuggled heroin for Mafia money.

As for the first possibility, that the shipment already was in Patsy's hands, this would mean that the suppliers, the Frenchmen, had left with short dollars. Police knew that the modus operandi in narcotics commerce resembled a pyramid. The connections to whom Patsy sold junk were given a price per kilo, pegged to current demand, and before the shipment they would give Patsy 'front' money, a down payment on the total to be paid, pending safe delivery and verification of quantity and quality ordered. After the day or two it usually required for these wholesalers to distribute the marked-up merchandise to their own customers, they would come back to Patsy with the rest of the 'bread.' And so it went down the line, to the pusher on the street corner dealing in consignments of 'nickel' ($5) bags of heavily cut heroin.

Meanwhile, at the top of the pyramid, where the big financing occurred, Patsy dealt in similar fashion with his suppliers. When they produced the shipment ordered, Patsy had to make a minimum down payment, and, after he had successfully delivered the goods to *his* preferred customers – never any more than five or six big operators – he would complete the payoff to the French manufacturers. The wholesale price to Patsy for such a formidable shipment as the rumored fifty kilos would have amounted to about half a million dollars at the going rate. Patsy would have been expected to put up about half, or perhaps even $300,000. Normally, after unloading their illegal cargo, the suppliers could either afford to relax and wait around to receive their full installment, or if the receiver were a particularly good and reliable customer, they could wend their way home, confident that full payment would be forthcoming. But if there were any conflict, as the police speculated there had been in this instance, the Frenchmen might be uneasy about departing with only partial payment from Patsy. The police also considered the recent rumors both that Patsy was having money troubles and that certain connections had been dissatisfied with the quality of his last delivery.

Frank Waters had one idea about where to look for the junk. It was still a very long shot but at least based on something more substantial than pure theorizing. 'Since last November,' the agent spoke up, 'I've been bugged by that Canadian car that Patsy drove over to Cherry Street and we sat on. Remember, it turned out to belong to this guy Maurice in Montreal, who happens to be a big peddler up there. And then it disappears.

'I felt sure then – we all did – that somehow that Buick figured in the shipment down from Canada. I know, we tossed it and found zip. But we didn't really have a chance to take it apart that night. And what happened right after that? The panic goes off. There's junk for everybody.

'Now, here we are two months later, and the word's out that a new load is coming in; and now people are bringing bread to our friend Patsy; and who comes to town but a bunch of Frenchmen. And where do *they* come from, two of them anyway? Montreal, Canada.'

'So you're suggesting that the key this time might also be a Canadian car?' Ben Fitzgerald asked.

'It's a thought,' Waters shrugged. 'Maybe even the *same* car. What was it, some light-colored Buick?'

'A tan nineteen-sixty Buick, an Invicta,' Eddie Egan answered. 'But I think different. I have an idea the junk will turn up at Patsy's old man's place out in Brooklyn.'

'And where do we look for this mystery car?' inquired Vinnie Hawkes, breaking the silence that followed Egan's speculation.

'I don't know,' Waters replied, 'in garages, in the streets.

The first place *I'd* look would be around Cherry Street, South Street, around there.'

'Christ, we could be looking till nineteen seventy,' Egan declared.

'Could be,' Waters agreed, frowning at Egan, 'but what the hell are we doing now? We're just sitting, twiddling our thumbs – since the *last* Frog skipped.'

Egan's ruddy face turned a shade whiter, a sure indication of a rise in his famous temper. 'I only let *one* get away,' he said with exaggerated politeness.

'All right, let's knock off the bullshit,' snapped Lieutenant Hawkes. 'We've all screwed up one way or another on this one.'

'What do you think, Vinnie?' Ben Fitzgerald interjected. 'Is it worth putting out an A.P.B. on a car of this type? I know it's way out, but . . .'

'Well, I can't see as we have anything to lose. Who knows what might turn up?' Hawkes scribbled '*All Points Bulletin – Buick*' on his pad. 'What else?'

'I have a suggestion,' Sonny Grosso leaned forward. 'Since all we can do is wait for somebody to make a move – assuming the thing isn't dead already – and,' he glanced at Egan, 'while we're looking for this Canadian Buick, I think we ought to cut back surveillance on Patsy. If we did scare off his friends, what with a couple of hundred fuzz running around, Patsy's going to be playing it real careful now.

'We might be better off just having a *light* tail on Patsy. We can keep tabs on him, but maybe in a few days he'll start breathing easier, and then make a move.'

'Everybody agree?' Hawkes asked, glancing around. 'Okay. Sonny, you and Popeye and Frank work out assignments.'

'I still say we'll find the shit at Joe Fuca's,' Egan growled.

Deputy Chief Inspector Carey and Federal Director

Gaffney, who had been holding their own private meeting in Carey's office, strode into Hawkes's office. Hawkes summed up the consensus of opinion for the two bosses.

Carey listened intently, frequently glancing at Gaffney, who nodded assent. When Hawkes had finished, Carey thought about the situation, pacing about among the detectives. He agreed to go along with continuing limited investigation for a few more days. Then, with a serious expression on his face, he pointed out that it was Monday, the fifteenth. At midnight, Thursday, the eighteenth, the search warrants for all the locations under surveillance would expire. They had been renewed twice for ten-day periods already, he reminded the men. If nothing conclusive happened by Thursday midnight – Carey's stern visage turned from one man to the next in emphasis – he and Federal Director Gaffney would have to pull the men off the case completely. So they had four days to crack the case. Tensely, the detectives and federal agents watched Carey and Gaffney disappear back into the inspector's office.

Later, as Sonny, Eddie and Frank Waters talked about the allocation of local and Federal personnel for the four days left them to hit Patsy's operation, Sonny was vaguely disturbed by a new undercurrent of animosity between his regular partner and Agent Waters, with whom he worked almost as often and equally as well.

That afternoon, Sonny assigned himself to watch 'lightly' over Patsy out in Brooklyn, and Egan made the rounds coordinating continued stakeouts of the Frenchmen's erstwhile hotels. Waters and Detective Dick Auletta meanwhile prowled the streets of the lower Manhattan area where two months before they had played hide-and-seek with Patsy and the Canadian Buick. And there, about 4 P.M., they made an interesting discovery. In a small, wooden garage on the property of a service station on South Street, just off Jefferson, the officers saw Tony Fuca's old Chevrolet station wagon. The entire bureau had been puzzled over what had happened to the Canadian car in the short time they had left it unguarded back in November. Tony, who frequently worked on the docks of the Mexican Line, virtually across South Street from where the car had disappeared, might have been the one who had disposed of the Buick!

No doubt it had been Patsy's responsibility that night to pick up the sedan and authenticate its having been loaded, or unloaded, but surely he was not willing to risk arrest for possession, that's what handyman Tony was for. It now appeared that Tony must have been waiting in this garage only a block and a half away when the detectives following Patsy had discovered the Buick. Waters and Auletta now guessed that Grosso and Egan probably passed within a few yards of Tony when they had cut through this very gas station, just after Patsy and the two girls took off in his other car. The little goon must have waited in the garage all those hours until he saw the detectives' two cars leave just before dawn. Then, gambling they hadn't left anyone behind, Tony had crept out and managed to drive the Buick off in the few minutes it had taken Waters to return to his office and send another agent back.

The officers decided that Patsy's brother needed more personal attention than had previously been tendered, so they sat on the old garage containing Tony's Chevy.

Most of Monday, Patsy did not stir from his store in Brooklyn. Detective Jimmy O'Brien had been watching the place alone when Sonny Grosso and Agent Jack Ripa joined him in mid-afternoon. They waited, not really sure what they expected Patsy to do; from time to time, one or another went into the luncheonette for a snack or to browse through magazines, but none of them gained any hints as to their subject's intentions or state of mind. Patsy seemed untroubled.

A little after 9:30 P.M. Nicky Travato arrived in his old Cadillac, which he parked outside the store. Minutes later, Patsy came out and got into the Caddy and drove off, heading toward the Williamsburg Bridge. Leaving O'Brien behind, Sonny and Ripa followed, excitement awakening in them now because this was the first time in three days that Patsy had shown any interest in leaving Brooklyn.

The detectives trailed him at a comfortable distance into Manhattan, off the bridge and uptown on the East River Drive. They saw him exit at 61st Street and turn up York Avenue. Patsy eluded them briefly, but then they spotted the gray Cadillac being backed into a parking space on York just north of 77th Street. By the time they had a chance to maneuver into a closer position, Patsy himself had been lost from view. Sonny and Ripa drove a few blocks up York, and through some of the cross streets, but, unable to find Patsy, they returned to keep watch on the Caddy.

About ten-thirty, Patsy was observed walking back down York Avenue toward the car. He swung the Caddy around and headed back downtown, reentering the drive at 62nd Street. Where had he gone for that half hour?

As Sonny and Ripa tailed Patsy south on East River Drive, Frank Waters and Dick Auletta were crossing the Manhattan Bridge toward Brooklyn behind the 1949 Chevy station wagon driven by Tony Fuca. After they had waited for some six-and-a-half hours with a patience that impressed even themselves, Tony had materialized out of the darkness by the little garage at the corner of the now darkened service station, and with a flourish had driven his car away and onto the bridge. It was a strange hour for Tony, who lived in the Bronx with his wife and two children, to be going out to

Brooklyn, Waters and Auletta noted; but in this investigation, strange things never seemed to cease happening.

Tony drove off the bridge onto the Brooklyn-Queens Expressway, northbound, directly to his brother's luncheonette in Williamsburg, arriving shortly before 11 P.M. Nicky Travato was alone in the store. Waters and Auletta pulled into the grounds of St. Catherine's Hospital across Bushwick Avenue, where by their radio they knew that Jimmy O'Brien was staked out, recently joined by Eddie Egan. Within ten minutes, Patsy drove up in Nicky's Cadillac, followed presently by Sonny Grosso and Jack Ripa in Sonny's white Olds. While the three in the store talked, the six officers brought each other up to date across the street.

Patsy locked up for the night about twelve. He and Nicky got into the Cadillac together, and Egan and O'Brien elected to tail them. But Waters for once stayed, more interested in Tony Fuca, because as he had come out of the store Tony had stuffed a small package into the slash pocket of his navy lumber jacket. When Tony wheeled his Chevy wagon around and headed toward the Williamsburg Bridge, Waters and Sonny were right behind him.

Tony didn't take the bridge. He went up on the Expressway and drove north to the cutoff to the Triborough Bridge, which he followed into the Bronx. The officers followed up Bruckner Boulevard to where Tony turned off to Westchester Avenue. At Southern Boulevard, he pulled into a small vacant lot, got out and – his jacket pocket still bulging – walked to a brightly lit hash house called Dave's. As Grosso and Waters came abreast of the place, through the plate glass window they saw Tony pass through a door into a rear room.

So Tony was making deliveries of junk even now!

While Grosso and Waters later tailed Tony to his apartment not far away on Bryant Avenue, in midtown Manhattan at

1:20 A.M., a sleek black 1960 Buick Invicta was being returned to the garage beneath the Waldorf-Astoria Hotel on 50th Street off Park Avenue. A very weary Jacques Angelvin walked to an elevator. He was worried because, contrary to François Scaglia's explicit instructions, he had spent half the day driving around New York in the new car he liked better than any mistress he had ever had.

Chapter Twelve

EVER since his arrival in New York Jacques Angelvin had been irked by the dictum laid down by Scaglia and Jehan against taking his Buick out of the hotel garage. How was he to survey the great city 'like a real American,' as he had promised his vast television audience before leaving Paris, if he were not permitted to move at will? Taxis here were very expensive. As for exploring the city on foot – hardly *comme il faut*. He understood what the auto contained, but he was sure there was no way it could be discovered. Would *le grand* Ed Sullivan tramp about Paris like a tourist?

But why had François and his friends not completed the transaction on schedule? That night, Jacques had reviewed the five days of his visit. So much had been frustrating. Arlette, the little girl from the ship, had left for Chicago on Thursday afternoon, only hours after the satisfying morning consummation of their shipboard flirtation. He had been forced to leave her at noon to meet Scaglia, which had not improved his disposition as he had walked uncertainly across the city to the bar of the Taft Hotel. Scaglia was awaiting him there, and they walked from the Taft to a small French restaurant in a street beyond the famed Broadway of which he had heard so many legends. This daylight glimpse of the avenue's brazen gaucherie was the first of his disappointments in New York.

At least his companion's conversation over luncheon was more encouraging. Scaglia and his associates hoped to conclude their negotiations by Saturday at the latest. Jacques was asked to be always available at the Waldorf, prepared to execute his simple assignment – to deliver the Buick to wherever he was directed. Meanwhile, the Corsican reiterated emphatically, his eyes hard, that the car was not to be moved.

Jacques asked almost plaintively when the transaction was a fait accompli, would he then be free to make full use of the Buick? *Mais certainement*, he was assured.

While he was waiting, New York had been made at least bearable by Jacques's chic guide, the lovely Lilli DeBecque. Thursday evening they had enjoyed cocktails and dinner at the Café de La Paix at the Hotel St. Moritz. In spite of the cold, he and Lilli had taken a walk in Central Park, and later he suggested a nightcap at the Waldorf. She sipped brandy with him, but when he invited her up to his suite once again, she declined with firmness.

On Friday Angelvin visited Peter Selliers, a French journalist, and Paul Crenesse, head of the New York office of Radio Télévision Française. They took him to NBC to see the studios and meet some of the American producers.

Again that evening he and Lilli went out, first to the Plaza for dinner and afterwards to the Maisonette of the St. Regis Hotel. And again that night, Mademoiselle DeBecque returned alone to her apartment on East 20th Street and Angelvin occupied his suite in the Waldorf without company.

On Saturday Lilli showed Jacques some of the sights of New York. Angelvin had been sorely tempted to take the beautiful Buick out for the trip around the city, but that morning Scaglia had telephoned him. François's voice rasped over the wire with tense urgency: there had been an unfortunate postponement, plans must be delayed.

But the car? Angelvin protested.

Leave the automobile untouched! And Scaglia rang off.

So by bus, subway and taxi Jacques and Lilli visited Greenwich Village, the Empire State Building, Rockefeller Plaza and even took the bus all the way uptown to see the George Washington Bridge. Angelvin was impressed with the New York subway system and amazed at the awesome size of the city it served. In spite of the thoroughly pleasant time they had together during the day, followed that evening by dinner at Trader Vic's, Lilli still refused to succumb to the blandishments of the French TV star. He slept badly that night. The Buick seemed at the core of all his growing discontent.

On Sunday his frustration built until finally he disobeyed Scaglia's orders. He went down to the garage, took his car out, picked up Lilli and drove all around New York, parking down at the Battery and taking a ferry boat over to the Statue of Liberty. The exhilaration of the drive did much for his spirits. Jacques hoped that perhaps 'le Jazz Hot' would do something to escalate his relationship with Lilli, and that night he took her to Basin Street East. But once more, Lilli went home and Jacques slept badly again.

As Angelvin had made ready to go out into the city Monday morning, he wished terribly that the entire ordeal were over. He looked forward to going to Niagara Falls for the day on Tuesday and then on Thursday night he would be in Montreal where things were French and the girls, he had been told, more amiable. Today he had further meetings with Paul Crenesse and other people who would help him take the pulse of American television. Also, he resolved that for the good of his spirit he would take his car out for another drive about town. He brooded at the cavalier treatment accorded to him by Scaglia, and made up his mind that when he returned to Paris, he would try to avoid Scaglia at all costs.

Lilli met Jacques at the Waldorf after lunch on Monday. Nervously, but buoyed by excitement, he led her down to the garage to his prized Buick and they drove out into the streets of New York. Occasionally he thought of the illicit cargo stuffed into the understructure of the vehicle, but the exhilaration of guiding his car about New York with the beauteous Lilli who at last seemed to be truly affectionate helped him to forget the dangerous crime he had taken on and the brutish Scaglia who had conspired to make his life so miserable.

They drove until nine o'clock, and then Lilli suggested dinner at Tavern-on-the-Green. They enjoyed dinner and wine. Lilli was warm and outgoing. Angelvin told her about his trip to Montreal, planned for Thursday, and seeing a shadow of disappointment flit across her brow he said that he would be back in New York to stay a while on Sunday, the twenty-first.

It had been a lovely afternoon and evening, she told him. They kissed in the car in front of her apartment, the first time in Jacques's life that he had owned an automobile spacious enough in which to kiss a woman with comfort, he thought proudly. Lilli promised to call him at the hotel to say good night and Jacques drove off to the Waldorf. Surely tomorrow night, he thought.

So, at 1:30 A.M., Tuesday, Jacques was back in his suite at the Waldorf. Except for the brief morning thing with Arlette on Thursday, he had led a painfully deprived sex life for the last two weeks. Jacques was emerging from the bathroom in his pajamas when the telephone rang. Lilli, he thought. But as he reached for the receiver realization struck: François. He had hardly thought of Scaglia since the afternoon. Did they know he had used the car?

The Corsican's voice was harsh. He had been ringing all evening: where had Jacques gone? *Oui, oui*, the car is quite safe, *ami*, still in the garage. He hoped he sounded convincing. Scaglia hesitated as if in doubt, then he told him: it would be tomorrow, or rather, now, today. No, do not interrupt, only listen most carefully. At 8:30 A.M. . . . and he dictated precise instructions.

When Scaglia clicked off, Jacques was trembling, his skin clammy.

Able only to doze, he was up at seven. He ordered a light breakfast sent to his room, then bathed and dressed. By eight-fifteen Jacques was fidgeting in the cavernous lobby, watching the clock. At eight-thirty, he descended to the garage and retrieved the Buick. Exchanging places behind the wheel with the attendant, he glanced quickly over the car's interior: everything appeared in order; no one would know that he had flaunted orders the previous days. Then he snorted at his own anxiety. How could they suspect his outing with the girl, any more than by looking at the car a stranger would suspect the immense secret it bore?

Following Scaglia's instructions, he drove out of the garage onto 49th Street, made a right turn on Park Avenue and proceeded slowly north in heavy morning traffic, eying each street sign intently as he passed, grateful for the simple numerical progression. At 79th Street, he turned right, east, and continued almost to the river. The last street to his left before the entrance to the river expressway was the one he was seeking: East End Avenue. Cautiously, his palms becoming moist, he drove left and then another block north. The apartment building was at the corner of 81st Street. Jacques pulled the car over to the gaping entrance of the building's basement-level garage in the middle of the block and verified the address – No. 45 East End Avenue. He rolled down the ramp and braked outside a small, neon-lit office. The attendant, a slim, middle-aged man with sandy hair, emerged and studied the Buick a moment, then looked hard at Jacques. 'When y' goin' out?' he asked with a trace of Celtic infection. Jacques shrugged helplessly. 'Okay,' the man said, 'we'll take care of it.' He went into his cubbyhole and tore a ticket stub off a panel of hooks next to the counter and gave it to Jacques. Take very good care of that ticket, François had emphasized. Jacques inserted the piece of yellow cardboard into his billfold and turned and trudged up the ramp to the street, aware of the man squinting at the back of his neck as he went.

On East End Avenue, Jacques waited a few minutes, ill at ease, until a cab came into view. He asked to be taken to the Waldorf-Astoria.

While Jacques Angelvin was delivering his 1960 Buick to the garage on East End Avenue, Patsy Fuca left his house in Brooklyn and again drove away in his friend Nicky Travato's gray 1956 Cadillac, observed at a respectful distance by Federal Agents Artie Fluhr and Bill Carrazo. Within minutes, however, the officers lost sight of the Caddy after it turned onto 65th Street, heading west. They were not overly concerned at first, figuring that they or some other team would soon reestablish contact. But they did not see Patsy again, nor did anyone else, neither near his luncheonette or his known haunts in Manhattan. As the morning wore on, the police grew increasingly anxious that their final link with whatever illegal activity was taking place, had disappeared.

That Tuesday morning, January 16, Detective Eddie Egan had been required to appear downtown before a Manhattan grand jury hearing about an earlier narcotics case in which he had been the arresting officer. When released shortly before noon, Egan learned about Patsy's worrisome disappearance. He was told that there were no leads and that detectives were checking every location in the city with which Pasty had been associated.

Egan walked to the municipal garage near Foley Square and got his Corvair. Driving out, automatically he reached down to switch on his portable radiophone, then remembered that he had left it in the shop for repairs. He missed it. The radio was probably more useful than guns to a policeman. Even when not involved in active investigation, those few times when there might be little else to think about, he enjoyed tuning to the all-police channel, listening to officers in other cars in the city chattering their staccato reports of a 'hot tail' here or a 'suspect observed' there.

What was it that had lodged in a recess of his memory about Patsy's involvements? It wasn't his girl at the Pike Slip Inn, nor any of the places they all had covered since the Frogs got away. It was like struggling to remember a person's name that should be on the tip of one's tongue; if only he could pin it down. It wasn't Patsy's use of Nicky Travato's Cadillac . . .

And then it hit him! Last night, Sonny and Ripa had tailed Patsy, in Nicky's car, up to 77th Street and York Avenue. Egan himself had followed Patsy and his wife to that same neighborhood only Friday! He recalled clearly now Patsy's mysterious visit to the luxury apartment house at No. 45 East End Avenue; that was only four or five blocks from 77th and York. Could there be a chance that he was up there again? Why not?

He drove over to the East River Drive and headed north, following the same route he had taken behind Patsy's Oldsmobile at about the same hour on Friday – only four days ago? It seemed like months.

Just as he made the turn into East End Avenue, two blocks ahead he saw a gray Cadillac swing across the sidewalk into the garage entrance of the building he knew to be No. 45. He could barely believe that he had seen Nicky's Cadillac. Patsy! He had walked right into him! Oh, mother, how lucky can one Irish cop get?

Egan pulled his car to the curb, tumbled out and ran toward the garage entrance. The Cadillac was halted down the ramp by the office cubbyhole. A man was getting out and handing his keys to an attendant. Egan edged into the dimly lit runway, and saw that the driver was *not* Patsy, nor anybody he knew. He walked closer to the rear of the Cadillac, reaching for his notebook. It *looked* like Travato's car, but it wasn't.

He was about to turn back up to the street when a voice alongside startled him: 'Can I help you, mister?'

Egan spun around to see a young Negro wearing the gray uniform of garage attendant. The detective grinned and flicked perspiration from his brow in exaggerated fashion. 'Hey, man, you scared me.' He flipped open his notebook and showed the man his police shield. 'Police. Listen, two guys just stuck up a liquor store a couple of blocks away, and they got away in a red Dodge. You seen any characters in a red Dodge?'

The young man scratched his head. 'No, I'm just back from lunch though. Ask in the office.'

Egan hadn't wanted to be seen here at all, much less turn the visit into a show. But he had committed himself and might as well carry the charade to the end. He might learn something that would serve him well if he ever were to look into this garage or building in the future.

Trailing the attendant, he walked into the small office with his bared shield still in hand. A sandy-haired, fifty-year-old man stood leaning over a high, narrow desk scattered with papers and parking checks. In the far right-hand corner, with his back to the door, a younger, dark-haired man wearing mechanic's coveralls persued a rack of road maps.

'Yes, sir,' the white attendant began.

'Cops,' the Negro interjected.

Egan showed his shield. 'There's been a holdup. I'm looking for a red Dodge.'

The dark man in the corner jerked his head around, then turned quickly away. Egan found himself staring at Patsy Fuca's back.

Chapter Thirteen

'WAS anybody hurt?' the one behind the counter asked.

Egan went back to his act. 'Oh, yeah, a coupla guys hit a liquor store. Nobody hurt.' He was a little short of breath. 'They were seen taking off in a red Dodge, 1960 four-door sedan. We're checking all the garages in the neighborhood. You come across any car like that, any strangers?'

The man lowered his eyes to the accumulation of chits on the desk top, as though concentrating on possible answers strewn there, then shook his head. 'Nope, not while I been on. You see anything, Jimmy?' he asked the Negro attendant.

'I just told him, I been out to lunch. I didn't see nothing.'

Egan pocketed his notebook and realized his hands were shaking. It was difficult not to glance over at Pasty, who was trying to melt into the corner. 'Okay,' Egan started to say and felt himself flush as his voice came out thinly. Straining to sound casual but official, he cleared his throat. 'Well, keep your eyes open, huh? And be careful. If anybody spots this car, call the station house right away, okay? See you around,' he said as he walked out of the cubicle and up the ramp, pressing his hands flat against the soft lining in his overcoat pockets to towel away the clamminess.

Egan's first impulse had been a defensive fear that Patsy must have recognized him. But by the time he reached the street, reason dictated that chances were a hundred-to-one, maybe a thousand-to-one, that Patsy had ever seen him before – at least not as a *cop*. In all of his surveillance of the past four months, the only times he had really exposed himself to Patsy was when he had posed as an intern from St. Catherine's Hospital and visited the luncheonette. Egan's knowledge of human nature told him that it was highly unlikely that Patsy had really observed *him* among all the other white-clad hospital personnel. And if Patsy had ever noticed him, it was improbable that he could identify the bundled-up cop searching for a getaway car in a basement garage in Manhattan as the 'doctor' in white from the store.

Egan hurried toward his own car, parked half a block south on East End Avenue. Whatever the probabilities, he had to get to a telephone and alert base that he had found Patsy Fuca. But, glancing back as he started to cross 81st Street, he caught a glimpse of a gray-overalled figure half hidden behind the garage entrance of No. 45. Egan paused and tried his best to effect the appearance of a cop on a street corner trying to calculate his next move in a robbery investigation. The figure in the entranceway edged a bit further back into the garage. He was watching Egan, all right. It was the sandy-haired one.

The officer figured quickly that if he left right now, Patsy might find reason to suspect that the police had caught up with him, and he would be gone again. The only thing to do was to carry out his pose of looking for a holdup car. Egan stepped briskly across 81st Street and went down into the garage in the building on the opposite corner.

In matter-of-fact fashion, he repeated the fiction about a robbery and a red Dodge to the attendant and then came back up to the street, and pausing only to check for traffic, walked across East End Avenue toward yet another apartment house with a garage in its lower level. The individual from No. 45 had come out of the entranceway and was on the corner of 81st Street now. Egan could feel his eyes follow him as he descended into the third building.

The sandy-haired attendant was still lounging outside when the detective emerged again. By now, Egan thought the guy could have slipped down into the second garage and checked the cop's story. Let's hope so; and the other one too. If the Dodge story keeps Patsy from panicking, I'm lucky. What the hell is he doing here, anyway? Egan made a note to pull the files on No. 45 East End Avenue to learn about its occupants, owner, renting agent, garage concessionaire and even its employees.

The detective entered a stationery store a block and a half away and found a telephone booth from which he could still observe the building. At any moment he expected to see Nicky's gray Cadillac speed out of the ramp, and he was ready to take up the tail. He dialed base control. Ben Fitzgerald answered.

'Fitz, I got Patsy!' Egan cried.

'Where?' Fitzgerald boomed.

In a minute and a half, Egan outlined what had happened from following one of his famous hunches. Suddenly he tensed:

'Hold it, Fitz. A car's coming out. Maybe it's Patsy.'

There was a silence as Egan squinted up the block. But it was not the familiar 1956 gray Cadillac that emerged. It was a black Buick Invicta that turned north as it gained the Avenue.

'No, Travato's car is still in the garage,' he said into the phone.

'Are you *sure* you saw Fuca?' the supervising agent persisted.

'Am I sure? Do I know Patsy? Look, scramble Sonny and Waters and the other guys, get them up here!'

While Egan listened, Fitzgerald switched on the all-cars transmitter and alerted available officers to converge on No. 45 East End Avenue.

'Fitz,' Egan called, remembering how some cops enjoy speeding to a scene of operations, 'tell them not to come on too strong and to fan out around this building. I'll be around some place close.'

Fitzgerald complied, then came back on the line. 'I sure hope you're right, Popeye,' he said, sounding a little quizzical. 'What the hell is Patsy doing in *that* neighborhood?'

'I don't know. But it's the same spot I tagged him to last Friday.'

'You did? I didn't know.'

'Look, I gotta go,' Egan cut him off. 'I'll talk to you later. Oh, wait. See if you can get me a rundown on the management and tenants of Forty-five East End Avenue, okay?'

Leaving the store, Egan climbed into his Corvair and eased it into a parking space near the corner of 82nd Street and East End, from where he could watch the comings and goings at No. 45. Switching off the motor, he sat back, content that Patsy had to come out sooner or later.

Assistance was not long in arriving. It was just past one-thirty when Egan spied Sonny Grosso approaching on foot along East End Avenue. Egan rolled down his window and whistled, and Sonny came to the car and got in.

By 2 P.M. every street in the vicinity was covered by narcotics officers, some in unmarked cars, others, in a variety of attire, on foot. Lieutenant Vinnie Hawkes headed the large surveillance unit. About 3:00 P.M. Sonny, who had left Eddie's car, returned, concern etched deeper into his already sad features. With his radio being repaired, Eddie depended on Sonny to bring him the latest news. The entire investigation team staked out around No. 45 East End Avenue had serious doubts that Egan had actually seen Patsy, Grosso reported.

Agent Waters casually ambled over to Egan's car, pulled open the back door and slumped inside. Eddie felt the skepticism in the aggressive little agent's eyes and tone as he expressed his disbelief that Patsy would be in this neighborhood at all. Egan struggled to hold his temper in check as the Federal agent needled him.

At 4 P.M. Dick Auletta approached. Lieutenant Hawkes wanted to see Popeye. Wearily Eddie slid out of the car and followed Auletta to a delicatessen around the corner. Hawkes, tall and spare, with the bleak look of Gary Cooper nearing a showdown, stood in the doorway. He was unmistakenly convinced that he was wasting the time of a large segment of the Narcotics Bureau following up Egan's alleged sighting of Patsy. He said as much.

Popeye staunchly maintained he *had* seen Patsy and suggested infiltrating someone into the garage to see if Nicky Travato's Cadillac which Patsy had last been seen driving might not be there. Hawkes mused aloud on who would walk into a garage for an 'inspection' and not seem out of the ordinary.

'Sanitation? Rent control? Welfare?' Egan offered.

Hawkes chuckled. 'Welfare? Around *here*?'

'You're right,' Egan agreed, grateful for a smile from the dour lieutenant. 'How about a fire inspection?'

Hawkes displayed immediate enthusiasm, remembering that Egan's stepfather was now a city fire chief. Hawkes and Egan repaired to the nearest telephone. Ten minutes later, Dick Auletta was dispatched to the fire station on East 75th Street. Auletta would be one of the inspecting 'firemen.'

It was nearing 5 P.M. and the streetlights had just blinked on, when a red fire truck rumbled around the corner of 79th Street, three blocks away from the garage. As the pessimistic surveillance team watched, rubber-booted firemen jumped from the glistening cruiser and began inspecting each garage as they came to it on East End Avenue. At 5:25 three firemen entered No. 45 and ten minutes later reappeared. Tense and worried, Egan watched from his car a block and a half up the Avenue as only two of the 'firemen' jumped back onto the cruiser; a third proceeded southward on foot, rounding the corner where Hawkes was waiting. After five more long, anguished minutes Hawkes appeared beside Egan's car and slid in.

'Well?' Egan blurted. 'Have I blown it?'

Hawkes's mouth softened. 'You were right, Eddie. Nicky's Caddy *is* in there.'

The detective slumped and looked at the lieutenant. 'Man, you guys had me talking to myself!'

'Go ahead and say it: "I told you so."'

Egan brushed off the gratuity. 'Who needs it?' Then he grinned. 'Anyway, I already said it – before.'

'The car is holed way down in the back of the lower level, Auletta says. It looks as though it's been there for some time.'

'That fits. What about Patsy?'

'No sign of him in the garage,' Hawkes related. 'He could be anywhere in the building, of course.'

'Just like last time I saw him here. He went up in the elevator. Did you get anything on the building or the tenants?'

'Yes. The *building* seems okay, tenants well-to-do, all apparently respectable – did you know Don Ameche, the actor, lives there? – but the garage itself, that shows promise.

'It's a concession,' Hawkes went on, 'and the guy who runs it, Sol Feinberg, has been through the mill more than once on suspicion of, let's say, under-the-counter enterprises, including possible interest in junk.'

'Hey, now—!' the detective smiled.

'We have never been able to nail him, and right now he's clean,' continued Hawkes. 'But he has a business partner who has a piece of this operation and also owns another commercial garage in the Bronx. But more than that he is an *active* suspect in a couple of major violations, also including narcotics . . . So does this make you feel better?'

'Beautiful!' Egan exclaimed. 'You know, I think I *will* say it again.'

'Say what?'

Egan grinned: 'I told you so.'

Before Hawkes returned to his own post, he told Egan that as soon as Auletta had reported confirmation of the Cadillac on the premises, Sonny Grosso had proposed setting up an observation and command post in the building facing No. 45 across East End Avenue. The lieutenant had charged Sonny with making arrangements with one of the building's occupants. 'And Sonny asked me to give you this message,' Hawkes added. 'Up the Irish!'

Egan was hungry all of a sudden. It was close to 6:30 P.M., and he had not eaten since breakfast. He accompanied Hawkes around the corner as far as the delicatessen where several hours earlier he had felt so demoralized as his boss chewed him out. His step was lighter now, buoyed by renewed confidence, and he indulged himself by ordering two roast beef sandwiches and two Pepsis to take back to the car.

Finding Patsy was the most important development in the past two days. The three Frenchmen were still missing, and a few hours earlier the Edison Hotel had received a handwritten note from Jean Jehan in which he enclosed $82.50 in Canadian currency to settle his room bill. The note asked that his belongings be forwarded to an address in Rosemont, Montreal. But even now Egan and the others had to face the possibility that any time during this long day of Patsy's absence he might well have been meeting the Frenchmen, finalizing the deal.

There was only one way to find out: wait for Patsy – and any other of his fellow conspirators who might happen along.

Egan munched his sandwiches, relaxed but alert and primed for anything.

Two more hours passed slowly, as the sharp wind whipped off the East River. Egan was grateful for the protection of the car, but still he felt chilled and cramped. He couldn't postulate what Patsy might be doing all this time. Probabilities and possibilities spun around in his head, but the only facts at hand were that Nicky's Cadillac was still in the garage and Patsy had not come out of the building. He would have to show himself sometime.

Patsy did appear, about five minutes later. But not from No. 45. He was walking up the far side of East End Avenue from the direction of 79th Street.

Egan started, and then watched tensely as the subject, still wearing coveralls, sauntered across 81st Street and, with scarcely a glance about, serenely turned into the garage.

Holy Mother! He must have been *out* all afternoon. Jesus H. Christ. Egan thought he knew when Patsy had slipped away: it had to have been when the detective had visited the other garages in the vicinity. Or it might have been during the few minutes he'd taken to telephone base, or while he was driving around the block to position himself on 82nd Street in view of the building. Patsy had enjoyed practically twelve hours of unobserved freedom this day.

It was a hell of a time to be without a radio, Egan swore, as the shock wore off. He shouldered the car door open and ran into East End Avenue, waving his arms and pointing to No. 45 across the way. Out of a doorway popped the lanky figure of Vinnie Hawkes, waving Egan back. Okay, at least everybody knew. He returned to his car and started the motor.

In five minutes the gray Cadillac loomed up from the garage and paused a moment, astraddle the sidewalk. Egan vowed to tail Patsy to the moon, if necessary. Just then, the right front door of the Corvair was yanked open and Agent

Luis Gonzalez tumbled inside next to him. He was carrying a portable radiophone. 'Good boy, *amigo*!' Egan cried.

He seized the microphone: 'Okay, Popeye here. I'm gonna take this bird, *wherever* he goes!'

Patsy turned right onto East End, passed Egan and signaled for a left on 83rd. Egan eased the Corvair out of 82nd and followed, Gonzalez barking the course into the radio.

Patsy drove through York Avenue and continued on 83rd Street to First Avenue, where he made a right and proceeded uptown. Egan and Gonzalez stayed with him as the Cadillac swung around into the downtown lanes of the East River Drive at 96th Street. 'Christ, he's still playing games,' Egan complained.

'. . . somebody get to Seventy-ninth and pick us up on the Drive!' Gonzalez was radioing smartly.

They glimpsed a car waiting in the 79th Street access as they flew past. It turned into the traffic flow after them, but Patsy now was veering off the Drive at the 73rd Street exit. He drove the block west to York Avenue, then went right, uptown again. At 82nd Street, Patsy made another right and, midway between York and East End Avenue – not a hundred yards from the spot where Egan had sat for some eight hours – squeezed the big Caddy into a space by the curb.

'He's parking on Eighty-second,' Gonzalez reported. 'We'll have to keep going past him. Somebody got him, kay?'

'We see him.' It was Sonny Grosso responding.

Egan drove down to East End and turned right and drew over in the middle of the block, directly opposite the garage from which Patsy had emerged a quarter of an hour earlier.

'Oh, ho!' – Sonny again, and gleeful – 'Guess who we found?'

'What's happening?' Egan shouted toward the radio.

'Patsy meets a guy on the sidewalk, and they're talking. And who is it but Mr. Mouren – Frog Number Three!'

So the ball game is *not* over! Egan exulted.

Minutes passed, the speaker crackling with the voices of officers in other cars crosschecking locations and logistics. Then Sonny broke through: 'The two of them are getting into the Caddy. They're moving out.'

The Cadillac came around the corner and passed Egan and Gonzalez in the Corvair. Egan waited until it had gone another block south on East End, then pulled out. Patsy turned up 79th Street to York. When the light changed, he made a wide left, and the Caddy stopped near the southwest corner of the intersection. Mouren got out and started walking west on 79th. Patsy drove on, headed downtown.

'. . . the Frog is out!' Gonzalez broadcast.

Egan tailed Patsy down to 63rd Street, where he turned onto the Drive again. They were making good speed downtown when word was flashed that Mouren had succeeded in melting into the night.

'One minute he was there, the next he was gone,' Vinnie Hawkes reported in discouraging tones.

Patsy led them over the Williamsburg Bridge to his luncheonette in Brooklyn. His father-in-law had been minding the store, and Patsy sent him home.

Egan and Gonzalez were soon joined by other cars, including one carrying Sonny and Waters and another with Dick Auletta. Gonzalez switched over to Auletta's car, and they left. Finally, at 11 P.M., Patsy closed up. Followed by the remaining officers, he drove the Caddy onto the Brooklyn-Queens Expressway and south to 65th Street. But instead of going directly to his own house, he scooted across 65th to New Utrecht Avenue, where, under the elevated structure, he rounded the block and parked in front of Nicky Travato's tenement building on 66th Street. Locking the Cadillac, Patsy went inside.

He was out again within ten minutes. He walked along

66th and entered an automobile at the curb fifty yards east of Nicky's house. Sonny recognized it as Patsy's own blue Buick compact.

Patsy drove over to 67th Street and into his open garage, and entered the house. The porch light darkened. Sixty-seventh Street was quiet.

At either end of the block, three tired detectives in two cars settled back in the silence and darkness.

'Who wants to sleep first?' Eddie Egan inquired into his radiophone.

Chapter Fourteen

TUESDAY HAD BEEN A LONG, exhausting day for Patsy Fuca. He looked over at his young wife Barbara, asleep in the bed across from him. He ought to rap her in the teeth. If the word ever got out she had been hooking him, he would he lucky if he could *get* a job sweeping the subways!

Patsy couldn't sleep. He rolled out of bed, pulled on a woolen robe and walked over to the window in his bare feet. Barbara stirred. He shrugged. She wasn't really a bad kid, he thought. With all that bread around, he couldn't blame her much for digging in. How much had she taken? A few grand? What *had* hung him up was the size of the load the Frenchies brought in. For fifty or fifty-one kilos, he had to front at least half, like $275,000. And he had been shy about fifty grand. As much a demand as everybody said there was for the stuff, it was tough getting his customers to put so much money together. Had he handled the business well? He wondered what Uncle Angie would think.

So he had to stall the Frenchmen. His mind wandered back over the past seven days. It was just a week ago that he had received the call from Giant to meet him the next day at the Roosevelt. Patsy hadn't been ready; he had needed maybe another week to get all the advance payment. He visualized the tall, elderly dandy. Slick as they come, but what a kookie old fart! *Mamma mia*, the way he dresses, alone, would be enough to get the cops on him.

But a real cool one, Giant. The other two Frenchmen, they

would have kicked the whole operation when they thought the fuzz had the big heat on. But not Giant; he just says let's go underground, the deal is too big to bury, nobody can touch us without possession, and who knows where the stuff is?

Patsy hadn't been worried about the law. Maybe they were on him, maybe not. He *always* assumed that cops were around; that way, you didn't get too careless. Were they tailing the other night – when was it, Friday? He didn't know. But he had been quick to encourage the Frenchmen to check out of their hotels: not only would that put off the cops, if they *had* been keeping tabs, but cooling the operation for a few days would also give him that much more time to collect the necessary front money.

At the first couple of meetings, the Frenchies had been talking about wrapping everything up by Saturday. And, going along with them, fearful of admitting that he needed more time, on Friday he had even driven up to East End Avenue to check the setup. But then came the long ride around town Friday night, and Patsy knew he had lucked into a grace period. The Frenchmen went up to the motel in Yonkers, and he had the whole weekend to push his contacts.

He grinned and congratulated himself on some fast thinking when Giant had called and said the heat was too much and maybe they should cut. Those cops, the Decency League or whatever it was, the city censor had sent in to take the dirty books out of his paperback racks had really done Patsy the favor of a lifetime. Could he have ever thought up such an alibi for heat?

Patsy didn't understand why they were so nervous. He had gone out Saturday night with Nicky to test for a tail, and there didn't seem to be any fuzz around; if there was, they weren't sticking too close, anyway. He wouldn't have any trouble moving the actor's Buick when the time came.

Besides, when the chips were down, he could always lose cops.

Giant must have pulled the other two Frenchmen together, because by Monday they were back talking about unloading the Buick the next day. Patsy actually still needed a few more days, but he had to go along. If he still didn't have all the bread by the time the car was clean, he would pay for as much as he could handle and try to make some kind of deal for the rest . . . Monday, he confirmed arrangements with his brother Tony to line up that garage in the Bronx where they would make the transfer, and with Tony Feola downtown at Anthony's Auto Shop to put the Buick back together after it had been stripped, just as he had back in November. That night he drove Nicky's Caddy – the cops wouldn't be watching for him in that – up to East End Avenue again to double-check the layout. Mouren met him there, and they rehearsed the schedule for Tuesday. Mouren even gave him a sample of the stuff – *madonna!* it was top quality! – which he magnanimously passed along to Tony back at the store. His brother deserved to make a few extra bills for himself.

Staring out the bedroom window into the shadows beyond the streetlights, he wondered if there were cops out there watching the house. In two more days he would have disposed of the largest single load of heroin ever brought into the city. This had been the most dangerous day, he thought.

Putting on sturdy work clothes early that morning, he had left home in Nicky's car and driven up the Expressway all the way to the Grand Central Parkway and then across the Triborough Bridge into the Bronx. Tony met him at Shulman's garage near Crotona Park. Everything was set there: they would have a nice secluded spot in the back to work on the Buick. Mouren would meet them there between twelve and one.

He drove downtown to the garage at No. 45 East End

Avenue and parked the Caddy deep in the hole. Then had come the snag: the French Buick was there all right, but Patsy didn't have a ticket for it, and the attendant insisted that only the boss, Feinberg, could release the car. Feinberg had stepped out for a few minutes with the keys to the Buick in his pocket. Patsy stewed in mounting impatience as he paced the cubicle office.

When that red-haired cop walked in showing his badge, Patsy almost fainted. He couldn't tell whether the guy recognized him. The cop had stared for a second like he had, but then it could have been because Patsy himself must have looked so startled. He relaxed when the attendant who had trailed the cop outside came back and confirmed that he *was* going to the different garages on the block looking for a holdup car. Still, it was no time to get careless. When Feinberg returned a few minutes later, Patsy drove out in the French Buick and headed straight uptown to the Bronx. He didn't see the cop again.

Tony and Mouren were waiting at Shulman's garage. Tony had a big steamer trunk that he had taken from the basement of his apartment house. Inside were two well-used suitcases. Mouren had a blue valise. Patsy himself had brought a black leather tool kit. Under an overhanging light far back in the garage, Mouren produced a single set of plans, which he spread out on the hood of the Buick.

It took them three hours to remove all 110 one-pound plastic-wrapped wrapped packages of white powder, plus a couple of dozen smaller packets, from the narrow cavities in the frame and underside of the Buick – in all, over fifty kilos of pure heroin. Tony kept stuffing the bags into his suitcases until at last Patsy, his face grimy, hands and forearms etched with red nicks and welts, stood and brushed himself off. Mouren checked the contents of several bags. The quality seemed to be excellent, as promised.

Then he and the Frenchman talked money. From his tool bag, Patsy removed $225,000 in large-denomination bills. He said he could make the full payoff by Thursday. How much could he handle now? Patsy calculated that he could take about forty kilos. They counted out eighty-eight half kilo (one pound) packages and a dozen of the little bags from the piles in Tony's suitcases; then Mouren transferred the remainder, twenty-three half kilos and a dozen more of the ounce-size packets, plus the neatly stacked cash, into his blue valise.

You know, said Patsy thoughtfully, staring at the blue suitcase, that bagful would be nice right now as working merchandise. The larger quantity could be stashed away as inventory for later use. Couldn't they trust him? The Frenchman said he would talk to Giant. Tonight, after Patsy had disposed of the Buick, they could meet – 9 P.M., on 82nd Street? Patsy agreed to pick Mouren up after he returned to the garage at No. 45 for Nicky's Cadillac.

Meanwhile, Mouren wondered, where did Patsy plan to store the goods on hand? That's our business, Patsy winked at his brother.

Tony stowed the steamer trunk containing the two packed suitcases in the back of the Buick, and Patsy threw in the tool kit. It was close to 4:30 P.M. when they backed out of the garage. Patsy dropped Mouren off on busy Westchester Avenue, and he and his brother watched as the Frenchman, carrying his blue valise, hailed a taxi and sped away. Then they drove the six blocks to Tony's apartment house on Bryant Avenue. In gathering dusk, the two lugged the trunk down a flight of concrete steps into the basement and on into an enclosed storage room. They cleared a space on a shelf deep against the rear wall and heaved the trunk up onto it. Tony found a piece of children's chalk and marked the black trunk in block letters: A. FUCA – 5/C. Then they went upstairs and had a drink with Tony's wife, Margaret, and Patsy played with their two children. At 7 P.M., he was in the Buick, on his way downtown to Anthony's Auto Shop.

He parked on East Broadway near Anthony's, leaving the key under the floor mat. The shop was already closed. Tomorrow, Wednesday, Feola would do his welding job, replace the splash pans and other panels removed from the underside, and leave the Buick back on the street for Patsy to pick up. There was even a jar of mud from France to be smeared over the reassembled frame. He would drive the Buick back uptown to No. 45 East End Avenue and deposit it in the garage, and on Thursday the actor, Angelvin, would come to retrieve it, and it would be all over.

Patsy had hailed a cab at East Broadway and Pike Street and directed it to 79th Street and York Avenue. From there, he walked over to East End and up two blocks to No. 45. As he drove out of the garage in Nicky's Caddy, he wondered again about the cop who had been nosing around earlier. He still had five minutes before he was to meet Mouren; so he wheeled northward to 96th Street and down the Drive to 73rd, just to make sure no fuzz were sticking to him. All looked clear. On 82nd Street, Mouren was waiting. They cruised a few blocks while the Frenchman told him that Giant might indeed turn over the withheld goods if on Thursday Patsy could produce at least the balance of front money. After all, he and his organization were valuable customers. Patsy dropped Mouren off at 79th Street and York and started home in high spirits. The bonanza was within reach.

Just one more day to go now. Patsy turned from the window and padded across the dark room to his bed. One more day. What could go wrong in one day?

After an interminable, cold, uncomfortable night in their respective cars outside Patsy Fuca's house, Detectives Eddie

Egan and Sonny Grosso and Agent Frank Waters bitterly watched the sun climb in the frosty blue sky over Brooklyn on Wednesday, January 17. Aside from sporadic grunts, wheezes and blasphemies, none of them said much. Sonny's dark beard felt raw on his throat; he could smell himself, and with a grimace he opened a window. Waters contacted base, but there was no news. Egan's own radiophone speaker sounded wan, and Sonny commented idly, 'You better get that juiced up.' Egan muttered, 'I'd be better off getting myself juiced up,' and his voice trailed off into mumbled obscenities.

With the aid of Water's ever-handy 'burglar's tool,' they had rifled Patsy's Oldsmobile during the night but found nothing. Now it was past eight, a clear sunny morning, and chattering schoolchildren, books in mittened hands, were coming out of the neat houses on 67th Street, walking or skipping toward Twelfth Avenue. The three officers slouched down in their cars, feeling very much like derelicts.

Patsy emerged alone from No. 1224 about eight-thirty, dressed in a thigh-length woolen car coat, and got into his Olds. 'Why don't you two take him?' Egan suggested into his radio to the others. 'I'll go up around the luncheonette and be there in case he shakes you.'

But Patsy didn't go directly to his store. Instead, he drove across the Manhattan Bridge to New York and went to a wholesale supply center at Houston and Forsyth streets. As Sonny and Waters waited outside, from a few minutes past nine until 12:35 P.M., Patsy rummaged the warehouse, purchasing nonperishable goods for his store – cigarettes, soda straws, paper cups, napkins, hard candies, stationery. He made several trips out to his car with bundles, and the rear seat was filled by the time he started back to Brooklyn. Arriving near the luncheonette just before 1 P.M., Sonny and Waters rejoined Egan at St. Catherine's Hospital across Bushwick Avenue and watched as for the next forty-five minutes Patsy and his brother Tony, who had made his appearance about eleven, leisurely unloaded the stores from the Oldsmobile.

At two o'clock, Patsy came out and again drove alone toward New York. This time he took the Williamsburg Bridge; he turned off Delancey onto Allen Street and then left onto East Broadway. Egan and Sonny, together now, watched him slow midway in the block and make a U-turn, pulling up before an auto repair shop whose sign over twin double-width overhead doors proclaimed the place as Anthony's. The detectives looked at each other in dawning interest. This was the same spot where that night in November Patsy, his wife and the girl Marilyn had stopped and Patsy had driven off in the Canadian Buick which he later left parked on Cherry Street.

Patsy stayed in Anthony's about twenty minutes. When he returned to his car at two forty-five, he was carrying what appeared to be a black leather satchel, like a doctor's bag, or a tool kit of some kind. Then, with the curious officers a safe distance behind, Patsy drove back to Delancey Street and onto the approach to the Williamsburg Bridge.

Midafternoon traffic was heavy toward Brooklyn, and Patsy's Olds became separated from Egan's Corvair by several vehicles. As they crawled along, Sonny had the right-hand door partly opened and, half-standing, he tried to keep the blue compact in view. When the flow slowed almost to a standstill, with a snort of disgust he threw the door fully open and jumped out. 'I'll run up ahead and make sure we're still on him,' he yelled to his partner. But in a minute or two, the cars began to move again, and Egan came upon Sonny jogging forlornly near the midpoint of the bridge. 'We'll never keep up with him,' Sonny puffed as he scrambled back into the Corvair. 'He was five or six cars ahead, and the way he drives, he'll be off the bridge and gone by the time we get across.'

'Well, let's hope he's headed back to his store,' Egan said, and he radioed the stakeouts at the luncheonette and at Patsy's house to watch for the subject. They themselves proceeded toward the luncheonette; and before they were within eight blocks of Bushwick Avenue, Frank Waters reported by radio that Patsy had just returned and was inside now with both his brother Tony and Barbara's father.

The detectives resumed their watch from the hospital grounds. The visit to Anthony's roused their imagination, as did the black bag that Patsy had brought away with him. If they could lend any credence to Waters's conjecture that, as the previous November, an automobile, perhaps again a Canadian Buick, was an integral part of Patsy's current action, the auto shop certainly could represent a pertinent link. As for the contents of the satchel, their theories ranged from special tools for stripping the mystery automobile, to the junk itself, to a bagful of cash with which the ultimate exchange would be made.

There were barely thirty-two hours left to the Narcotics Bureau before the search warrants expired. The fevered theorizing of the police was becoming more like wishful thinking than hard deduction. But they would have been stunned to realize how close their shotgun suppositions were to the truth. Emotion and primary instinct impelled them to hit now, hit Patsy before it really was too late – and still they held back. Perhaps it already was too late; in that case, it wouldn't matter much anyway. But essentially they clung to the hope, bolstered by well-practiced intuition, that the climax was yet to come; and a precipitous move, even if only an hour premature, could ruin what slim chances remained. They had to stay on Patsy and not let him out of sight for a moment.

At 4 P.M., Patsy and Tony left the luncheonette together and entered Patsy's Oldsmobile. Again, Patsy drove out

Grand Avenue toward the bridge into New York, but now, instead, he swung onto the Brooklyn-Queens Expressway and raced south. A fresh pair of Federal agents having arrived to take over at the stakeout, Waters in his white Olds and Egan and Sonny in the Corvair all took out after the Fuca brothers. They followed them to Patsy's home neighborhood. There, Patsy parked his car near his house, then the two walked around the corner of Twelfth Avenue – where they got into Nicky Travato's gray Cadillac, which was sitting at the curb, empty. Something's up now, the officers told themselves.

Now Patsy and Tony retraced their route on the Expressway. At the Manhattan Bridge cutoff, however, Patsy exited toward New York. He came off the bridge at Canal Street, made another right at Pike, and drove straight down to South Street, along the river, where he swung around and stopped in front of the Pike Slip Inn. Tony got out and went into the bar. Patsy eased the Caddy back up Pike toward East Broadway.

'He's going back to that Anthony's,' Egan guessed.

But a block before East Broadway, Patsy turned right into Henry Street.

'This is where we sat on him the other night when he came to play cards,' Waters said. 'It's kind of early, though . . .'

'Don't forget,' Sonny noted, 'his grandmother lives in this street, too.'

Not wishing to enter the congested street behind Patsy, Egan and Sonny continued up Pike past Henry before pulling over, while Waters navigated around on East Broadway, intending to circle the block and cover Henry Street from the other side.

But by the time the three of them had positioned themselves at either end of Henry Street, the Cadillac no longer was there. While Sonny and Waters waited at each corner,

Egan strode briskly through the tenement block from Pike to Rutgers streets. The Caddy just was gone. The only answer could be that while they'd been maneuvering so cautiously, Patsy had either roared straight through Henry or turned off into yet another street. Now he could be anywhere. They dashed back to their cars and, first, radioed an alert, then sped around to East Broadway, converging on Anthony's auto shop. The gray Caddy was not in sight. Sonny went into the garage and looked around. Approached by an Italian-looking mechanic, he said he had a faulty gasket that needed fixing. The man told him they were just closing, to come back tomorrow. He came out shaking his head: Nicky's car was not there.

Next they sped back to the Pike Slip Inn, and Sonny went in. He returned in a few minutes and slid in next to Egan, his expression doleful. 'Tony's gone, too,' he grumbled.

They drove through Henry Street again . . . and East Broadway. Nothing. Patsy had slipped through their fingers once more. And, judging by the manner of his evasion, it could have been their last crack at him.

At 5:30 P.M., Old Slip and the other narrow lanes girdling the 1st Precinct station house already were dark and fast becoming lifeless. The lower tip of Manhattan, at night, is one of the few sections of the pulsating city virtually devoid of motion. Now, on the perimeter of the area, along South Street, cars were still trickling out of all-day parking enclosures, and on the Viaduct overhead bumper-to-bumper traffic crept toward the Staten Island Ferry and the entrances to the Brooklyn-Battery Tunnel; but in a couple of hours solitude would settle over the streets below. Isolated footsteps would echo among blackened buildings, and the most noticeable sign of movement would be an occasional sweep of headlights. Even at five-thirty, on Old Slip itself, the only apparent outposts of activity were a yellowish glow emanating from the tall windowed doors of a fire station and, across Front Street, the pale green globes flanking the dimly lit entrance of the 1st Precinct.

Inside, the police building was quiet. Clocks ticked and radiators hissed and sometimes clanked. The uniformed desk sergeant sat alone behind his high desk, reading. Two young patrolmen, their collars open and without gun belts and shields, in plain blue from neck to toe, looked strangely out of place as they stood by a bulletin board talking in hushed voices. The four-to-twelve shift had only marched out ninety minutes before, and it would be hours before the midnight crew would begin straggling in for assembly. On the second floor, in the squad room, one detective wearing a sweater lounged in a swivel chair reading a magazine while another in a white shirt and brown tie hunched over a desk, writing scratchily on a lined pad.

By contrast, on the floor above, there was an odd sense of purpose even without much more motion. There were only a few men at scattered lamp-lit desks in the big bullpen to the right of the stairway foyer, and they were quiet; most of the room was in shadows. Chief Carey's office in the far corner was dark, but light blazed from the one next to it. Hawkes was not at his desk, however. He and five other grim-faced men were seated around a conference table in a tiny room at the other end of the floor where the Special Investigating Unit operated.

Also seated around the table with Hawkes, in various attitudes of weary tension, were Eddie Egan, Sonny Grosso, Agent Frank Waters, and Sergeant Jack Fleming and Detective Jack Gildea of S.I.U.

The men were silent for the moment. Egan's drawn face was fuzzy with red bristles. He wore a blue and yellow plaid flannel shirt; his black, thigh-length leather jacket was hung over the back of his chair. Sonny tugged at the throat of his black turtleneck shirt; he too was unshaven, and his eyes were puffy and red-streaked. The others were dressed in ordinary shirts and ties, but all collars were open, ties loosened, sleeves turned up to the forearms. Suit jackets hung on doorknobs or lay rumpled on a desk top. It had been a long day. They were supposed to be reviewing the Fuca case, but there was little to say, really. The simple, nettling factor was that they had finally bumbled surveillance of Patsy Fuca.

Hawkes cleared his throat. 'Well, have we had it?'

There was a rustle of nervous shifting in seats, but no one spoke at first. Then Frank Waters drawled: 'Speaking for my office, I'd say it sure looks like the thing is scratched. What have we got? No Frenchmen, and now no Patsy, and he sure looked like he was moving out today.' His glance flicked toward Egan.

The detective slumped in his straight-backed chair and merely scowled. Waters was beginning to annoy him. Everything the agent said lately seemed to imply oblique criticism of the police, or of Sonny and him, or was it just of *him*?

'He had to be up to something,' Sonny offered listlessly.

Egan roused himself. 'He's been "up to something" every day. I say let's use the warrants and hit every place now,' he growled.

'Hit who, *what*?' Waters questioned. 'We got nobody!'

'He's right, Eddie,' Hawkes said quietly. 'We know Patsy's not home or at his store. Tony's not home – he *is* at the store. Travato's home, but his car's out, and that doesn't mean anything unless we have Patsy. The Frenchmen – who knows where *they* are? Where would you hit?'

'The warrants expire tomorrow night,' Egan persisted.

'We still got more than twenty-four hours.' The usually pessimistic Sonny surprised his partner with this bright observation.

'We'll just have to hope for a break,' Waters added.

'We can always use the warrants tomorrow, whatever happens,' Hawkes said.

'Even if there's only a slim chance,' Waters went on, 'we got to save the warrants until the last possible minute. They could mean our whole case—'

'*Our* case – Sonny's and mine, the N.Y.P.D., not Federal!' Egan snapped and immediately regretted his pettiness.

Jack Fleming spoke up: '*That* kind of stuff is not going to get us anywhere at all.'

Sonny stood up and stretched. 'Well, unless somebody has got some hot idea, I tell you where *I'm* going. I've missed my Wednesday night bowling league three weeks in a row now. Instead of going around in any more circles, I think I'll just go roll a few. You can always reach me . . .'

Jim Gildea clucked, 'I wouldn't mind a night off myself. My kids won't even recognize me.'

Egan rose abruptly. 'Well, I really hope you guys can get your entertainment plans squared away.' Egan scooped up his jacket and strode to the stairs and out of the 1st Precinct.

It was 6:35 P.M. Egan picked his way through the darkness of Old Slip to his car. Carol Galvin made her way into his mind. She would be on duty now. He hadn't seen her in more than a week. Tonight would be a very good time.

Chapter Fifteen

THE tavern where Carol Galvin worked as a barmaid was located at Nassau and John streets, just five blocks north of the New York Stock Exchange and Wall Street. Leaving the 1st Precinct, near the East River, Eddie Egan decided to bypass the narrow, challenging one-way lanes of the financial hub. He aimed his Corvair up South Street – almost deserted now except for a few trucks still at riverfront loading platforms – planning to cut over west on Fulton Street to Nassau. He was tired, a little numb from disappointment and didn't want to think about complicated things anymore. He would concentrate tonight on patching things up with Carol.

Not that *that* was going to be easy. He hadn't spoken with her since just before New Year's. Then, she had still been interested in the rich old patron from Jersey and couldn't understand how Egan could be so violently opposed to what promised to benefit both of them. But the few moments he had had to himself during the past hectic week, he had found himself missing her. Just the thought of her golden beauty filling his arms now sent a tingle skittering up his backbone. But that too gave him pause: was it *just* a physical desire that drew them together? Well, if that's what it was, he would be a sucker not to make the most of it. Tonight he would try to lose himself in Carol.

It was not until the Brooklyn Bridge loomed before him that Egan realized he had already driven several blocks beyond his intended turnoff at Fulton Street. Another half mile ahead the familiar Manhattan Bridge passed over South Street and the Viaduct – the Manhattan Bridge and Pike Slip and Henry Street and East Broadway, Patsy Fuca's playground. Force of habit, he chuckled sourly to himself. Well, as long as he'd come so far, just for the record he might as well continue and take one more look around. There still was plenty of time to get to the Nassau Tavern. It was only 6:45 P.M., and Carol didn't get off until eleven.

He made a left on Pike Street past Blair's Inn, then drove through Henry Street. The dingy block was quiet. At Rutgers Street he swung up to East Broadway and turned downtown. Anthony's auto shop came up on his right, the only clearing in an almost solid line of parked cars. Anthony's was dark, closed for the night.

And then he saw Nicky Travato's gray Cadillac, parked two cars the other side of Anthony's driveway.

Egan almost jumped on his brakes, but he caught himself and continued on to the intersection of Pike Street. Patsy or his friends could be around, watching to see if some excitable cop would pounce on the Caddy. He circled the block and back to East Broadway, nosing the Corvair into the curb behind another auto, half a car length into a bus stop.

Switching off the headlights and motor, he reached for the radiophone. 'This is Popeye, calling base. Popeye to base . . . does anybody read me, kay?'

'Ten-four. We read you.'

'I just found the car our friend was driving, the gray Cadillac.'

'Repeat. Your signal is wavy. What about a Cadillac? Repeat, please.'

Egan twisted the volume dial as far as it would turn. 'I said I am sitting on the Cadillac that we lost this afternoon. I am now on East Broadway, the west side of East Broadway, near the corner of Canal Street. The car, the Caddy, is parked beyond Anthony's auto shop, halfway between me and Pike Street, on the same side as me. I am going to wait here and see if the subject comes back for it. Who you got around to help? Do you read, kay?'

There was a hissing, static-filled pause, and Egan, breathing an obscenity, was about to repeat the message when base responded: 'Hold it a second. Yeah, we got you. Your signal's real weak though. Look, there's hardly anybody here. Everybody went home, or they're out someplace . . .'

'Well, *find* somebody!' Egan bellowed. 'We can't risk another screw-up. With all the agents in New York—'

'Okay, okay. We'll get somebody over there. We'll let you know.'

'Ten-four.'

That was about seven P.M. Egan's eyes scarcely left the front of Anthony's. From his location, he couldn't see the Cadillac itself, but he had it placed roughly twenty-five feet along the building line past the auto repair shop. He could spot any movement within that focal area. Egan wasn't tired or depressed anymore, and he wasn't thinking of Carol. He was all cop again.

At seven-forty, the radio gabbled: 'Popeye? Ripa here. On Park Row coming up to East Broadway. Are you still in the same location? Acknowledge.'

'Ten-four,' he answered. 'You alone?'

'Eddie Guy's with me. What's with our man?'

'Nothing yet. Look, try to grab a space by the corner of East Broadway and Pike Street; then we'll have the Caddy in between us. Somebody's got to show. Glad you guys are here.'

'Ten-four. Hey, by the way, we don't read you too good. Signal's in and out.'

'Yeah, I know. Hope it holds out. Kay.'

Egan relaxed a little, knowing that the two Federal agents would be covering the other end of the block. He sat back and lit a Camel. Before he finished the cigarette, Ripa reported again:

'Okay, we got a spot the other side of Pike. What's happening?'

'Still the same,' Egan replied.

'Ten-four.'

Hardly had the detective turned his gaze back to East Broadway when his attention was caught by a pale blue-and-white two-door coupe moving slowly past him. Egan jerked as though lanced. There were three men in the front seat, and one was Patsy Fuca.

The two-tone coupe, a Chevrolet at least six or seven years old, slowed down. One of its taillights was not working. Egan pressed the radio mike to his mouth: 'There's a blue and white Chevy in the middle of the block. He's in it!'

Egan leaned out his window to follow the progress of the Chevy. It eased to a halt abreast of the spot where he estimated the Cadillac to be parked. 'He's getting out,' he alerted the other agents by radio.

'We make him . . . but we can barely read you.'

'He's talking to the guys in the car,' Egan continued. 'He's going to the Caddy . . . Now he's back by the other car . . .' Egan ducked his head inside. 'He was looking back this way. I wonder if one of them made me?' Cautiously he again tilted his head sideways toward the window. 'Uh-oh! Now he's going around and getting into the driver's seat of the same car! The sonofagun is on to something.'

The Chevrolet started to move away. 'Watch them, watch them!' Egan warned the agents. 'They're coming your way.'

He backed the Corvair into the bus stop, shifted gears and lurched forward along East Broadway.

'– they're making a left on Pike,' Jack Ripa advised.

Egan pressed down on the accelerator. As he approached the intersection, he barked into the phone: 'If you read me – you guys stick right there and don't take your eyes off that Caddy. I'll take—'

'Are you gonna take him?' Ripa's voice was urgent. 'You want us to sit on the Caddy?'

'Great!' Egan snorted aloud. 'Now they're not reading me at all!' He was cornering on Pike. As he went by, he gestured furiously toward the agents' car.

Ripa responded: 'Okay, ten-four. The Chevy turned into Henry Street.'

Egan wheeled the bouncy Corvair down wide Pike Street and made a screeching left into Henry. The other car, traceable by its single taillight, was still moving about a block ahead. There was little doubt in Egan's mind that Patsy, the master driver, was testing surveillance. The Chevy continued three more blocks along Henry, then cut sharply right on Clinton Street, through the LaGuardia housing project. Egan rounded that corner just in time to see the single taillight disappearing onto Cherry Street as though circling back in the same direction from which it had come. He followed, maintaining distance of about a block; it was too late now to be subtle. At Jefferson, the Chevy went left, toward the river. Egan swung around the corner, and applied his brakes. Near Water, the next cross street, the Chevy had stopped and was idling as one of the men left the car and was clambering into another at the curb. It was not Patsy.

The Chevy started up again, only two men in the front seat now, moving rapidly down toward South Street. Egan accelerated after them. But before the detective reached Water Street, the car at the curb swerved out broadside to his path. 'Dirty bastard!' Egan cried, stamping on his brake pedal. It was a bright green Valiant, about a sixty-one. Egan recognized it, and the driver as well. He was a pal of Patsy's from the Pike Slip Inn named Solly DiBrasco, called 'the Brass,' a thug whom the police had guessed was one of Patsy's 'connections.'

Egan pressed a long blast on his horn. The Valiant remained lengthwise across the street in front of them. Egan backed the Corvair a few yards, then crept forward, edging to the left. DiBrasco moved the Valiant just enough to prevent any passage around his front end. 'You dirty moth—!' Egan choked.

He grabbed at the radiophone. 'Popeye here. I am being blocked off by one of his friends while he takes off in the other car. This is a deliberate act of obstruction! The car must be loaded with junk! If anybody reads me – *HIT* that son of a bitch!' he pleaded viciously, disregarding the dictum that radio transmissions should not contain profanity.

'Where are you?' Jack Ripa's voice returned. 'We're coming!'

Egan growled directions. He had jerked into reverse again. Now, as he veered ahead to the right, he snapped his .38 from its belt holster with his left hand and thrust it out the window toward the Valiant. 'You let me past, you guinea bastard!' he roared at Sol the Brass. 'Or you're gonna get one!'

Still waving the revolver, with his other hand Egan maneuvered the car behind the Valiant, partially up onto the sidewalk, and clear.

Jefferson Street, of course, was empty. Muttering curses, Egan squealed around the corner of South Street. The only vehicle in sight had two red taillights. At Pike, he hesitated, then whipped right past Blair's Inn, up toward East Broadway.

The moment he turned that corner, Egan knew he had been beaten. Outside Anthony's Auto Shop, there was a gaping space in the line of parked cars where the gray Cadillac had been.

Egan did not pause. He raced the Corvair up East Broadway to Clinton Street again and back down toward the river. At least maybe he could nail Patsy's confederate. But when he reached Jefferson and Water streets, the Valiant was parked, silent, in the place it had originally been. DiBrasco was nowhere to be seen.

Still bristling, Egan snarled at the radio: 'We better have a meeting.'

The offices of the U.S. Bureau of Narcotics were located in the huge, block square Federal Office Building at 90 Church Street, one long block west of Broadway. Three blocks further west was the Hudson River. Two blocks to the east was City Hall Park and Plaza. Although the streets were wider here, and the buildings taller and more impressively businesslike, at night the area was almost as desolate as Old Slip on the eastern tip of Manhattan.

The few elevators running at night in the Federal Building were operated by night watchmen. On the sixth floor, a glass door in a corner was numbered 605, and lettered FEDERAL BUREAU OF NARCOTICS. Beyond the door was a sparsely furnished reception room with two lounge chairs and an end table; behind a partition there was a receptionist's desk. Inside, a long room, partitioned into six sections, demarked the six groups into which the bureau's New York office was divided. Each group normally comprised twenty agents; each had its own stenographer-secretary and its own radio communications setup. Each section was furnished with eight or more comfortably spaced desks, usually more than adequate to accommodate the number of agents who might be in the office at any one time. Its atmosphere of spaciousness and comfort was in marked contrast to the near squalor of the New York Police Department's Narcotics Bureau. Unconsciously or otherwise, when a city detective had occasion to visit his Federal counterparts an imprint of discontent remained with him when he left 90 Church Street.

Eddie Egan usually felt this way, and tonight his pique cut deeper because the case had deteriorated the past several days. Egan still was simmering over the brazen way he had been obstructed by Patsy's *paisano*, Sol the Brass. But at least he knew where to find Solly when this was over – which might well be already.

Waters was senior agent in No. 4 Group, and by nine-thirty he had managed to round up seventeen other agents, following the alert by Jack Ripa relayed from Egan. The only New York police narcotics officer who had so far responded to the call from base radio was Detective Dick Auletta. Twenty of them gathered now in the group section, some perched on desks, some straddling chairs, others standing. Coffee and sandwiches had been sent up. Once again jackets were off, ties loosened. They all looked tired.

Egan, Ripa and Eddie Guy related how Patsy had again eluded surveillance. 'I'm convinced that the car Patsy was driving tonight must have been loaded,' Egan declared. 'Having that punk block me was an *overt* act against the law. I say hit Patsy's house, his old man's place, and all the other places we got warrants for, *now*, or else we might as well forget the whole operation!'

'Eddie, I know how you feel,' Waters said, 'but we went through all this before over at your office. If you *had* bagged Patsy tonight with the stuff on him, great. But now that he's faded again, I don't think there's a prayer.'

The telephone on Waters's desk jingled. 'Four-seven-oh.' He listened a few seconds, then said, 'Okay. Is somebody staying on him out there? Okay. Thanks.' He replaced the receiver and turned to the others. 'That was radio control. Patsy got home a little while ago – in his own car, the Olds.'

'He must have switched with Travato again someplace,' said Egan. 'I still say let's hit them all, now.'

'Look,' Waters countered, 'it's a cinch he didn't bring the stuff into his own house, assuming he did have it on him tonight. And we don't know where he stopped between the time you saw him and he got home.'

'I know, I know,' Egan waved him off, 'like you said, we went around this track before. But my point is this: I honestly think we've screwed this whole thing up. The Frenchmen, the key guys, I don't think we'll ever see them again. I think they probably already made their deal, and they're gone. Maybe they even called the deal off because of the heat, but I don't think so. From everything we heard, it was too big. The mob *needs* this shipment. All right, so the Frenchmen I can do without. But Patsy? Him I care about. And the *stuff* I care about. And I say if we don't get smart and hit Patsy and every place else right now, by tomorrow that stuff is going to be distributed and we're going to wind up with nothing. We can't wait anymore!'

The telephone rang again. Waters picked it up. 'Egan? Who's calling? Just a minute.' Smirking, he held the receiver out to the detective. 'It's a "friend" – a lady. One of your stools?'

Egan took the phone and sat on the edge of the desk, turning his back to Waters. 'Popeye here. Hey, Carol!' He stood erect. 'Wait a minute, will you?' Egan twisted around to Waters. 'It's not a stool. Is there another extension I could use?' Waters pointed toward a desk across the room, then pressed the Hold button on the telephone and reached for the receiver.

Egan picked up the other phone. 'Okay, I'm back. So what's new with you? God, I wanted to see you so bad tonight. No kidding, I was really on my way to your joint when I got tied up.'

'Honey,' Carol interrupted, 'I would love to see you and talk and everything – but I think I better tell you first why I called. I tried your office, and they said you were at this number. I don't know, it seemed like it might be important . . .'

'Well, what's the matter?'

'Well, a little while ago this man came in the place, and I recognized him. He's been here a few times before, but I also know he's a friend of that fellow you've been working on – you know, Patsy?'

'Where you talking from?' Egan asked.

'It's okay. I'm on my break. Nobody can hear. This fella, an Italian type, he sits at the bar with some other man, and they have a couple of drinks, and he's laughing about how he made a monkey out of some cop tonight. And honey, it sounded like you!'

'Why me?'

'Well, he didn't give any real description or anything. But he said there were a couple of cars, and he got out and blocked off this cop – the cop was Irish, he said – and this cop was blowing his top. But the thing that really got me interested was when he mentioned Pasty.'

'What did he say?'

'Well, he said something about Pasty "got away," and then he said something I don't understand, but since I was interested at this point, this is what I thought might mean something to you.'

'Yeah?' Egan tensed.

'He said, this is exactly what he said: "They're chasing him all over town, and they don't know he's clean."'

'He's clean?'

'He thought that was a big joke too. But wait. He said something else. Something about tomorrow morning, nine o'clock, Pasty and some other people will wrap up the whole deal. Of course, I didn't know what they were talking about.'

'Tomorrow at nine? But where, baby – did he say *where?*'

'No.'

'Balls!'

'Well, thanks a lot. I try to help, and—'

'No, no, I didn't mean *you*. It's just that, well, never mind. . . . You are just something else! I've really got to come see you. Maybe later tonight?'

'Could be.'

'Look, babe, I'd love to talk to you some more now, but you have been a great help, and I've got to go to work. See you later, huh?'

'I'd like to see you . . .'

When Egan told the others the information he'd received, there was a hubbub of speculation. 'Well, I'd say this brightens the picture,' Frank Waters announced. 'Patsy's got a meet tomorrow morning at nine, obviously with his French friends. So we still do have a crack!'

'Great,' Egan said – 'but where?'

Waters, behind his desk, looked at the detective standing before him with an expression of exaggerated pity. '*Where?* Where else have they always met? The Hotel Roosevelt!'

Egan frowned. 'No . . . I think you're wrong.'

The other officers began to press around. 'Where then?' Waters challenged. The room had hushed.

'I put my money on East End Avenue,' Egan stated flatly.

'East End Avenue. *Why?* The only time we had Patsy up there, we sat on our asses for a whole day, and then he just drove home!'

'I got a hunch.'

'Look, the only consistent factor in this whole mixed-up investigation is that when Patsy meets the Frenchmen, he meets them at the Roosevelt. It's the *only* place we have to go on!'

'No,' Egan controlled his voice with effort. 'We probably

burned the Roosevelt. But this number forty-five East End Avenue – we seen Patsy there, he met one of the Frogs there the other night, he's been driving cars in and out of the garage there, and my hunch is they think we don't know about it.'

'You and your hunches!' Waters snapped. 'Maybe I shouldn't say this, but it's your hunches that have got us up the creek right now. If you'd acted more as part of the team instead of like a private eye—'

'*Whose* team?' Egan roared. '*Yours?* For Chrissake, me and Sonny had this thing in our back pockets until you Feds screwed everything up! Who the hell scared the Frenchmen away? Your hot tracking team! You guys wouldn't know surveillance from a loud cheer!'

Waters's fists were balled; but he swallowed and cleared his throat. 'I say the Roosevelt.'

Egan leaned on the desk, his two hands flat on the blotter. 'Frank, you do just whatever you want; go when you want and take whoever wants to go with you. As for me, I feel there is only one place this meet will be and that's at East End Avenue. That's where I'm going, even if it's by myself. The way things went the other night, I would feel a lot more secure if your small army stayed home anyway.'

Waters exploded out of his chair and punched Egan across the left side of his jaw. The detective staggered backwards. Waters, shorter but, for his size, almost as husky as the burly Egan, lunged around his desk. He ran into a hard chop to the mouth which stopped him. Egan leveled his right fist again for a plowing drive into Waters's midsection, but the agent recovered and whipped his left hand across the other side of Egan's face. Then the two grappled, arms flung wildly. The other officers, startled and shrinking back at first, now swarmed around them, several grasping Waters's shoulders and arms and others tugging at Egan's waist.

The two glared at each other, breathing hard, straining

against the arms which held them back. A spot of blood smudged the corner of Waters's mouth. Egan's normal ruddy complexion was even pinker on the cheeks, where the agent had struck him. Now he shook off the arms and smoothed his rumpled clothing deliberately.

'Okay, Frank, so that's the way it is,' he said through set teeth. 'Tomorrow morning, my cops are going to East End Avenue, and you guys can go any damn place you please. Just stay out of our way.' Egan put on his jacket and started for the door. Then he turned. They all were watching him. 'And if any cop,' he looked directly at Dick Auletta, who stood bewildered among the agents, 'decides to go with *you*, he's going to answer to Sonny and me.' With that, he walked out of the Federal office.

When Patsy Fuca had arrived home, he was still shaken by his wild getaway downtown. That *skoonj* of a cop! What the hell had he been doing around Anthony's? Did they know about Anthony's? For the first time, he'd felt fright. Did they know about No. 45 East End Avenue, too? If they did, tomorrow he could be walking straight into a trap. But there hadn't been any sign of cops up there when he had returned the French Buick.

Everything had gone without a hitch earlier. He had made sure there was no chance of a tail when he drove into New York with Tony after having received the word from Anthony's that the traps had been closed and the Buick had been put back together again. First, he switched to Nicky's Caddy. Then, at Pike Slip, he let Tony off at Blair's, and went on to Henry Street.

At the corner of Rutgers, Solly was waiting. Patsy got out of Nicky's car and walked up to East Broadway, while Solly the Brass hopped in the Caddy and drove it back behind Blair's. There, Tony took over. He would cruise around awhile, then later, after Anthony's closed, leave it outside the garage. They didn't want to use Sol's flashy green Valiant – that probably was too well known to the fuzz, so Solly had got another friend from the Inn, Johnny Frasca, to come along in his beat-up Chevy.

Finally, Patsy drove the French Buick out of Anthony's and sailed uptown to the garage at No. 45 East End, followed by Solly and Frasca. He had walked out to Frasca's waiting car, they went and had a drink at the Inner Circle Bar at 63rd and York, then made their way easily downtown, where Patsy was to retrieve the Cadillac and return home.

But then Solly had spotted that guy down the block from Anthony's, sitting alone in a little red car. It looked too much like a plant. Suddenly concerned, Patsy decided to test it. Sure enough, the sonofabitch came after them. That was not good. Had the guy been tailing them the whole time, uptown and everywhere? Patsy had to get out of there, get time to think. Maybe it was stupid to have let Solly pull that bit of blocking the street, but it did give him the chance to hustle back to the Caddy and beat it.

Nobody had followed him home, he was pretty sure of that. And he didn't see anybody around his house. If the fuzz did have a tail on him, *that's* where he would have expected to find someone. But by Anthony's?

Barbara asked him what was wrong when he came in, but he said nothing, everything went okay. She went back to the television, and he poured himself a stiff whiskey and went back over the night in his mind. It could have been just a crazy accident, tripping over that cop. Maybe the cop thought Patsy and his friends were acting suspiciously. He might even have known them from Blair's. But that he had tumbled to Anthony's, or the rest of the operation, no, it really didn't figure.

Patsy relaxed with another drink, persuading himself that the scare had been groundless. And as the liquor spread its gentle euphoria over him, his mind drifted to tomorrow, and the payoff.

Late Wednesday night Jacques Angelvin returned to his new room at the Commodore Hotel. He had enjoyed a pleasant dinner with Jacques Sallibert, who had taken over as head of the New York bureau of Radio Télévision Française from Paul Crenesse. The small, dingy room at the Commodore Hotel depressed him, but the dinner, wine, and good masculine conversation had been warm and hearty. This was the second evening he had not seen Lilli.

Jacques was disgruntled. All his plans for exploring television in New York were to be wiped out. He couldn't even tell Lilli that their date for the next week would not happen and, worse, he had been granted an appointment with David Rockefeller's representatives at the Chase Manhattan Bank for two-thirty on the afternoon of January 22. But Wednesday morning Scaglia had ordered that following the conclusion of the transaction on Thursday, Jacques must leave with him for Montreal.

François must be truly worried. Jacques was to meet him at that garage at ten tomorrow morning, and they were to drive all the way to Montreal. He had planned to visit French Canada after New York, but hardly this way. The new plan was that they would meet Scaglia's friends at the Hotel Queen Elizabeth in Montreal, then return to Paris by air the following morning. The Buick? – someone else in Montreal would dispose of that, François had said.

He looked around the cramped room to which he had moved from the Waldorf-Astoria. All this scuttling about depressed him; it was foreboding. Scaglia and his associates also had moved from their hotels, apparently. There must be great danger from the police. Jacques ached with regret over having let himself be drawn into such madness. He had kept assuring himself that there was no possibility that the police could be aware of *him*. But what of tomorrow? If Scaglia were truly in a precarious position, then Jacques himself must be exposed for the first time.

He went to the dresser, took a half pint of cognac from a drawer and gulped from the bottle. The brandy stinging sweet in his throat, he looked around at his belongings; his bags were still largely unpacked. Scaglia had insisted that they could not even take their clothing; there should be no cause for suspicion that they were actually leaving New York. They would have time in Montreal to acquire new things, François promised.

It had definitely not been a pleasant week so far for Angelvin. Lilli had been busy Tuesday evening and he had dined with his friend Pierre Olivier. During the day, Tuesday, he had visited with Mr. Deck at the Perrera foreign currency exchange to make discreet arrangements for the exchange of a large number of dollars for French francs. The rate of exchange was more favorable in New York than back in Paris.

Angelvin was also running low on money, and he had been trying – unsuccessfully – to secure a loan from Scaglia against the money he would receive when the deal with the Americans was consummated.

On Wednesday Angelvin took Lilli to lunch. Later he walked despondently back to the Waldorf in the cold, sad and frustrated that Lilli had not accepted his plea to join him in a siesta. He knew he must check out of the Waldorf that afternoon after his nap and go to a smaller room at the Commodore Hotel. He arrived in his room tired, a little drunk, and cold. The maid was there, cleaning the bathroom. How I want to take a *pipi*, he thought to himself disconsolately. He also wanted a girl, and the chamber maid looked as though she were a hundred years old. Everything was so bad. Glaring at the tiled bathroom he pulled off his pants, climbed into the bed and petulantly urinated between the sheets.

Later, after meeting with Crenesse of Télévision Française, he checked out of the Waldorf, paying his bill of $228.71, and checked into the Commodore. This left him with little money, although he looked forward to the ten thousand dollars promised for tomorrow.

Jacques poured down the rest of the cognac and fell on his new bed fully dressed to wait for the morning.

On Thursday, January 18, he woke up with a hangover and a general feeling of uneasiness. To cheer himself up, he sat at the table and wrote optimistic words in his diary: 'Tonight I will be at the Queen Elizabeth in Montreal . . . touch wood!' Jacques couldn't know it would be the last notation ever made in this diary.

About 10 P.M., Wednesday night, Sonny Grosso had been called to the telephone at a cashier's desk in a bowling center in the Bronx. Frank Waters was at the other end. 'What's up?' Sonny asked.

'It's your buddy Egan,' the agent began acidly. 'He made a goddamn ass of himself here a little while ago.'

'Yeah, how?' Sonny grinned.

'No, I mean it.' The detective's smile faded as, in terse, bitter words, Waters described what had occurred at the Federal Bureau. 'I've had it with him,' the agent concluded. 'He's got a lousy attitude, like he's God Almighty or something, and when he starts throwing his weight around in our office, well, that's too much!'

Sonny was thoughtful a moment, the crash of bowling pins thundering across the lanes. 'Well, I'll tell you,' he said at last, cupping his hand around the speaker, 'you may not get along with my partner, but he happens to be one hell of a detective, and frankly I think he's right about where to go tomorrow.'

'You go along with him?'

'And what's more,' Sonny went on grimly, 'who the hell

are you to take a swing at my partner? How would you like me to come down and bust one of *your* people in the mouth?'

'All right, all right,' Waters conceded. 'But what about you?'

'I'm going to string along with Popeye, and so will the rest of our guys. He's been right too many times before to kiss him off now. So you and your agents go where you want.'

Eddie Egan spent a restless night. He had forgotten completely about getting back to Carol, so tense was he with aggravation and uncertainty. The fight had been a bad scene. Maybe he *had* pushed too hard, but that wise-ass Waters! When he got home, he started to call Sonny at the bowling alley, but then decided not to ruin *his* night too. He would speak to him first thing in the morning. The morning – he might damn well turn out to be the Lone Ranger at that, if everybody went along with the Feds. Private eye, Waters had called him.

Thursday, January 18, Egan's alarm buzzed him awake at 6:30 A.M. He made coffee, showered and shaved and dressed warmly. By 7:05 A.M., wearing a brown porkpie hat and a bulky-knit blue and white cardigan beneath his leather car coat, he was in his Corvair, headed toward Manhattan. All night he had wrestled with the temptation to go straight to Patsy's house in the morning and put the collar on him there and then. *That* would eliminate all the discussion about where to play hide-and-seek with the bum and his friends. But he had discarded that idea finally. The only thing to do, really, was to head downtown to the Narcotics Bureau, round up what men he could, and get situated around No. 45 East End Avenue well in advance of Patsy's supposed meet.

He drove west on Myrtle Avenue, aiming to get onto the Brooklyn-Queens Expressway at Marcy and Kent avenues. Several mornings recently, he had arranged to pick up Agent

Luis Gonzalez there and drive him into town. Luis was a nice little guy, kind of new to the job, and he didn't have his own car. Last night, before the blowoff, Luis had mentioned that he would appreciate it if Egan could pick him up again Thursday morning. After what happened, though, it was a cinch Luis wouldn't be waiting.

But as Egan swung the Corvair toward the Expressway, he spied the slim Puerto Rican standing at the entrance to the ramp. He looked like a mugger: peaked cap low over his brow, black crew sweater under a worn Army field jacket, baggy trousers, black sneakers. Egan pulled up and the agent jumped in alongside him.

'Well, this is a surprise—' the detective started to exclaim. Gonzalez was flashing a wide grin at him. 'What the hell is so funny?' Egan demanded.

'The luck of the Irish strikes again,' the agent chuckled cryptically.

'What does that mean?'

'It means you won.'

'Won? Won what?'

'Last night,' Gonzalez said, 'they finally decided you were right. Everybody is going to stake out East End Avenue.'

Chapter Sixteen

On Thursday morning Eddie Egan and Sonny Grosso had exactly sixteen hours left before the case they had so painstakingly developed would have to be aborted by the Narcotics Bureau. The revised strategy for this day was simple, but it had to be handled with precision. When Patsy left his house in Brooklyn, word would be flashed; but once it could be established that he had driven onto the Gowanus Expressway, as was expected, normal visual surveillance was to be reduced to a minimum. Instead, an unmarked police car would be positioned at the side of the roadway, its hood up, at the vital junction where city-bound traffic either proceeds into the Brooklyn-Battery Tunnel or veers right and continues on what at that point becomes the Brooklyn-Queens Expressway. Should Patsy choose the tunnel, which seemed unlikely, the information would be relayed ahead, and detectives would be waiting at the tip of Manhattan to trace his route from there. If Patsy stayed on the expressway, the officer in the 'stalled' car was to fall in behind and notify base wherever the subject turned off – the Brooklyn Bridge, Manhattan Bridge, or even if he were to go all the way north to Williamsburg. For maximum security, one car was staked out at Patsy's luncheonette, and another at his parents' home on 7th Street in Brooklyn. In Manhattan, a radio car would be situated at the terminus of each of the bridges from Brooklyn. One car would patrol the Pike Slip area, specifically watching Anthony's Auto Shop. Another was to cover the Hotel Roosevelt uptown at 45th Street, on the chance that Frank Waters may have been correct after all. The rest of the investigators would blanket the area around 81st Street and East End Avenue. The observation post in the cabinetmaker's shop on the third floor of the building across East End Avenue from No. 45 had been reactivated, and stationed there would be Sonny Grosso, Lieutenant Vinnie Hawkes, Sergeant Jack Fleming, and Waters.

The orders were given with the caution: Do Not Press. Patsy was to be given free rein. Wherever the meeting might be, it would probably be the last, and the lawmen could not permit overzealousness to alarm Patsy or the other principals before an overt exchange could be observed. Then, and only then, could they move in. They had to be *sure* this time. They doubted there would be any more chances to break this case.

At the 1st Precinct, other narcotics detectives already had dispersed or were moving out the door. The station house proper was busy, as the midnight-to-eights reported in and the day-watch assembled. After all logistics were confirmed, Egan and Gonzalez left before eight-thirty, driving up South Street to park under the Brooklyn Bridge and wait the first word of Patsy's movements. There, they were in position convenient to any of the three downtown bridges Patsy might cross. Egan wanted to be the one to pick up Patsy whichever way he came into the city. Patsy was *his* baby.

At about eight forty-five, the radio crackled the alert: Patsy was leaving his house, driving his blue compact Oldsmobile, onto the Gowanus Expressway, northbound. Egan and Gonzalez listened eagerly. Patsy bypassed the turnoff to the tunnel, was proceeding north on the expressway, swinging off and making for the Brooklyn Bridge.

'This is it, kid!' Egan exclaimed to the youthful agent. He shoved the Corvair into gear and raced up Pearl Street to Chambers, then over west to the official parking area alongside the Municipal Building, overlooking City Hall. It was a perfect observation point. All traffic coming off the Brooklyn Bridge must pass this spot, and furthermore, any cars aiming to transfer from the bridge to the East River Drive had to curl back east immediately in front of the parking area.

Less than ten minutes later Egan recognized the small blue Oldsmobile curving down the ramp and past the Municipal Building, toward the approach to the Drive. He and Gonzalez moved out, the agent reporting by radio to the others listening throughout the city. Patsy turned uptown on the Drive. Egan held the Corvair well behind, maintaining the lightest possible tail. All they needed to ascertain at this stage was the point at which Patsy would leave the river highway. If he were to exit at 42nd Street, it would indicate that his destination was most likely the Roosevelt, and then they would have to alert the bulk of the investigating force posted around East End Avenue to scramble back to midtown. The only alternative which could not be anticipated was the possibility that the meet would turn out to be some *other* place altogether, so it remained imperative that Egan and Gonzalez never lose sight of Patsy.

The subject was driving easily, apparently unconcerned about surveillance. Though the day was overcast and damply cold, there was little morning haze along the river, and with the uptown traffic moderate, the two officers had no difficulty in keeping the blue compact in view. Coming up to 42nd Street, Gonzalez radioed all cars to stand by, but Patsy made no move toward that exit ramp. 'Okay, he's going on by,' the agent reported. 'Next exit: Sixty-first Street.'

He replaced the microphone on its hook when the receiver squawked: 'Did you say he's exiting at Sixty-first Street, kay?'

Gonzalez looked at Egan in exasperation as he reached for the mike again. 'I don't have no accent, do I?' he smiled sadly.

Egan chuckled. 'No . . . it's the goddam sender. It was all screwed up last night, too. I forgot about that.'

'Repeat,' the agent said firmly into the phone – 'subject did not, repeat did NOT, exit at Forty-second Street, is proceeding northbound, will advise if he turns off at Sixty-first. Do you read, kay?'

The response was a clutter of tinny voices; finally one dominated: '—your signal is very poor. If it goes before we mark subject, we're in trouble . . .'

Gonzalez exhaled a grim 'Ten-four.'

Egan, shaking his head, muttered, 'Damn!' His eyes were fixed upon the little Oldsmobile perhaps a quarter of a mile ahead. 'He's moving over toward the left lane. Looks like Sixty-first, all right. Yep, he's getting off! Tell them!'

'Sixty-first, Sixty-first!' the agent cried, the mike tight to his mouth. 'Subject off Drive at Sixty-first! Do you read?'

'Sixty-first. Ten-four.'

Gonzalez and Egan grinned at each other. But they still couldn't lose Patsy. It was not an absolute certainty that 81st Street and East End Avenue would be the precise rendezvous site, because it could be anywhere in that neighborhood. With luck there would be a car with detectives stationed near the Drive exit at 61st Street and York Avenue, noting which way Patsy went from there. But Egan still wanted to follow him through personally to the final setting.

He was edging the Corvair toward the 61st Street cutoff when the radio announced: 'Subject turning uptown on York . . .'

'At least the receiver is working good,' Gonzalez commented happily.

'Yeah, that's something . . . Well, Louie, it looks like we guessed right.'

* * *

At 9:30 A.M., the four officers positioned in the third-floor cabinet shop on the west side of East End Avenue were startled to see that two of the three missing Frogs had materialized in front of No. 45 across the way – François Barbier and J. Mouren.

Neither Sonny, Waters, Hawkes nor Fleming had actually seen the Frenchmen appear; they had no idea where the two had come from or whether they arrived together or separately. The detectives had been intent on following the radioed account of Patsy Fuca's progress into Manhattan and uptown, and rooting for Eddie Egan's sender to hold out. One or another had been stepping to the window to scan the avenue below, but it was not until the report was confirmed that Patsy was moving north on York Avenue and evidently into the immediate area that they turned full attention to the building opposite. And, suddenly, disconcertingly, Frogs Two and Three were just *there*.

'These birds slip in and out of sight like they had a magic lamp,' Waters marveled, as Sonny returned to the radio to alert all officers in the vicinity. The undercover men were everywhere, on East End Avenue and in all the connecting streets from 79th to 86th and west as far as Second Avenue. Even the four in the cabinet shop command post couldn't be sure who was where or, for that matter, who was *who*. Not knowing what to expect, many were on foot in general proximity to No. 45, and these had adopted various guises – building handymen, clerks in stores, Con Edison street diggers, fathers walking baby carriages, neatly dressed door-to-door salesmen. Others were spotted in automobiles at key locations, where they could quickly relay radio communications to the 'pedestrians.' A couple even were driving special taxicabs through the neighborhood. For his part, Sonny, clad in a woolen lumber jacket, slacks and chukka boots, already had arranged with the proprietor of a liquor store nearby to borrow his delivery bicycle if necessary. Waters, in business clothes, could be anybody.

Their job, they kept reminding themselves, was to observe. They would make no overt moves until definite grounds for a felony arrest could be established, such as exchange and possession of suspected goods.

Barbier and Mouren stood in front of No. 45 about fifteen minutes, talking and occasionally looking up and down the avenue. Sonny watched them through field glasses. Both were dressed conservatively, in black overcoats, dark suits, white shirts and colorless ties; Mouren wore a gray Homburg; Barbier was hatless, his full brown hair breeze-blown. Certainly they must be waiting for someone – who else but Patsy?

Nothing further had been heard from Egan; at last report he had Patsy coming north on York Avenue. Then, the radio crackled: 'Subject driving up East End from Seventy-ninth, moving slow.' The officers bunched at the third-floor window. They could see Patsy's car now. As it neared 81st Street, it hesitated, then made a wide, slow left turn. Across the avenue, Barbier tipped Mouren's arm, and both looked toward the opposite corner; Barbier flipped a hand in a gesture of recognition. The Olds left the officers' field of vision. 'Subject going west on Eighty-first,' somebody advised. 'Who's got him over there?' another voice queried. There was a staticky, garbled reply. Waters grabbed the microphone: 'Did somebody say they got him?' After a few seconds, a voice volunteered: 'I can see him, making a right on York. Anybody up around York?'

'Oh, goddamn!' Sonny growled.

'Hey, look!' Vinnie Hawkes called from the window. The two Frenchmen had started across the avenue toward the corner beyond which Patsy's car had slid out of sight. But in the middle of the street they stopped, exchanged a few words, and Mouren turned and strode rapidly back to No. 45, where he went down into the garage. Barbier continued to the opposite sidewalk. He ambled to the corner and glanced around on 81st. Then he walked slowly the other way, toward 82nd, keeping so close to the building line that he was lost to sight from the window above.

'Somebody better get down there before *they* go up in smoke,' Jack Fleming suggested.

Sonny and Waters tumbled down the stairs to the street. Barbier stood in front of the adjacent apartment house, his back to the wall, gazing over at No. 45. As Waters strolled toward 81st Street, Sonny dashed into the liquor store just off the building entrance. In a minute he came out with a brown paper package and placed it in the bin of the three-wheeled delivery bicycle standing by the curb. Then, without apparently noticing the man in black not fifty feet from him, Sonny wheeled the bike into the gutter and began to pedal up East End. He went only as far as 83rd before he pulled over behind a parked truck and turned his attention back down the avenue.

Waters, meanwhile, had walked around into 81st Street. He saw no one nor anything identifiable with the Frenchmen. The agent returned to the corner cautiously. A peek assured him that Frog Two still stood by the next apartment house. Waters waited just around the corner. In a few minutes, Frog Three came up the garage ramp across the way. Now he was toting a blue valise, the same type – perhaps the same one – that Jean Jehan had carried to a meet with Patsy that night a week ago. Waters wondered if Frog One would show today.

Mouren crossed the avenue and rejoined Barbier. The two chatted a moment, then started walking toward 82nd Street. Waters followed. Up the avenue, he could see Sonny returning on his bicycle. The Frenchmen turned into 82nd. As Waters reached the corner, Sonny was swerving into the street and pumping the cumbersome vehicle against the uphill slope.

In the middle of the block, between East End and York

avenue, a small blue car was double-parked. As Barbier and Mouren came abreast of it, the driver leaned to his right and opened the right-hand door, and when he straightened to his sitting position again, Waters recognized Patsy. Sonny was pedaling past the car as the Frenchmen got in, Mouren still gripping the blue valise. Waters kept walking toward them. The Oldsmobile moved past him, down toward East End. There were only the three in the car. Where was Jehan? Waters, and Sonny farther up the street, watched the blue compact turn on East End, going uptown.

Back at 82nd Street and York Avenue, Eddie Egan and Luis Gonzalez in Egan's Corvair had seen Patsy double-park midway in the block; they had observed two men approach and enter the Olds, one of them carrying a suitcase of some kind. From that distance the officers could not visually identify the men, but from the radio reports they knew it was Frogs Two and Three and that Mouren had the bag; and they saw the car take a left on East End. Now, a voice on the receiver blared that the Olds was turning left again on 83rd Street, westbound. Egan drove to the next corner, 83rd and York. To the right, the trim blue car was nearing York. On an impulse Egan swung the Corvair left into 83rd and headed west. They were almost to First Avenue before Gonzalez, watching the rear, reported that the Olds, having waited for a change in traffic signals, had crossed York and was coming over on 83rd.

Egan turned uptown on First Avenue, moving slowly. The signal light just ahead at 84th Street changed to green, and he drew to a stop at the corner of 85th. The Oldsmobile bearing Patsy and the two Frenchmen had not yet appeared in his rearview mirror.

The radio was a babble of negative confusion. 'Where are they now?' 'Last we saw them was on Eighty-third . . .' 'Has anybody got 'em?' 'Doesn't *anybody* have them?'

'Louie, try it again,' Egan said. 'Tell 'em where *we* are.'

The agent shouted into the mike, then listened. From the response it was plain that they were not being received. Gonzalez frowned at Egan.

The detective, shaking his head, regarded the faulty radio dourly. 'Gee, what a kick in the ass!' he muttered.

Suddenly Gonzalez slid from his seat to a crouch on the floor. 'Watch it – don't look around!'

'What is it?' Egan froze, eyes straight ahead.

'It's them! Right next to you! Waiting for the light. Man, that Irish-luck bit of yours is working overtime! They're *all* in the car now – the big Frog, too!'

'Jehan?' Egan had to make a real physical effort to keep his head straight forward. 'They must've picked him up somewhere between York and First.'

'They're moving.'

The light had changed, and Patsy's Olds pulled away uptown. Egan grasped the radio mike. 'Popeye here. Is anybody on them?' His tone became desperate. 'They're going north on First Avenue. Is *anybody* on them?' He flicked the switch, and the voices of other officers rattled in the receiver – all asking one another if anyone had the Olds in view. 'Can anybody read me?' Egan pleaded. The blue compact ahead was turning right on 86th Street.

'Well, Louie, sounds like we're on our own.' He released the hand brake and the Corvair jumped forward. Rounding the corner of 86th, they saw the Olds making another right heading downtown on York. 'Let's keep trying,' the detective said to Gonzalez. 'Keep a running report going in case somebody picks us up.'

While the agent radioed their progress back downtown, Egan alternated between watching the blue car ahead and looking down each passing street for some sign of assistance. It seemed incredible, with so large a force of men covering a relatively small area, that the conspirators had managed to elude surveillance in the first place and would be riding free right now were it not for his and Gonzalez's 'Irish' luck. The radio channels remained a confusion of urgent voices.

The Olds slowed to a stop at the northwest corner of 82nd Street. Frog Two, Barbier, got out alone. The car moved away, and Barbier crossed York, walking east toward the river. Gonzalez practically shouted the report into his mike. But again there was no indication that it had been received.

A few minutes later, at 79th Street, the Olds edged to the curb again. After a moment, Frog Three stepped to the sidewalk. Mouren no longer carried the blue bag. He waited at the corner while Patsy held for a red light, then, as the car resumed its course downtown; started walking west.

'Well, there goes another one,' Egan moaned bitterly. 'Unless some of our guys are around, we'll never see that bird again! Goddammit!' he slapped the wheel. Gonzalez flashed his report. But from the receiver's chatter, it was clear that they had not been heard and that nobody else had seen Mouren.

'Here's Frog Two again!' Sonny's excited voice burst into the car. 'He's alone, crossing East End toward Forty-five . . . He's going up to some guy who's been waiting there. Where are Patsy and the other Frog? Is anybody on them yet?'

Egan snatched the mike from Gonzalez. 'Cloudy? Popeye. *I'm* on them! Can you read me? I'm on the guy from Brooklyn and Frog One is with him! Cloudy, do you read me?'

'– Frog Two and the other guy are getting into a car that's been brought out of the garage!' Sonny exclaimed, obviously unaware of his partner's plea. 'It is a black Buick sedan, I'd say a sixty . . . hey! It has foreign plates! Eighteen-l-u-seventy-five, repeat, one-eight-l-u-seven-five . . .' Suddenly the transmission became garbled, with a number of voices shouting in the background.

The only thing Egan and Gonzalez could do was stay on Patsy and Jehan. These were the key guys, anyway, Egan told himself. And, perhaps most important, the blue valise still was in that car . . . By now, the blue Olds had passed 70th Street. Before the intersection of 63rd Street, Patsy swung over and stopped. As he and Jehan sat talking for a few minutes, Gonzalez kept trying frantically to raise some response from the radio. Then the door of the Olds opened, and Frog One emerged. In his hand was a black satchel; it looked like the leather tool bag Patsy had been seen with the day before. Jehan pushed the door closed, bowed low to tip his black Homburg to Patsy, and, straight and regal again, marched around the corner and disappeared going west on 63rd Street.

'Oh, God!' Egan wailed, two blocks behind. 'Now there goes the top guy, and all the bread with him in that black bag, I bet! Jesus, Mary and Joseph!' He shook his fist at the radio.

'And there goes Patsy too,' Gonzalez added. 'He's making a left there at Sixty-third, going downtown on the Drive. What'll we do? Jehan is walking off with the loot, but Patsy's still got the blue suitcase with maybe a load of junk!'

Egan shook his head. 'We got no choice anymore. We got to stay with Patsy.' He accelerated down York toward 63rd Street.

'I hate to lose the Frenchman, but Patsy's the one with the shit. *Him* we gotta nail at least.'

'Popeye! If you read me, get back here to East End, *quick!*' It was Sonny, and he sounded shrill.

Egan cried futilely into his own defective mike: 'Sonny, I *can't!* Louie and I are on Patsy! The blue suitcase is still in the car!'

'– Popeye, *please*, if you read me, come here! We bagged two Frenchmen!'

‘Oh, no!’ the detective thundered. ‘They didn’t *hit!* They collared the wrong guys! God*damn* it!’

‘He sounds like there might be trouble,’ Gonzalez said with concern.

‘Screw ’em!’ snapped Egan. ‘What should we do, drop Patsy now? Just because they panicked?’

They were at the 63rd Street intersection.

‘But maybe they need help,’ the agent persisted.

Egan looked at him, frustration contorting his features. With a great aching sigh, he murmured ‘Yeah,’ and wheeled the Corvair around in a tight U-turn to head back uptown. Patsy’s Olds sped away, downtown.

The officers in the cabinet shop overlooking No. 45 East End Avenue had been beside themselves, at first with disbelief, then the anger of humiliation, and finally, as Egan surmised from afar, the frenzy of panic rising out of the growing realization that they had blown *everything*. Sonny and Waters, on top of the scene when Patsy’s car, with the two Frenchmen as passengers, drove out of 82nd Street and north on East End, both had dashed back to the command post, where Hawkes and Fleming told them that the Olds had been placed westbound on 83rd Street. And then – nothing. There were detectives in vehicles and on foot spotted at each intersection and some in between, all the way to Second Avenue, and yet, somehow, inexplicably, the subject car apparently had been able to slip through unnoticed!

But, realistically, they knew that the stunning evasion was not at all mysterious. Similar disappearances had happened to each of them in other supposedly airtight surveillance situations. The effectiveness of a surveillance depended upon the alertness of the officers involved and the accurate relay of the subjects’ movements to the next possible point of observation. Any one of several unforeseen things were liable to have happened this time: one detective team along the skein may have been distracted for the mere seconds it would require for an automobile, which some of these officers had not seen before today, to pass them by. Or perhaps, through some misfortune in logistical timing, a man on foot patrol might have been switching positions, or exchanging notes with a cruising radio car, at just the moment that Patsy and the Frenchmen swept past. Whatever, once the relay was broken at one point, odds would multiply rapidly that detectives farther along the line of flight, in any direction, might also miss observing the subject vehicle. When a pattern is no longer in effect, the officers don't know which way to look, and in such conditions often even the obvious is ignored.

The mortifying reality magnified with each passing minute that they had three or four suspected major felons in their net, and might well have scooped up the fourth along the way, and suddenly the whole catch had disappeared. And then, shortly after 10:00 A.M., the radio spluttered: 'One of the Frogs is back – Frog Two! He's alone, walking down Eighty-second to East End . . .'

The officers again crowded to the window. For several minutes past, they had noticed a rather handsome man in a striking black leather overcoat pacing expectantly in front of No. 45; but other than Fleming's remark that the fellow had a certain 'foreign' air about him, no particular significance had been attached to his presence. The neighborhood abounded in well-turned-out gentlemen and fashion-conscious women. But now, as they watched, Barbier had reappeared at the corner of 82nd Street and was striding directly across the avenue toward this stranger. They shook hands and talked.

'Another one!' Waters exclaimed, his field glasses trained on the two. 'Who the hell is *this* guy? I've never seen him before. About five-ten, looks in his forties.' Waters broadcast the new suspect's description on to base radio and the men patrolling the area. 'Solid build, good head of brown hair.'

Then Barbier drew a small piece of paper from his coat pocket and handed it to the other man. Waters said it looked like a ticket stub, maybe a garage ticket. The newcomer stepped to the mouth of No. 45's garage and motioned to someone inside. In a moment, the Negro attendant appeared to take the ticket or slip and then turned down the ramp.

'I don't like this,' Waters complained. 'They're getting a car out of there. Barbier's going for a ride. We can't let him take off again!'

'Let's see,' Sonny breathed at his elbow. The hulk of an automobile loomed out of the shadows of the garage. They watched, Sonny fingering the radio mike, describing the scene for detectives listening throughout the area.

Barbier and the stranger climbed into the sedan, the latter taking the wheel position. 'Frank!' Sonny cried. 'It's a *foreign* Buick! Remember the Canadian—!'

'Christ, let's get out in the street!' Waters bellowed. 'This could be the delivery!'

The two ran down the stairs. As they reached the sidewalk, the black Buick was turning out of the driveway across the avenue and driving off uptown. Waters's white Oldsmobile was parked at the corner of 81st Street, facing downtown. They piled into it, and almost before the doors slammed shut the agent had the engine racing, and then he was hauling the hardtop around in a screeching U-turn. The Buick now was beyond 83rd Street and picking up speed.

'We're not gonna hit them yet . . .' Sonny's remark was half-statement and half-question.

'We'll have to see how it plays,' Waters replied uncertainly.

'They're going fast,' Sonny observed. 'They broke the red light at Eighty-fourth!'

'Barbier's looking back. Look, he's telling the other guy to move it.'

The Buick was approaching another red signal at 85th Street, but instead of braking, the big sedan raced through and ahead on East End.

'Look at that!' cried Waters.

'They're making a run! There *must* be something in that car!'

'Barbier's still watching.'

Waters stomped on the accelerator. 'Should we hit?'

'I don't know.'

'If we stay with them like this, they're gonna make us anyway . . .'

'I hate to burn it too soon . . . Oh, hell, we better hit!'

With a burst of speed, the Oldsmobile roared through the stoplights at 84th and 85th streets, gaining rapidly on the Buick. They passed 86th, 87th. Barbier appeared increasingly agitated as the white car closed the gap. Crossing 88th Street, the nose of Waters's Olds was just off the left rear fender of the Buick. Waters was pressing hard on the horn now, warning the other car to the side. Sonny, leaning out the window, waved at the other driver to stop. The Buick slowed abruptly, and Waters swerved and cut it off with a squeal of brakes just before 89th Street.

Sonny was already on the radiophone: 'Popeye! If you read me, get back here to East End Avenue, quick! We bagged two Frenchmen!'

It was not until the officers had hopped out and were flanking the Buick with guns ready that they realized that the scene was being acted out directly in front of the mayor's residence, Gracie Mansion. The driver looked frightened and was jabbering in French. His companion, Barbier, glared at the detectives sullenly.

'All right, quiet down,' Sonny said. 'Let's see your identification. Your *identification*!' The detective took out his own wallet and displayed it. 'Identification, both of you,' he repeated. The driver reached into his inside jacket pocket – Sonny pointed the nozzle of his .38 at him – and, slowly, he pulled out a billfold, which he offered to the officer. 'No, empty it on there,' Sonny instructed, indicating the shelf atop the dashboard. Waters gestured similarly to Barbier. Now other cars were pulling up, and detectives clustered around them.

'Jacques Angelvin,' Sonny read awkwardly from one of the papers, all written in French, which the driver nervously had extracted from his billfold. 'Looks like this one is on the television over in France. He's even got clippings on himself.'

'And our friend Mr. Barbier here,' Waters commented, 'is not Barbier after all. His passport says his name is Scaglia, François Scaglia.'

Scaglia stared at the agent. 'I am known to you?'

'He speaks!' Waters exclaimed.

'My English is little,' the Frenchman said thickly. 'But *pardon*, how it is that I am known?'

'We know plenty about you, fella,' Sonny said, leaning in the opposite window. 'And you know we do.'

Scaglia spoke sharply in French to Angelvin. Then he turned to Sonny: 'We are of France. For what is it you stop us? We are in arrest?'

Sonny glanced across at Waters, whose eyes had been scanning the interior of the car. They didn't have a warrant to search the vehicle, nor did they even have the right to frisk the subjects yet; to do so without a warrant would make even damaging evidence inadmissible in court. Waters, his expression glum, shook his head. 'You went through two red lights,' Sonny said. 'We are going to hold you for questioning.'

'We wish to have interpreter,' Scaglia demanded.

'Yeah, sure . . .'

* * *

Such was the uncertain scene as Eddie Egan and Luis Gonzalez drove up, among Federal agents and city police officers appearing from all quarters. Egan ran from his car to the crowd of detectives around the Buick and elbowed through to Sonny's side. 'What happened?' he cried. 'Are you okay?'

'Eddie!' Sonny took his arm and, turning him away from the captured car, told him what had happened.

'So, what'd you come up with?' Egan asked anxiously.

Sonny's face sagged. 'Nothing.'

'Nothing? You pull me off Patsy for *nothing* . . . ?'

'What do you mean, 'off Patsy'? You were *on* him?'

Waters had come around to join them. 'Not only Patsy, all of them!' Egan declared. 'I even had Frog One.'

'That's crazy,' Waters scoffed. 'There were only the two Frenchmen with Patsy.'

'Well, between when you guys lost them and I found them, they picked up Jehan. The whole four were together. I kept trying to tell you, but my transmitter is shot.'

'But where *were* you?' Sonny insisted, eyes wide.

Egan described tersely his pursuit of Patsy's car and the agony of watching one after another of the suspects walk away unmolested. 'I saw this bird get out,' he said, tossing his head toward Scaglia, 'and then Mouren, and finally Jehan, and it was killing me, but at least I still had Patsy with the Frog's suitcase still in the car. And then you call like you're getting raped, and I leave Patsy go. I got to be the prize dummy of the year!' He spat disgustedly into the gutter.

'But how were we to know—?' Sonny moaned.

'I don't know. I also don't know how so many Feds and cops could lose these guys in the first place. Well,' Egan looked at his wristwatch – it was 10:20 A.M. – 'there's no use standing around here shootin' the shit. I'm gonna go find Patsy.'

'Where?' Waters demanded.

'I don't know, but I'll find him, and I'll hit him. It's probably too late now, but I'm gonna use those warrants before the day's out, I guarantee you.'

'What do you think *we* should do?' Sonny beseeched.

Egan eyed the crowd of men around the French Buick and then turned his glare directly on Agent Waters. 'You can start out by telling them it's normal procedure for seventeen cops to stop a car for going through a red light.'

As Egan and Gonzalez piled back into the Corvair, Grosso and Waters herded the two Frenchmen into Waters's car. They placed a guard over the Buick, then took Angelvin and Scaglia back to No. 45. By now, Lieutenant Hawkes had commandeered the office at the garage there as temporary headquarters.

'You want an interpreter?' Sergeant Fleming asked.

Both Angelvin and Scaglia nodded solemnly.

Fleming, Grosso and Agent Waters went to the back of the office and conferred with Hawkes. The lieutenant shook his head dourly. 'I don't know. We've got two French nationals and we got nothing on them. This could be embarrassing.'

'We haven't tossed the car yet,' Agent Waters pointed out.

'We do that without a warrant and we're in even deeper,' Hawkes growled. 'But let's hold them as long as we can.'

Waters nodded. 'I'll call our office for a French interpreter,' he offered.

'Tell him to take his time,' Hawkes cautioned.

'Of course,' Waters said, picking up the phone. He contacted the Federal Bureau and talked to Agent Martin F. Pera, a French translator. 'Now take these directions how to get here, Pera.' Waters outlined a route for the translator which would take him winding through lower Manhattan, out through Brooklyn to Jamaica and back through Queens, past LaGuardia Airport and then back downtown. 'If you get lost, call us and we'll give you new directions,' Waters counseled. Sonny, at his side, laughed grimly at the circuitous itinerary.

'O.K.,' Waters said, hanging up. He sighed wearily. 'I knew we shouldn't of hit.'

'What do you mean?' Sonny yelped. '*You* said to hit these guys!'

'The hell I did,' Waters contradicted. '*You* wanted to hit.'

'Come on! Let's still try to save this case,' Hawkes interjected gruffly.

Meanwhile, Luis Gonzalez and Egan raced downtown on the East River Drive. Egan was angry but remained hopeful. They would all be mental cases before it was over. Patsy had about a fifteen- or twenty-minute head start, but that was sufficient time to get rid of the stuff. There was only one real hope: that Patsy felt free and easy and was not in a big hurry to dispose of the merchandise. But this too was a slim hope, considering the presumed magnitude of this particular transaction.

Egan had decided that the first place to look was Blair's Pike Slip Inn. That's where the man always seemed to go when things looked bright and he was relaxed. Besides, it wasn't much out of the way to any of the bridges to Brooklyn. If Patsy wasn't at Blair's or elsewhere around his old neighborhood, the only other place to go then was Brooklyn and hit every place with the warrants, which were fast running out.

It was 10:45 A.M. when he turned off the Drive at Grand Street, and, maneuvering through side streets, aimed the Corvair down South Street toward Pike. It was a different thoroughfare by daylight: the warehouse piers were bustling with the loading and unloading of small trucks and massive vans backed against the platforms, some cutting the wide avenue in half with their bulk. At night, it was eerie down here, the shadows of the silent piers deep and forbidding under cover of the broad Viaduct overhead. It was a stretch of riverfront that could look and feel as ominous as any fictionalized Barbary Coast. But, by daylight at least, it was alive; the only smell was of fish.

Egan slowed near Pike; the Inn was just around the corner. He made the turn cautiously.

Gonzalez gasped. 'You're making me a believer!' the agent croaked.

Patsy was standing outside Blair's, chatting with Iñez, the barmaid. His blue Oldsmobile was parked a few feet away.

Egan could not repress a grin as he drove past, up Pike Street. 'Sonofabitch!' he gloated. 'Sonofabitch!' Two blocks up he drew over to the curb. 'Don't look,' he told Gonzalez. 'I got him in the mirror.'

'Do you think he still has the stuff on him?' the agent wondered.

'He could've dropped it in the joint there, or any place in between. We hit him now, and he ain't got it, we can kiss it off. All we can do is stay with him and hope he shows it. This case goes up, down, up, down, like a roller coaster,' Egan marveled.

It wasn't two minutes before Patsy reentered the compact and, with a wave at the girl on the step of Blair's, drove up Pike toward East Broadway. Another couple of minutes and they would have missed him again, Egan mused.

They followed Patsy up onto the Manhattan Bridge and across into Brooklyn. Gonzalez continued to report to the radio in the vain hope that some act of mercy by the electronic gods would make it work. In the excitement they had forgotten to exchange it for a new one, and now there was no time.

The trail led south through Brooklyn, to 65th Street. Patsy was going home. Egan pulled up to the corner of 12th Avenue as Patsy turned into his driveway on 67th Street.

The detective tried the radio again: 'Popeye here. If anybody reads me, I have just tailed Patsy to his house in Brooklyn. Does anybody read me?' There was no reply.

'It's no good, Louie. Look, there's a garage around on Sixty-eighth. Why don't you hustle over there and telephone base where we are, while I sit here and see what happens?'

'Right.' Gonzalez slid out his side and strode quickly toward the next corner.

Egan realized in a moment that Patsy had not left his car. It was still idling in the driveway, straddling the sidewalk. And then Egan saw Barbara Fuca, wearing her furry car coat, come down the steps from their house and get into the front seat alongside her husband. The detective searched Twelfth Avenue for signs of Gonzalez, but the agent already had turned the corner of 68th Street. Now Patsy was backing the Olds out of the driveway, and he started off east on 67th. Egan had no choice: he had to follow alone.

Patsy drove back to the Gowanus Expressway, northbound. Egan stayed close, taking no chances. The blue compact exited at Third Avenue and 16th Street, still in Brooklyn. He was going to the parents' house!

Patsy found a space for the Olds only a few yards from the entrance to No. 245. Egan, turning off Third Avenue into 7th Street, which was one-way eastbound, spotted him and Barbara just as they were getting out of the car. The officer drove slowly past as the couple walked to the front door. Patsy was *not* carrying the blue valise which Frog Three had carried into the Olds two hours earlier. Either he had stashed it somewhere during the twenty minutes he had been missing, Egan calculated, or it was still in the car. Egan pulled over near a fire hydrant on the opposite side of the street, about two thirds of the way toward Fourth Avenue.

Fifteen minutes passed, and twenty, and the detective shifted in his seat with irritation. Impatience urged him to take a crack at Patsy's car, for which he also had a warrant. He could grab the heroin if it was there and burst into the house in a dramatic single-handed confrontation. But the rules of the narcotics game insisted that no less than two officers effect a seizure and arrest, so that there would always be one corroborating witness. At the same time, anxiety prodded him to chance a dash to a public telephone – he could see a glass booth outside a service garage near the corner of Fourth Avenue. But, finally, prudence counseled him not to take his eyes off the car and the house until Patsy made some kind of move.

And then he saw Patsy come out of the house – not from the front door, but up hidden outside stairs from the basement. In shirt sleeves now, he went to his car, glancing up and down the street before unlocking it. He bent into the rear, and when he straightened up he was gripping the blue valise. Patsy relocked the left door, looked about him again, and disappeared into the basement down under the main entrance.

Flushed with excitement, Egan scrambled from the Corvair and hurried up the street to the sidewalk telephone booth. With No. 245 only partially in view, he dialed base radio with quick, nervous fingers.

'This is Egan. What's happening?'

'They're all running around like crazy, trying to salvage something,' the communicator answered.

'The Frenchmen?'

'Dry. Not a thing.'

'Where is everybody? Still up around East End?'

'Yes. They've set up temporary headquarters at that garage. Where are you? Luis Gonzalez called, and then he called back, saying . . .'

'Patsy took off. I couldn't wait for Louie. I'm sitting on old man Fuca's house on Seventh Street in Brooklyn. I need help.

I think Patsy just moved the goods in the house. Get some guys out here! And listen, you got a number up there? I wanna talk to Vinnie Hawkes.'

No one had stirred outside the Fuca house. Egan dialed the number for the garage at No. 45 East End Avenue. He briefed Lieutenant Hawkes, urging his boss to expedite reinforcements. He also begged that someone bring him a portable radio set. Then he asked:

'How's Sonny doing, and Waters?'

'I'm afraid I might have to lock them in cages,' Hawkes said dryly. 'They're fighting like a pair of cats over who's responsible for calling the hit on the Frenchmen.'

'Tell them not to scratch each other's eyes out. Popeye will save their skins yet.'

'You watch out for your own skin.'

Egan walked back to his car. It was quarter past twelve. Rays of pale sun were trying to force through the layers of moody gray above. Seventh Street was quiet; there were few pedestrians on the quiet block. Egan sat in the right front seat of the Corvair, chin resting on his left forearm on the back of the seat, looking behind at No. 245 and the small blue Oldsmobile at the curb. The fingers of his right hand played with the holster snap of the .38 Police Special at his hip.

A number of vehicles came through the block from Third Avenue in the next twenty-five minutes, but at twelve-forty Egan sensed something different about one car now crawling past the Fuca house. It held Detective Dick Auletta and Agent Artie Fluhr. Egan grinned, leaned across to the driver's side, and playfully flattened his nose against the window, goggling at them like a clown. Auletta noticed him as they came up alongside and smiled broadly. Fluhr stopped the car next to the Corvair, but Egan motioned them to keep going farther up the street. He got out and walked along the sidewalk after them, glancing back toward No. 245 every few strides.

Fluhr had nosed in near the corner. As Egan climbed in the back and flopped down with a grunt, Auletta greeted him: 'Well, has the little man had a trying day?'

'Don't ask,' Egan wheezed. 'What a mess, huh? You know about my radio crapping out? Christ!'

'Your worries are over,' Fluhr smiled. 'We brought you another portable unit.'

'Beautiful!' Egan twisted around to gaze a long second out the rear window. Turning back to the others, he said: 'I wouldn't say our problems are necessarily over, though.' And he filled them in on his observations and suspicions.

'So what's the play?' Auletta asked. 'Do we go for the collar now?'

'I been thinking about that,' said Egan. 'And I think I'd rather wait until Patsy comes out again. I want to see if he still has that suitcase with him. If he does, we'll have to split up and you guys tail him. If he comes out clean, we hit. I'd sure like to have some guys around in any case. You never know what can go wrong.'

'Hold it!' Fluhr warned, eyes focused back on 7th Street. 'Patsy and Barbara, they're coming out.' The three officers, hunched low, watching carefully as the couple got in either side of the Olds. Patsy did not have the blue valise with him.

'Boy, you guys got here just in time!' Egan exclaimed. 'Look, Artie, we'll let them pass by here, then you two go get them. I'll run back to the house. I've got to get the warrants out of my car first. Give me that radio, in case we have to talk.'

Fluhr handed over the flat, gray rectangular walkie-talkie. They all ducked down out of sight as Patsy's blue compact approached and rolled by to the corner.

Egan waited until the Olds turned right on Fourth Avenue before he clambered out and broke into a sprint back to his own car. Behind him, Fluhr's tires screeched as he and

Auletta swept around the corner after the Fucas. The detective fumbled with his keys, opened the glove compartment and began to sort through the wrinkled sheaf of documents stuffed inside. He snorted impatiently and crammed the entire pile inside his jacket. Radiophone under one arm and his .38 in hand, Egan marched across the street to No. 245.

Chapter Seventeen

JOSEPH FUCA answered Egan's ring. He was a short, scowling old man with untidy gray-white hair and a day's growth of beard, wearing a soiled white shirt with the sleeves rolled to the elbows. 'Yeah?' he glowered suspiciously at the burly redhead at the door.

With his free hand, Egan flipped open his shield case. 'Police officer. I have a warrant to search this house. You are Joseph Fuca?'

'Policeman? Whatta you wanta? I no—'. Fuca's mouth hung open and he blanched as he noticed the revolver in Egan's other fist.

'Just take it nice and easy and we'll get along fine,' Egan said evenly, shouldering through the doorway into a small foyer. 'Now, you're Joe Fuca, right?' The man was still staring at the gun. 'Who else is here?' the detective inquired. Fuca only shook his head dumbly. 'Okay.' Egan shoved the .38 back into its holster under his leather jacket. 'That better?'

He looked the little man over again. His shapeless gray trousers were splotched with old paint, and there also seemed to be traces of a white dust of some kind. His scuffed brown shoes were covered with a powder also. 'Okay, old man,' he commanded, 'let's go inside.'

'I no got nut-ting you want,' Fuca protested. 'Whatta you come—?'

'Fluhr here,' a tinny voice echoed out of Egan's armpit. Fuca jumped, startled.

Grinning, the detective brought the transmitter to his mouth. 'You got them?'

'We got them.'

'Any trouble?'

'Negative.'

'Bring them back, kay.'

'Ten-four.'

Pushing Fuca before him, Egan made his way into the front parlor. The furniture was old-fashioned, mostly stuffed and much of it threadbare; faded white doilies masked arms and headrests and the floor was covered with worn green linoleum. The place looked reasonably tidy, but somehow there was a fetid atmosphere of uncleanliness. Egan could smell the unmistakable, slightly stale aroma of Italian spices.

'Where's your wife?' he asked.

'She's out.'

'Too bad. We're going to have visitors – your boy Patsy and his wife.'

'Whatta you mean, they justa left.' Now the old man glared at Egan. 'Why you maka this business? I gotta nutting here!'

'You got somethin' here all right,' Egan snapped. 'And in a few minutes we're gonna find it – and mister, you're going to have real trouble.'

The doorbell rang. 'Stay here!' the detective ordered. He went to the door. Standing outside were Detective Jim Hurley and Agent Jack Ripa. 'Hey, gang!' Egan welcomed them. 'Come on in. We're about to have a party.'

'We heard on the radio,' Hurley said. 'Any other guys show yet?'

'Not yet.'

'Well, there's more coming. You think this is the drop?'

'I think so,' Egan said, 'but we'll soon find out. Start looking around.' As he stood aside in the doorway to let the two officers in, another car drew up outside. It was Fluhr and Auletta with their captives. 'Well,' Egan exclaimed, 'here's our prize package!'

A very sullen Patsy crossed the sidewalk ahead of Barbara and Auletta, then Fluhr followed behind them. The man whom Egan and his partners had been shadowing for months, whose every move had been watched and studied and analyzed and often worried about, somehow appeared slighter to the detective now, less menacing. Patsy's eyes were downcast yet wary. He moved like a trapped animal which fears the finish is near but which still may make one last clawing attempt at freedom should an opening present itself.

Egan propelled Patsy into the parlor, trailed by Barbara, chewing gum, wearing her gaudy blonde wig. Then as Auletta and Fluhr entered, two more cars double-parked on 7th Street and four more detectives joined them. They began to examine the house.

Egan confronted Patsy head-on: 'Okay, you can make it easy all around if you tell us right off where the stuff is.'

'What stuff?' Patsy snarled. 'What the hell is going on here? You better have—!'

Egan brandished his fistful of official documents. 'We got warrants for you and practically every place you been the past three months. You, your wife, your house, your two cars, your store, the Travatos, their car, your brother Tony and his house and his car, this joint, your father and mother—' he paused, pleased to note that Patsy had visibly paled, his eyes blinking in obvious surprise – 'even your French friends back in New York!'

Patsy was unable to speak for a moment. He shook his head, and looked up. 'What French friends? I don't know no French – except Denise Darcel . . .'

'Yeah? Well, then you don't care that they have all been arrested – right after you left them today.'

'I don't even know what you're talking about.' He was going to try to brazen it through. 'What do you want from me?'

'You got a load of junk stashed in this house,' accused Egan, aware that he himself was partly bluffing, for he could not be sure that Patsy had not really disposed of the heroin elsewhere and the suitcase he had brought into his parents' house was not clean.

'What's junk?' Patsy asked with the eyes of an altar boy.

Egan, fists on hips, legs planted apart, studied the shorter man with undisguised contempt, his gaze deliberately picking Patsy apart from his face down to his feet. The shoes bore a film of whitish powder, like his father's. The detective glanced over at the elder Fuca's shoes again, then, looking up at Patsy, he snapped to the old man: 'Okay, Pop, which way to the cellar?' The minute flicker he saw in Patsy's eyes might have been one of apprehension.

Joe Fuca was clearly reluctant, but he showed them to a door in the narrow corridor connecting the parlor with the rear of the apartment, 'Open it,' commanded Egan. It was dark below. 'Lights!'

Fuca flipped a switch just inside the door. Egan looked down. At the foot of the stairs, lying open on the cement floor, was a blue suitcase. He looked around at the old man and then to the son, a smile beginning to show on his mouth. 'If we have to, we'll, rip this place apart until we find what we're looking for.' Patsy's face was expressionless. His father just glared. 'No? Okay. Keep them up here,' he told Auletta and the other officers, as he disappeared down the wooden steps.

For a basement, the area below was about as neat as the parlor upstairs. It was a narrow rectangle, extending from the street side of the house to the rear. There was the outside door at the front end and two boarded-up windows. Two other small windows high in the rear wall opened on a backyard. At that end, the basement was separated by wood-plank partitions into three compartments, like large bins, apparently for storage use. In one corner, by a yellowed washtub, were an electric washing machine and a dryer, in another corner a blackened boiler and water heater. Overhead were the usual grimy pipes and asbestos-covered hot water ducts. The floor was chipped in spots, but it was swept very clean – a little unusual for even a tidy basement, Egan thought.

He knelt by the open valise. It was empty, but in the corners he noticed filmy traces of a white powdery substance. He explored it with his forefinger, then placed the tip of his finger on his tongue. The taste was acidly bitter. One test of heroin.

Grinning, Egan looked up the stairs to Patsy, standing on the top step, Dick Auletta at his shoulder. 'Right *here* there's enough shit to put you away. With your record, you oughta get ten years. But I'll tell you what: for *you*, I'm gonna go for triple that! Put the cuffs on him, Dick.'

As he looked up from his crouched position, Egan's attention was caught by a cluster of large dark stains in the faded plaster ceiling over the stairs. He rose and stood on the bottom step and felt gingerly at one of the spots. It was damp, as though recently replastered. There were four such spots, of varying sizes, one more than a foot across. Then, behind the stairs and almost directly below them, for the first time he noticed that all four jets of an ancient gas stove were burning – as though to speed the drying of fresh plaster.

'Well, well!' Egan grinned up again at Patsy, whose expression now was sagging. The detective went over to one of the storage bins in the rear and found an empty wooden crate, and he brought it back to the stove and climbed up onto it. Carefully, he probed one of the wet spots with his fingers, pushing up into the mushy plaster. Now, having tugged his sleeve back from the wrist, he shoved his hand all the way through. His fingers closed around a smooth, lumpy package. It was a plastic-wrapped bag, about the size and shape of a long bag of rice, but filled with white powder. It weighed about a pound – half a kilo of heroin!

'Dick,' he called up to Auletta. 'You got a field tester?'

'Artie's got plenty.'

'Tell him to come down. I think we struck gold!'

Fluhr clattered down the stairs. He whistled when he saw the bundle in Egan's hand. 'Look at *that*!'

'Let's give it the treatment.'

Fluhr produced a small tin, like a pillbox, and extracted a tiny glass vial containing a clear liquid. He snapped off the top and handed it to Egan. The vial contained a few drops of sulfuric acid and formaldehyde, called a Marquis reagent after the chemist who had developed the test for opium derivatives. Contact with any opium derivative would cause the liquid to turn a purplish color, the depth of shade depending upon the strength, or 'purity,' of the narcotic sample. Egan dipped his fingers into the package just taken from the ceiling. He rubbed some of the white powder into the test tube. Almost instantly, the mixture became a deep purple.

'Good Christ!' the Federal agent gasped. 'Have you ever seen such a reaction?'

'Never,' Egan murmured in awe. 'This has got to be the purest stuff anybody's ever seen around here!'

A sullen Patsy Fuca and his wife Barbara, concealing her nervousness by furiously chomping her gum and snapping profane remarks at the officers, were led by Agent Bill Bailey and Detective Dick Auletta to Bailey's car and driven back to 67th Street for a search of their house.

Eddie Egan skipped exuberantly up the rickety steps from the basement to the kitchen, where old Joe Fuca was being interrogated by Detectives Jim Hurley and Jimmy Gildea. Fuca was sitting at the kitchen table steadily working a bottle of whiskey, as the detectives tried to make him tell all he knew about the contents of the blue suitcase. Egan tossed two plastic bags each containing half a kilo of heroin on the table in front of Fuca. 'Nothing in the house, huh, Joe?'

Fuca stared at the bags and cried: 'Thatsa dynamite. Pasquale tell me that is *dynamite*.'

With a disdainful snort, Egan turned to the telephone on the kitchen wall and dialed the number of the police temporary headquarters in the office of the garage back in Manhattan. Sergeant Jack Fleming answered.

'I'm at Fuca's on 7th Street in Brooklyn. I've got a kilo and the shit's still comin' out of the ceiling. Call Chief Carey and ask him to call me here.' Egan read off the Fuca number and told Fleming to have Carey ring twice and hang up, then once and hang up.

Egan went back to the basement. He dug into the ceiling, removing one bag of heroin after another. Then, to his surprise, his searching fingers felt cold metal. He pulled out a submachine gun.

'Hey, Joe,' he shouted up the stairs, 'you got a blueprint for this joint? There won't be any ceilings and walls left when we get through down here.'

The telephone in the kitchen rang twice, was silent, rang once, was silent again, then began to ring again. Egan stamped up the steps, hugging the half-kilo bags to him. He threw them down on the table and jerked the phone from the hook: 'Popeye here.'

'What have you got there, Eddie?'

'Six kilos and a machine gun and still counting.'

Chief Carey whistled. 'Six kilos? Could there be more?'

'Could be *forty*-six. We'll need a lot of men over here with axes and crowbars.'

'I'll be there myself,' Carey answered.

'Yes, sir.' Egan hung up and turned to Fuca and his two inquisitors. 'The big man himself is coming over. Better sober Joe up.' Egan's beefy hand stabbed across the table, snatching the bottle of whiskey.

Fuca screamed in rage: 'Giva my drink!' Fuca's eyes blazed as he shambled to his feet. 'You lousy, dirty bastid cop! Bust up my house!' The old man made a clumsy lunge at Egan, trying to strike his face. Egan, with a short, sharp jab to the jaw, sent him sprawling back across the table. Fuca stumbled to the floor and lay still, spittle spewing from his mouth as he breathed heavily.

Sonny Grosso and Frank Waters were standing morosely in the lobby of the Hotel Commodore adjacent to Grand Central Station. Having made the impulsive move to stop the Frenchmen, under stress that perhaps overrode both their better judgments, only to find nothing substantially incriminating, both were acutely embarrassed and well aware that their precipitousness would probably lead to harassment of the bureau from officials all the way up to the U.S. Department of State.

François Scaglia and Jacques Angelvin continued to protest ignorance of any wrongdoing and were still waiting in detainment at the garage for the French interpreter. Agent Martin F. Pera had obligingly lost his way twice and still hadn't arrived at No. 45 East End Avenue.

The only items of interest found on either Barbier-Scaglia or Angelvin were two hotel room receipts in the pocket of the television performer, who seemed to be near tears as he proclaimed that this could only be a misunderstanding. One of the receipts was for a room at the Waldorf-Astoria; the faded carbon showed the arrival date to be January 10, 1962. The other, less crumpled and plainer, was from the Commodore, and the check-in date was January 17, 1962, just the day before.

After the arrest, Sonny and Waters had driven down to the Waldorf, where they confirmed that Angelvin had stayed for several days. He had kept his auto in the hotel garage, and he had checked out Wednesday morning, settling his bill in cash. The detectives then went to the Commodore. An assistant manager let them into Angelvin's room, a low-priced, unadorned bedroom which was crowded with twin beds. The Frenchman had unpacked only a few of his clothes and his toiletries. There was some correspondence from Radio Télévision Française and from a TV production firm in New York; a mildly affectionate note from a woman named Lilli DeBecque; several tourist folders and a map of the city; a copy of a short letter Angelvin had written to the U.S. Lines about his planned return voyage to Le Havre aboard the *America*, and a ticket for his passage. They also found a small diary, filled with cramped French. There was nothing else among his things that seemed of immediate importance. Downstairs, the officers inquired about Angelvin's car; but the front desk reported that when the gentleman had checked in he had mentioned nothing about garage service.

They telephoned back to Hawkes at East End Avenue that the Commodore appeared to be a blind alley. Then, barren of immediate direction, they stood by the assistant manager's desk, pondering glumly what to do next.

'We should never have stopped them,' Sonny complained. 'We've probably blown it for good now.'

'Well, *you* said to hit,' Waters remarked.

'*I* did? Why, you silly bastard, *you* wanted to hit! I was afraid that—'

'Officer?' It was the hotel manager. 'Telephone for Detective Grosso . . .'

Hawkes was calling, shouting into the phone.

Sonny leapt straight up with a whoop: 'Six kilos and still coming!' He danced about the desk, almost yanking the telephone to the floor. 'Popeye! Fantastic!' he cried. 'What a score! Okay, right, we'll be up.'

Slamming down the receiver, Sonny turned to Waters, his pale and tired face now a grinning beacon. 'Popeye did it! He got Patsy and his old man!'

The agent's eyes were popped and shining bright. 'Where?'

'The old man's cellar. And there's more coming out of the ceiling.'

Waters did a little jig, pounding Sonny on the shoulders. 'Oh, boy! Oh, *boy!*'

'How about that!' Sonny cried, hugging the smaller man. 'And we thought we blew it!' He placed his hands on the Federal agent's shoulders and leaped over his back. Not to be outdone, Waters leapfrogged over a crouching Sonny. 'And now we got Patsy *and* the Frenchmen!' Waters spun a pirouette in the center of the lobby, oblivious to the people staring at their uninhibited antics.

'It's a good thing we did hit them,' Sonny gloated.

'I kept trying to tell you that,' laughed Waters.

'*You?* You were the one who wanted to lay off them!'

'Me? Are you kidding? I wanted to bust 'em all the time!'

'*I'm* the one said let's hit,' Sonny blazed. 'Come on now, Frank!'

At 2:00 P.M., after his conversation with Egan, Chief Carey called Chief of Detectives James 'Lefty' Leggett at the 240 Center Street headquarters of the New York City Police Department, and advised that a seizure had been made at 245 7th Street in Brooklyn. This necessary bit of police procedure was responsible for Jean Jehan, 'Giant,' escaping from the city with what the police later estimated could have been as much as half a million dollars of Mafia money. This was in the black satchel which Egan had seen him carry away earlier in the day. The money would have gone to the policemen's widows' fund had he been apprehended.

At the chief of detectives' desk there is a direct line to the pressroom, and within minutes of the call from Chief Carey every newspaper, radio and television station in the city had reporters rushing out to Joe Fuca's house. Radio and television sets were blaring reports by midafternoon and the late editions of the afternoon papers carried the full story. Presumably Jehan heard the news and left the city instantly, even as detectives were searching in the sixties and seventies from York Avenue to East End for the recognizable dapper Frenchman who was close to the top of the crime syndicate hierarchy.

Meanwhile, thirty minutes after talking to Egan, Chief Carey arrived at the Fuca house, even while the press and television cameramen were gathering. The detectives had turned the Fuca basement into a shambles, clawing not only bags of heroin from the ceiling but rifles, pistols, bayonets, and hand grenades. Chief Carey strode into the kitchen, threw a look of disgust at the drunken Joe Fuca and went down to the basement. He picked his way through the rubble toward Eddie Egan.

'Eleven kilos of heroin – and enough guns and ammunition to wipe out a rival "family," Chief,' Egan boomed in satisfaction.

Carey shook his head in disbelief. 'This is the biggest haul we've ever made in one place!'

Chapter Eighteen

DICK AULETTA and Bill Bailey had by this time escorted Patsy and Barbara Fuca to their house. A surprised and frightened maid who had been baby-sitting watched in shock as the two narcotics officers began a thorough search of the house; Patsy and Barbara watched glowering. After an hour's search yielded nothing incriminating, Agent Bailey, looking about for any hiding place they might have missed, found himself staring at the squawling infant in the baby carriage. He guestured at the carriage and told Barbara to pick up her child. At first Barbara refused, and Auletta approached the carriage with the obvious intent of removing the baby himself. Barbara hastily picked up the baby.

Auletta carefully stripped off blankets and mattresses. There was a finger hole in one corner of the plywood bottom; pulling it up, Auletta found himself staring at two .38-caliber revolvers. He grinned at Bailey, who took a look and flashed a wide smile. They both turned to Patsy and Barbara. Patsy maintained a sullen silence.

Auletta next called Joe Fuca's house and asked for help in searching Nicky Travato's place. Egan told him to get over to Travato's and whatever detectives he could spare would meet him there.

A minute search of Travato's dingy flat, four blocks away on 66th Street, turned up two one-ounce plastic packets of heroin in the pocket of Barbara Travato's coat hanging in her clothes closet. Nicky took the blame for the presence of the drug, and the detectives agreed that his wife probably was blameless.

'Hey, Nicky,' Auletta grinned sardonically as they led the swarthy longshoreman downstairs to their car. 'What would Little Angie do if he knew you and Patsy were running an ounce business by cutting the family's inventory?' The look of fear on Travato's face answered the question eloquently.

At the Fuca house back on 7th Street, Eddie Egan handed Jim Hurley the search warrant, with only hours of validity left to it, for Tony Fuca's place in the Bronx.

Hurley telephoned Tony's apartment and his wife answered. Tony wasn't home. They needed him – chances were Peggy Fuca didn't know what was going on, and the warrant was only good once. The officer hung up without identifying himself. Then, over the radio, Hurley called the car that was supposed to be sitting on Patsy's luncheonette. Sure enough, Tony Fuca was there, still oblivious to what had been happening.

Hurley and two other detectives made the twenty-minute drive from Brooklyn, up through Queens, to the Bronx and parked outside Tony's building. They sat there for two hours, wondering nervously whether Tony would come home before their search warrant expired at midnight, when a radio call from the car outside the luncheonette reported that Tony had just been relieved by Joe Desina and had left.

Twenty minutes later Hurley watched Tony pull his car up in front of the shabby building on Bryant Avenue and walk into the front door and up the stairs. The detectives waited another fifteen minutes, then made their move. They pushed their way through the lower door, walked up the stairs to the fifth floor and pounded on the door marked 5-C. Tony Fuca opened his door, and the detectives burst inside.

While Hurley read the search warrant to the scowling Tony and a thoroughly cowed Peggy Fuca, the others began a methodical search. After every closet, cupboard and recess had been searched, they began on the furniture. Inside the seat cushion of the sofa, they founded a loaded .38 revolver and three one-ounce bags of heroin and another glassine envelope containing half an ounce more. 'So Patsy's put you in the ounce business,' Hurley sneered. 'Kind of dangerous, isn't it, Tony?'

Peggy Fuca seemed genuinely astounded at the discovery. Tony, confronted with the evidence, absolved his wife of any guilt, and the detectives decided that she, like Barbara Travato, had no knowledge of the conspiracy.

Meanwhile other detectives had been dispatched to pick up Barbara Fuca's father, Joe Desina, at Patsy's store. And in Manhattan, a platoon of city and Federal officers still were scouring the East End Avenue area from the sixties to eighties for Jean Jehan.

At Joe Fuca's house, Egan was triumphantly destroying the walls and ceilings of the basement, when a detective came to the door and called down, 'Eddie, there's a call for you.' Egan made his way through and over the dusty mounds of debris and up to the kitchen. At the sight of the redheaded detective, the animal snarls of Joe Fuca reached a crescendo of hostility. Egan cocked a threatening backhand and picked up the phone. It was Vinnie Hawkes.

'Popeye, we're still trying to find the big boy in this operation. And now we find there's another Frenchman lives on the fifteenth floor of No. 45 East End.'

'Hey—!' Egan remembered the first time he had followed Patsy to the address and observed him getting into the elevator which, the indicator revealed, had stopped on the fifteenth floor. 'What do you want me to do?' he asked.

'Hustle downtown and get a search warrant for Apartment 15-C here, and come on up.'

'I'm still taking this place apart,' Egan protested. 'Why me?'

'You're the expert on warrants. This could be important now. Let the other guys finish the wrecking job.' There was authority and finality in the lieutenant's tone.

'Okay, Vinnie,' Egan murmured, fighting back his annoyance. 'So far the count here is eleven kilos, by the way . . .'

As Egan left the Fuca house, 7th Street was becoming clogged with vehicles, television and radio equipment, reporters, spectators and more cops. This haul ought to be good for great spreads in the papers, Egan thought as he shouldered his way to his car. Chief Carey would be in his glory.

Egan drove to the bureau at Old Slip, parked and went up to his cubicle of an office where he sat down to write out the necessary affidavit to authorize a search of the premises of Apartment 15-C at No. 45 East End Avenue. Painstakingly, he composed the affidavit. There was reason to believe, he wrote, that there was a direct connection between Apartment 15-C at No. 45 East End Avenue and Pasquale Fuca, who had just been found in possession of eleven kilos of heroin. Fuca had been followed by police officers and seen to be consorting with certain French nationals suspected of conspiracy to smuggle heroin into the United States from France. Fuca had been traced making at least one visit to the fifteenth floor of No. 45 East End Avenue. Apartment 15-C was occupied by a French national.

Egan went on for three quarters of an hour detailing the reasons for the search warrant, then hurriedly telephoned State Supreme Court Judge Mitchell Schweitzer and asked if his honor would remain in his chambers a few minutes. The judge agreed. But by the time Egan left the 1st Precinct it was 5:30 P.M., and when he reached the courthouse at Foley Square, Judge Schweitzer was walking out of the elevator on his way home. Egan quickly reiterated the importance of the case, and the judge, impatient, returned to his chambers and signed the search warrant. By six, Egan was on his way uptown to East End Avenue.

At temporary headquarters in the garage office at No. 45, the interpreter, Agent Martin Pera, had just arrived and was questioning Angelvin and Scaglia. Fleming and Hawkes pumped Egan's hand, congratulating him. Sonny and Frank Waters banged him on the back as though he had made the winning touchdown. Egan handed Fleming the warrant, and they went to the office of the supervisor of the building, a woman, who took them up to 15-C.

The occupant was in Mexico on vacation; he had been away for a week. It interested the police that the last time the gentleman had been away was precisely the week in November when Egan and Grosso had followed Patsy downtown and discovered the Buick belonging to the Canadian narcotics connection, Maurice Martin.

A careful search of the luxurious apartment turned up nothing of interest, until Egan picked up a book of matches from an end table. It was from La Cloche d'Or. The cover had caught his attention because he had tailed Jehan to the same chic French café the previous Friday night. Now his interest quickened: inserted on the back cover was a small souvenir photograph. It showed two men, and one of them was Giant. He showed the small photo to the building manager. She was unable to identify Jehan, but she recognized the other man as the occupant of the apartment. Controlling his rising excitement, Egan slipped the matchbook into his pocket.

This required a little calm thought, and he didn't want to alarm the woman. Excusing himself, he went into the expensively appointed bathroom. As he sat contemplatively, he pulled his package of Camels and some matches from his pocket, lit up, and smoked for a few minutes. Was it possible that they had stumbled upon the *real* top boss of this operation? *Was* this where Patsy had come that day? It had to be: the picture of Jehan seemed to verify it. O.K. Play it cool. He walked back into the living room. The others had given up on finding anything incriminating. All the detectives followed the manageress out of the apartment, down the elevator and out to the street.

'Well, we *got* something,' Egan said outside, fumbling for the matchbook.

'What?' the discouraged Lieutenant Hawkes inquired.

'Could be big. At least it should be good enough to get the guy in for some questions.' Egan dug deep into one pocket and then another. The matchbook wasn't there. Stricken, he realized he must have dropped it in the bathroom. And now there was no way he could go back into the apartment. The search warrant had already been executed, he knew another one would not be granted – certainly not before someone would have gone through the apartment to see what the police might have found . . . and discovered the matchcover beside the toilet. Frustration knotted inside his stomach as it had so many times during the case, but there was nothing he could do now.

Hawkes checked in with the Narcotics Bureau and found that all the suspects in the case had been rounded up and taken to Old Slip for questioning. They left additional officers in the area to be on the lookout for Jehan, and then he, Fleming, Egan, Grosso and Waters cruised down the East Side Highway to Old Slip.

By the time they arrived at the Narcotics Bureau, it was bedlam, with two stenographers desperately trying to record the confusion. Patsy and Barbara Fuca had been the first prisoners to arrive. From their house, they'd been taken to Brooklyn's 61st Precinct, then in midafternoon downtown to the 1st Precinct. When Joe Fuca's wife, Natalie, returned to her home, to find it surrounded by curious passersby and a gaggle of reporters, she was detained with Joe. The old Italian couple with some difficulty had been maneuvered, hysterical and screaming, from the house on 7th Street into police cars and sped across the bridge to lower Manhattan and Old Slip. Nicky Travato and Tony Fuca were also brought in after being booked at their local precincts; but both their wives had been allowed to stay home. Scaglia and Angelvin had been taken to the 24th Precinct on 68th Street in Manhattan for booking and then were also brought downtown. Now the Narcotics Bureau was more active than it had been at any time since its inception. The largest single confiscation of heroin yet made in the United States had been brought in as evidence against the suspects.

It was almost nine P.M. when Egan and his group arrived and pushed through the mob of photographers, television cameramen and reporters clamoring for more news about the arrest. As they struggled to get up to the third floor of the old 1st Precinct building, Joe Fuca could be heard still screaming in a frenzy. At the landing between the second and third floor, Fuca broke away from the detective holding him and kicked the cameraman who had just taken a flash picture of him. This knocked the camera out of the photographer's hands, and it fell down the stairwell to the marble ground floor with a crash. Egan started toward the old Italian, but Joe, spying the redheaded Irishman moving on him, shrank back and quieted down.

The Narcotics Bureau officers had managed to separate the suspects, holding each one in a separate cubicle office. Those who had been active in the case went from one office to the next, asking each prisoner questions, trying to fit the facts of the case together. Natalie Fuca's hysterical shrieks knifed through the building. They reached a crescendo whenever she caught a glimpse of her son's wife, Barbara, who acted the 'tough broad' role, chewing gum, swishing her hips and swearing profusely at everyone.

'She's the who-er, the cheap who-er!' Natalie screamed. 'It's you what got us in thisa mess. Pasquale, why you marry thisa cheap bum who-er?'

Egan and Grosso finally maneuvered Barbara and Patsy Fuca into the same cubicle and began questioning them. Not unexpectedly, Patsy was a tough customer to crack.

'What are you talkin' about?' he shouted. 'I don't know no Frenchmen. Why don't you go catch a murderer instead of buggin' me?'

'Don't tell us you weren't driving Nicky Travato's Cadillac up around Forty-five East End Avenue,' Egan bellowed. 'Remember seeing me in the garage office?'

Patsy stared at the detective. 'I *thought* you looked familiar.'

'And how about this: the doctors?' Egan taunted.

'Sonofabitch!' Patsy exclaimed. 'You guys used to come into my place from the hospital!' He turned to Barbara. 'I always thought there was something funny about those fuckin' guys!'

But although obviously surprised at the officers' knowledge of his activities, Patsy would admit nothing. The detectives gave him very convincing arguments that at that moment Nicky was incriminating him, but still he refused to weaken. Teams of detectives moved from one suspect to the next, trying to squeeze out every additional bit of information they could, with little success.

And then Chief Carey called a meeting of all detectives involved in the case in the front office. In all there were almost ninety city detectives and Federal agents on hand. For an hour he patiently pieced all the facts of the case together, still trying to find out where Angelvin fitted in, dismissing the officers one by one as they told what they knew and had seen. Finally there were only five men left: Detectives Egan and Grosso, Lieutenant Hawkes, Sergeant Fleming and Agent Waters.

'O.K.,' Carey announced at last, 'I've got the story. Two assistant D.A.'s, Bob Walsh from Brooklyn and Irving Lang from Manhattan, are waiting downstairs. We're going to present the case to them and see which one wants to prosecute.'

Carey and the five officers went downstairs to the office where the district attorneys were waiting. It was almost midnight by now. For over an hour, they laid out their case in detail. After listening carefully, Irving Lang stated that he felt the case was not strong enough to be prosecuted in Manhattan. The policemen's faces dropped.

Robert Walsh, however, said that on behalf of Kings County District Attorney, Edward Silver, he *would* accept the case for prosecution in Brooklyn. Elated, Egan, Grosso, Waters and their superiors went back up to the third floor and proceeded with the formalities of arresting the suspects, who until now had officially been 'detained.'

Since Sonny was a second-grade detective waiting to make first, it was decided that he should officially make the arrests of Patsy and Barbara Fuca and Egan officially arrest only Scaglia. Other detectives active in the case were assigned the official credit for Nicky Travato, Joe Fuca, Tony Fuca and Joe Desina. Angelvin was held as a material witness.

It took the weary detectives all the rest of the night of the eighteenth and the morning of the nineteenth to finish questioning and booking the prisoners. The official forms were endless. In addition, for convenience's sake, each prisoner's booking had to be recorded in the section of the city in which each had been arrested.

At 10 A.M., Friday, the nineteenth, the arresting officers took six of their prisoners back to Brooklyn – all but Tony Fuca, who was returning to the Bronx, where he had been apprehended – where they were presented before Judge Ruben Levy in Kings County Criminal Session. For the preliminary hearing, a court-appointed counsel stood up for all the accused. First, Detective Eddie Egan went before the bench and voiced his formal complaint against François Scaglia: conspiracy to smuggle into New York and sell illegal narcotics. Sonny Grosso then stated his complaint against Patsy Fuca: conspiracy as well as possession of narcotics. In turn, each of the arresting officers stepped forward and filed their charges: against Joe Fuca, accessory to a felony; against Nicky Travato, possession; against Barbara Fuca, accessory. As for Jacques Angelvin, Brooklyn Assistant D.A. Walsh recommended to the court that for the time being he be held as a material witness in the case against Scaglia and the Fucas.

The arraignment lasted less than fifteen minutes. Angelvin was committed to Civil Prison in Manhattan, notorious as the 'alimony jail.' Barbara Fuca was sent to Manhattan's Women's House of Detention in $50,000 bail. Patsy Fuca, his father, Scaglia and Travato were remanded to the Raymond Street jail in Brooklyn, all but the old man held in $100,000 bail. Joe Fuca's bond was set at $50,000.

Early Friday afternoon, their long hunt finally completed, Eddie Egan and Sonny Grosso went to their respective homes and slept through into Saturday.

Chapter Nineteen

On Saturday morning, January 20, Egan was requested by Chief Carey to accompany a police photographer to the Fuca house on 7th Street and assist in taking pictures of the basement where the heroin and arms had been found. To Egan's astonishment, the hopeless mess of rubble had been cleaned up so thoroughly that the only signs of the wreckage of two days before were the stripped walls and ceiling. The floor was spotless. Egan speculated that some Dons must have come by, looking to see if the police had missed anything. He cursed their negligence in not keeping a guard on the place.

Then, as the photographer was busy snapping pictures, in a dark corner of the cellar Egan noticed a large, square sheet of plywood on the floor which he had not seen before. He turned it over and found himself staring into an earthen pit about two feet deep, roughly the size of a grave. It was empty. But, it occurred to Egan, there was room in this excavation for a lot more heroin than the twenty-four pounds they had discovered in the ceiling. The detective began to wonder if in fact there wasn't one hell of a lot more heroin around someplace. This could have been the 'bank" where it was scheduled to end up.

Since Thursday the investigators had been unable to shake a nagging skepticism that Patsy and the French narcotics overlords would have taken such risks for what amounted, in their league, to a paltry eleven kilos. Then there were the questions of how they had moved the stuff into the country, and how many other hands were involved. What was the role of this French TV performer, Angelvin – he had no criminal background; where did he fit in? And what about the two Frogs still unaccounted for?

And no money had been found. The police calculated that the going wholesale rate for 'H' was about $10,000 to $12,000 per kilogram; so, presumably up to $120,000 was floating around somewhere, or in somebody's pocket, just from what had been intercepted so far. On the open market, after being 'cut' (diluted) and turned over from dealer to dealer, by the time it reached the individual buyers eleven pure kilos could be worth thirty times the wholesale price. And it was a sellers' market, crying to be exploited. It was reasonable to assume, then, that such a tempting potential would have prompted far more ambitious enterprise among this crowd than the mere twenty-four pounds confiscated.

But if there was more, where could they have stashed it? Had it already been distributed? That *was* a possibility. The subjects had had enough time, nearly a week, in which to parcel out quantities to various connections. Yet, on the basis of all their observation, information, and the judgment of experience, the investigators doubted that. Police informants had not come up with even a hint that any new junk had yet made it to the streets; the 'panic' was still on.

If they could find out how the Frogs had brought the stuff in, that might offer a clue as to its present hiding place. And to be able to convict the foreigners along with Patsy and the others, it had to be proved that they had in fact participated in the illegal delivery. As it was, the two Frenchmen in custody, Barbier, now identified as Scaglia, and Angelvin, were being held on suspicion of conspiracy, a tenuous charge that might not stick unless the law could establish possession and intent-to-sell. Neither had been found with any heroin on his person. Both were continuing to insist that they were innocent.

On Monday, January 22, after two good nights of sleep, Sonny Grosso was sifting through the papers and effects he had confiscated from Angelvin's room at the Commodore. There were some copies of correspondence with the United States Lines. Angelvin had declared the weight of his Buick and baggage at 4,685 pounds. Shortly after his arrival at the Waldorf he had received a form letter from United States Lines requesting a confirmation of his return trip January 25 on the S.S. *America* and information on any new items to be declared on the homeward voyage. Although he had come over tourist class, Angelvin was planning to make the return trip in style: first class. His reply to United States Lines, of which he had thoughtfully made a copy, struck an immediate chord of suspicion in Sonny's now rested mind. Confirming his return reservation, Angelvin added that he had miscalculated the weight of his automobile and personal effects and that now the Buick would weigh 4,573 – 112 pounds less than he had originally stated. Ordinarily when a person takes his automobile with him on an overseas trip, he files just one shipping declaration covering both legs of the voyage. Now he requested a reduced freight charge for the eastward crossing. The weight differential amounted to a saving of about $33.00 for the French TV star, Grosso estimated.

But why 112 pounds lighter? Didn't most visitors return home with *additional* poundage in purchases and souvenirs? Everything else on the manifest seemed to be the same as he'd originally declared. How could he have anticipated a reduction in weight more than a week before departure?

Sonny was stunned as he contemplated the possibility. If the 112 pounds represented the total weight of heroin that had been smuggled in, it would be the largest shipment ever attempted at one time in New York. And this meant that eighty-eight pounds, forty kilos more of heroin – perhaps eventually worth, at retail, twenty-five or twenty-six million dollars more – were still to be found. The damage which could be done to the international dope network by the confiscation of such a load and the conviction of the principals could be extremely significant.

The vacant hole in Joe Fuca's cellar, added to the possibilities aroused by Angelvin's second declaration of weight for his car, thus led the investigators to conclude that the medium of delivery had to be the actor's automobile. Sonny secured a warrant to search the Buick on Thursday, January 25 – ironically, the day that Angelvin was to have sailed aboard the *America*. In the meantime, rather than trust the police pound on Hudson River Pier, the detectives had hidden the Buick in an old abandoned sanitation garage out in Brooklyn on Meeker Avenue. The Mafia would not be able to find it there.

Once the warrant was official, the Police Department's Motor Transport Maintenance Division mechanic, Irving Abrahams, went over the Buick inch by inch, panel and upholstery, stitch by stitch. He found no trace of narcotics nor any hiding place for a large shipment.

Buick engineering experts next were called in to work with Abrahams, and they finally found what the police were looking for. There were a series of bolts under the front fenders which were caked with dried mud, seemingly undisturbed. But when flakes of the mud were scraped off and examined, it was not crumbly and dusty as might be expected but still retained a certain cohesion, as though it were relatively *fresh* mud. The samples were tested in the police lab, and it proved to be mud from a known variety of French soil, all right. But it was of recent vintage and, more significantly, had been applied to the underside of the car recently, probably within the past week or two.

The engineers went to work on the bolts, which, apparently attached splash pans to the fender bottoms. They were immovable. Then a Buick technician checked with his plant in Detroit and learned that there were models of General Motors cars with certain bolts that could be fastened or loosened only when the electrical system was operative. The ignition was switched on. The unusual bolts were unscrewed.

The tinny plate covering the splash pan under the left front fender was removed first. There was a hollow trap inside – a detective was able to shove his entire arm into it without obstruction. The secret trap seemed to extend from the front of the car all the way to the back. Now they uncovered more traps on the other side of the Buick and behind and under the headlights. There was easily enough space for 112 pounds of heroin in small packages, and then some.

Using powerful vacuum tubes, the police investigators cleaned out the traps in the Buick and examined the residue. A small amount of white powder, perhaps as much as half an inch of cigarette ash, was found in the vacuum cleaner and tested. The Marquis test showed this residue to be an opium derivative.

Eddie Egan and Sonny Grosso had a hunch where to start looking for clues to the hiding place of the eighty-eight pounds of junk which were still missing. Several times during the investigation they had observed Patsy in or near Anthony's Garage on East Broadway. Maybe that place was a drop for either the missing dope or the 'bread' or both.

The two marched into Anthony's on January 27, assuming a pseudo-official air of stern suspicion, although of course they had nothing more incriminating than the fact that a key figure in a major arrest was known to have patronized the auto shop. Their bluff interrogation paid off to the extent that an intimidated Anthony Feola, owner and chief mechanic, nervously admitted that Patsy had paid him fifty dollars to replace the splash panels under the fenders of the 1960 Buick, and coat the bolts with some kind of mud from a jar that Patsy had given him. Then Feola parked the car outside on East Broadway and left it there. But this information produced little more than the satisfaction of filling in a few more details in the overall picture.

A thorough examination of the garage at No. 45 East End Avenue had turned up nothing more enlightening than confirmation that Angelvin's Buick had been checked there for a couple of days. It had been deposited on Tuesday, January 16, by a foreign type (Angelvin) and driven out on the eighteenth by the same person. Between times, Patsy Fuca had brought Travato's Cadillac in, left it, and gone somewhere in the Buick; it had been out all one night (Tuesday) and was returned late the next day by Patsy, but where he had driven was still unknown.

The police decided that it was unlikely that Sol Friedman, owner of the garage, whom they knew to be a shrewd, cautious individual, would have risked permitting the actual transfer of so large a load of junk on his premises, sensitive as he had to be about his already shaky relationship with the law. They had small doubt that Friedman *knew* what was going on – though, again, this would be difficult to prove sufficiently to prosecute even a conspiracy charge. But they reached the conclusion that No. 45 East End Avenue had been only a relay station in the disposal operation. Patsy had transported the Buick somewhere else to unload.

Then, checking their files, they were reminded that Friedman had a near-silent partner, Arnie Shulman, a hoodlum who was known to have been involved in narcotics. Shulman had a share of the No. 45 East End Avenue concession and he also owned another commercial garage on Tremont Avenue in the Bronx in which Friedman had no interest. And this garage was only six blocks from where Patsy's brother Tony lived.

Egan and Grosso drove to the Bronx. With a picture of Angelvin's car they casually wandered into Shulman's garage and found an old mechanic working on a wreck at the rear. They showed him the picture and asked if this car had been in the garage. The mechanic looked at the picture and Egan thought he detected a flash of recognition – but the garageman at first was noncommittal. Egan bore in on him, and after a few moments of tough talk the mechanic remembered that the Buick had been brought in the week before by three men, one of whom he thought he recognized from the neighborhood. The men had worked on it for most of an afternoon and then driven it away. Egan patted the old mechanic on the shoulder soothingly, commended him on his public-spirited attitude, and he and Grosso departed, winking at one another.

The detectives made for Tony Fuca's house. They had never figured that Tony was an important cog in the Angelo Tuminaro apparatus. Like Patsy's friend Nicky Travato, longshoreman Tony was roughhewn, little educated and, as far as the police could determine, not particularly bright. They had no past record on him. He had been around Patsy a great deal and obviously had been helpful to his brother, like tending the Brooklyn luncheonette on weekends. Even after the raid on his apartment which had turned up the three-and-a-half ounces of heroin and a loaded pistol, the police had regarded Tony as little more than a muscular stooge, an accessory surely, but hardly one to whom the Mafia might entrust a fortune in responsibility and goods.

But now Egan and Grosso reassessed probabilities. They remembered a monitored telephone conversation between Patsy and 'Uncle Harry' the night before the arrests. Talking about some clothing that Patsy was supposed to have just acquired, 'Uncle Harry' suggested that Patsy could 'only use a few suits at a time' and that he ought to 'put the rest away' in storage. The 'few suits' could have been the eleven kilos seized in Joe Fuca's basement which was to have been current inventory for the local organization, as administered by Patsy for Little Angie. The 'rest' could be hidden away in some reliable place, to be drawn upon according to the demands of the marketplace.

Put the rest away, 'Uncle Harry' had advised, and Patsy had assured him that he had. But, beyond a few odd ounces, no big stuff had been found in Patsy's own house, in his luncheonette, in Nicky Travato's apartment or in Tony Fuca's flat. But then one of the detectives who had arrested Tony returned from a brief holiday and revealed that only Tony's *apartment* had been searched the night of the arrests; the rest of the building had been untouched. This opened a new vein of thought to Egan and Grosso. Tony's house was not far from Shulman's Garage, where they were sure the transfer from Angelvin's Buick had been made.

Tony Fuca lived with his wife Peggy and their two small daughters at 1171 Bryant Avenue in the lower Bronx in a building that was a half-step away from being a firetrap. It was a drab five-story walk-up of dirty brown brick, indistinguishable from adjacent buildings or, for that matter, from thousands of other walk-ups in lower-class sections of New York. The streets and sidewalks were littered with debris and scraps of garbage. The neighborhood was tucked in a dreary residential pocket bounded by busy thoroughfares such as Westchester Avenue and Southern Boulevard. At one time it had been shared largely by Italian and Eastern European Jewish immigrants, but now there had been an influx of Puerto Ricans, and few of the Italians and Jews remained. Tony was one of the few Italians. He and his family lived in a three-and-a-half-room flat on the top floor.

While Egan was scouting the neighborhood, Grosso went to see the janitor. At the side of the building was a ramp down into an alleyway separating No. 1171 from the adjacent apartment house. An ill-fitting wood door with glass panels in its upper half led into the basement. Inside, a narrow corridor off the entryway led to the boiler room, where Sonny found the janitor, stoking the hot water heater. A lean, sharp-eyed man of fifty or more, he listened expressionless as the officer identified himself. Sonny explained that there had been a recent series of burglaries in the vicinity and that the police were quietly investigating each apartment house in an attempt to uncover a possible hiding place for the stolen goods. 'We don't say it's this building,' the detective said, 'but in case it might be, where around here could people stash things that nobody would be likely to find?'

The janitor pointed behind Sonny back along the corridor. 'Well, there's a closet for paint, and a storage room, for old trunks and things people leave' – his accent was slightly Germanic or Slavic – 'and a room for the carriages, baby carriages, you know. But I don't think—'

'Don't worry about it,' Sonny smiled wanly. 'There'll be no trouble. We'll handle it nice and quiet. You just cooperate, and everything'll be fine. We don't want *nobody* to know we came down here – get it?'

The gaunt man nodded, his blue eyes now open very wide.

One hour later, on a dusty, filth-laden shelf in the so-called 'carriage room,' a cramped, cobweb-covered enclosure near the entrance to the cellar, Grosso and Egan came upon a heavy, large steamer trunk. On it in chalk was scribbled, Fuca. Together they hefted the trunk to the floor and forced it open. Inside were two battered suitcases. Egan and Grosso opened them – and gasped at the sheer bulk of their find. The bags were crammed with plastic packets containing white powder. They counted out a total of eighty-eight packages weighing about a pound apiece, each, if the heroin proved to be as pure as the stuff seized at Joe Fuca's, worth more than a hundred times its weight in gold.

Egan repacked the bags while Grosso ran outside to his car and called in the information to the Narcotics Bureau. An hour later, Lieutenant Hawkes arrived at the basement with Agent Waters and, after a conference, it was decided to put the junk back where it had been found and mount surveillance over it until someone came to claim it. Somebody *had* to come for a load that size.

That same day, in Naples, Italy, sixty-five-year-old Charles (Lucky) Luciano, the deported Italo-American vice king who was believed to have continued to reign as a top Mafia boss of the United States even from his palazzo in exile, collapsed and died of a sudden heart attack.

Luciano may or may not have been aware that at the time of his death American and Italian narcotics agents, with the help of French police, were poised to arrest him on charges of having directed the smuggling of more than 150-million dollars' worth of dope into the U.S. over the previous decade.

It is doubtful in any event that Patsy and Tony Fuca, sulking separately in New York jail cells awaiting indictment, could have understood immediately that it was the busting of their own operation which may have crystalized the international operation against Luciano's ring and perhaps even worried the *capo*, as he was known, to his grave.

Chapter Twenty

THE Fucas and Scaglia were arraigned and in jail, and the heroin traces found in the Buick now definitely implicated Angelvin, who was being held only as a 'material' witness to the conspiracy until he could be proved part of it. Assistant District Attorney Michael Gagliano, representing Kings County District Attorney Ed Silver, was given the assignment of presenting the case to the grand jury.

Before a criminal case could be brought to trial, an indictment by a county grand jury had to be obtained. A grand jury is made up of twenty-three citizens – twenty-two jurors and a foreman. Qualifications for grand jury duty are more stringent than for trial juries. The panel consists entirely of volunteers, most of them professional or retired people of relative affluence and, generally speaking, of wider intelligence than 'conscripted' jurymen. Of the twenty-three panel members – of whom no more than six may be women – a quorum of sixteen is required on any one case, and to obtain an indictment at least twelve must vote in favor. In the event of an eleven-eleven tie, the foreman casts the deciding vote. In Brooklyn, each selected grand jury is expected to sit for one month every two years. However, once empaneled, a panel will continue to sit on a case it has accepted until either an indictment is handed down or the people's evidence is deemed insufficient to prosecute.

The Brooklyn grand jury met in a sealed room on the sixth floor of the antiquated Kings County Court House. The panel members were at all times securely removed from public scrutiny and possible harassment. Special elevators took the jurors from the ground floor of the court building to their hearing room, which was off a corridor inaccessible to the public. During hearings, the only outsiders present are the district attorney, or an assistant, and one witness at a time. There is no judge. Because the sole aim of the proceedings is to afford the attorney for the people an opportunity to establish cause for indictment, witnesses must appear without counsel, and there is no cross-examination. However, witnesses – except for the accused – are granted immunity against self-incrimination, and presumably one could confess to a murder before a grand jury without it being used against him. As for the accused, it is rare that a prisoner personally appears before a grand jury, for to do so he must waive all immunity and civil rights, and his defense counsel is barred from the hearing.

Kings County Assistant District Attorney Michael Gagliano, intent upon the importance of securing indictments in the Fuca case, was pleased to discover that Grand Jury No. 1 was still in session, just finishing up its month's hearing. The foreman of Grand Jury No. 1, Jack Champagne, was a man in whom Gagliano had great faith for his integrity and justice. Champagne himself had served on grand jury duty for fifteen years, and the panel he now headed was, Gagliano knew, composed of particularly experienced jurors.

On February 7, late in the afternoon of the day when he was assigned to the case, Gagliano hurried over to the courthouse in time to catch Jack Champagne as the foreman came out of the lobby elevator from the upstairs hearing room. Gagliano found that Champagne had only moments before dismissed Grand Jury No. 1. Hastily the assistant district attorney explained the case to Champagne, a stocky man in his late fifties, with wavy gray-white hair, who peered through extra-thick tinted glasses as he listened intently. Champagne was a construction man who had also been an officer in city and state penal institutions, and previously done undercover work for the district attorney's office in such cases as the prosecution of the top mobsters of Murder, Inc. Champagne showed immediate interest in this latest narcotics case and its international ramifications, so he and Gagliano stepped back into the grand jury elevator. On the sixth floor, in the jurymen's private corridor outside the hearing room, they found most of the members of the jury preparing to leave. With all the considerable persuasiveness at his command, Champagne rapidly convinced his fellow jurors that this was the hottest narcotics case ever to come before a grand jury. The hitch was, he explained, that the case had to be opened immediately, because the following day a new grand jury would sit. At 6 P.M., the members of Grand Jury No. 1 filed back into their hearing room.

Gagliano opened the case by having Detective First Grade Edward Egan state that he had arrested François Scaglia on January 19. Egan then outlined the details of the complaint. The case thus now belonged to Grand Jury No. 1, and it would be theirs until disposition one way or another.

Since Patsy Fuca's detainment on January 18, and his official arrest on January 19, he had been increasingly concerned about his wife and his father. The thought of their having to go to jail finally caused him to pass the word to Detectives Egan and Grosso that he might be willing to be cooperative if they could see that Barbara and old Joe were left out of it. The detectives made no promises. Would Patsy *talk*? Patsy responded by confiding that the Frenchman, Jean Jehan, originally had planned to meet with him at the Inner Circle Bar the night of the arrests, January 18. He also indicated that Giant must have made off with a large bundle of cash.

Hopeful, Egan and Grosso called in Grand Jury Foreman Champagne and Assistant District Attorney Gagliano to join in the interrogation.

But it quickly became apparent that Patsy had given the law all the help it could expect from him. Under direct questioning by men who were aware of his almost every move over the past four months, he failed to provide a single item of new information or even, for that matter, of what the officers already knew to be truth. Either he avoided answering incriminating questions or he lied outright. Finally, when Champagne pressed him about his specific activities in the overall Mafia narcotics operations, Patsy quailed. 'Are you kiddin'?' he whined. 'I answer stuff like this and I'm dead. If they even knew I talked to you guys, I'm a dead man!'

Realizing at last that Patsy had intended his 'cooperation' to be a sham from the start, the voluble Jury foreman rose, scowling, and went to a window, where, turning to the prisoner, he challenged: 'Then you might as well jump right now!'

As the grand jury hearings opened, the Narcotics Bureau received an anonymous letter from France. The writer said that the Mafia and the syndicate were desperate at the loss of the heroin shipment and, more important, were so concerned that Scaglia, Fuca, or Angelvin might talk that a contract for their deaths had already been let. The hired assassin was identified in the letter as the maître d'hôtel of one of New York's most exclusive and expensive restaurants, which was not named.

As a result of this cryptic warning, Scaglia was immediately moved to the new maximum security prison in Kew Gardens, Queens, and Angelvin to another high security jail on the lower west side of New York. Since Scaglia was apparently the priority candidate for assassination, the police speculated that any killer who understood the New York City prison system would think that the police would have Scaglia in a

Manhattan jail since it was customary to keep a man in the same borough in which he was arrested. By the same reasoning, Patsy, who had been arrested in Brooklyn, was sent to 125 White Street, Manhattan, better known as the Tombs.

During the first month of the grand jury hearings, Detectives Egan and Grosso were shuttling from the courthouse in Brooklyn to the basement of Tony Fuca's house in the Bronx. When the heroin found in the carriage room of the basement, forty kilos, was added to that seized earlier, the total came to something over fifty-one kilos, or about 112 pounds: exactly the underweight so meticulously declared by Jacques Angelvin preparatory to his return voyage to France.

There was no question that the total seizure was the largest ever accomplished by law enforcement agencies in the United States, surpassing the previous record of fifteen months before when a South American diplomat to the United Nations was caught with some one hundred pounds in his sole possession. But there remained one particularly unsatisfying aspect to the Fuca case from the narcotics officers' point of view. With respect to the last cache of forty kilos, how were they to establish possession? In narcotics, that was the name of the game, and now that the Fucas and two of the Frenchmen were already in jail, as Eddie Egan put it they had 'nobody left to pin the *big* rap on.' This dour estimate included Tony Fuca, for, regardless of how reasonable it was to *assume* that it was he who had squirreled away the bigger load of junk in his own apartment house cellar, it still could not be proven.

Meanwhile, police informers throughout the city had begun to advance reports of a growing restlessness 'around.' The lowly addicts, the pushers and the small-time connections in the streets all were feeling the pinch of a short supply of heroin. But perhaps more important, the higher-echelon wholesalers and distributors also were beginning to snarl and, it would seem, plan drastic action to safeguard if not to recover their investments. These were the hoodlum 'business men' who had paid Patsy Fuca substantial monies for imports that were already contracted at customary incredible profit margins.

The police reasoned that one or more of these disappointed Mafia connections would try to retrieve the eighty-eight pounds from Tony Fuca's basement. And so, the decision was reached to leave undisturbed the findings at 1171 Bryant Avenue, the Bronx. The basement, the building and the surrounding area would be watched around the clock. The narcotics officers would wait.

Chapter Twenty-One

ON Sunday, February 4, 1962, seventeen days after the first arrests, the permanent stakeout of Tony Fuca's Bronx tenement began. Tours were divided into eight-hour shifts, with two New York detectives and three Federal agents on each tour. The core of the operation was the cellar where the stuff still reposed on the shelf in the carriage room. This locked room faced the entrance to the cellar, from the alley. To the left of the entry, outside in the alley, were stairs leading to the lobby of the building. Within view of the carriage room was a closet which served as a paint locker. To the left of the carriage room, out of sight of the door to the cellar, was a dingy, musty alcove littered with sundry discards from apartments upstairs, including crippled furniture, mattresses, toys, rugs and ragged trunks. Deeper into the cellar, a narrow whitewashed corridor led to the boiler room in the rear, which was cramped with machinery, pipes and flues. The back area was the only warm spot in the cellar, and the boiler room was chosen as the retreat for any who felt the need of a nap during the long hours of winter vigil. A worn, discolored mattress was laid on the concrete floor behind the clanking water heater. The men on duty were armed with a small arsenal, which included machine guns, shotguns and tear gas grenades, as well as their service revolvers and hundreds of rounds of ammunition. Nobody knew who or how many hoods might show up looking for the hidden fortune in junk. There was little firm information about what might happen; but things were stirring.

Egan, Grosso and Agent Waters slipped in and out of the location through back alleys of adjacent buildings, exchanging and coordinating reports and what few tips were forthcoming from Lieutenant Vinnie Hawkes and Sergeant Jack Fleming of S.I.U. downtown. Egan and Grosso had been augmented by Detectives Dick Auletta and Jimmy O'Brien; Waters headed a rotating team of twelve Federal agents. The prospect of days or even weeks of sitting in a dismal, filthy basement was enough to stretch the temper of the most seasoned law officer, but, the police detectives observed sourly, the Feds assigned seemed woefully short on hard experience. Except for the tough Waters, most of the agents appeared young and impatient.

As it turned out, the combined surveillance details experienced more harassment from other law officers than from any sinister enemy forces. The investigators decided not to inform the local police precinct of their mission, because they believed that anything less than total security would compromise their position. This decision led to complications almost immediately.

The stakeout team was still relaxed and unapprehensive when on Monday, the second day, a scrawny, sour-faced elderly man wearing the spattered white coveralls and cap of a professional painter walked into the cellar. Two detectives were in the gloomy alcove beyond the carriage room, playing gin rummy by a dim overhead bulb. A third was back in the boiler room, stretched out on the mattress near the boiler. The painter didn't notice any of these at first. After a few moments of massaging the cold from his hands, he affectionately packed and lit an ancient curved-stem pipe and went to the paint locker. When he opened the door, he jumped back as though he had touched a live electric wire, and his pipe clattered on the floor. Seated there, glaring at him within the lighted paint locker, a paperback book in one hand and a huge shotgun across his lap, was a burly, tough-looking redhaired stranger.

Eddie Egan said nothing; he just stared. Shaken, the painter recoiled into the corridor leading to the boiler room. Then he saw the two sweatered men hunched over an old steamer trunk in the storage alcove. They had laid down their cards and were looking at him. He started to speak – but his eyes went wide, and his mouth hung open. Propped against the wall near these two were machine guns. One of the men stood. Around his waist was a bulky cartridge belt. There was a movement down the passageway inside the boiler room, and another figure appeared there, standing silently, looking at the painter. In fright and bewilderment, the old man's eyes jumped from one to another of the menacing-looking figures. He backed toward the door to the alley, tore it open and was gone.

The card players glanced at each other, and the one who had stood ambled to the open door of the paint locker, where Egan was on his feet now, stretching.

'I guess that was the house painter,' Egan grinned, half yawning.

'He looked surprised as hell. I thought Grosso gave the super a cover story.'

'He did. This was another guy. The super must have forgot to brief him. Good super.'

'I don't know,' the agent shook his head. 'This looks like it could get kind of hairy.'

Doubt as to the wisdom of keeping their vigil secret from the local constabulary spread quickly. Later the same day the incredulous old painter returned twice more to the cellar, as if to verify his fears. Each time, to his obvious distress, he found four armed and silent men, and when he came the last time, that evening, there was a different set of four men. The detectives were beginning to feel sorry for the poor old fellow because it was plain that his consternation had led him to the bottle and that his composure was disintegrating. When he tottered from the cellar that night, again without a word having been offered, he might have been one in shock.

But a few hours later the third team of narcotics investigators had their first taste of how complex their undercover situation could in fact become from restricted communication. The cellar was dark, except for a slit of light under the closed door of the paint locker, where a Federal agent sat doing a crossword puzzle. The others were in the alcove and boiler room trying to relax in the dank early-morning chill. After the painter's last visit, they had decided to rig up a crude warning signal against night callers: a length of supple wire was hooked to the top of the door from the alleyway, strung along the ceiling down the corridor into the boiler room, over a pulley screwed into the ceiling and attached to a pail full of plaster of paris. When the alley door was opened, the heavy pail would drop with a clunk onto the cement floor; the sound probably would not be noticed by anyone entering the cellar, but it would be enough to prepare the detectives in the rear.

It was shortly after 2:00 A.M., Tuesday, when the agent up front in the closet heard a faint shuffle of footsteps outside. He doused the light and opened the door of his hiding place a crack, hands gripping the shotgun. The cellar door creaked open, letting in a rush of cold night air, and he strained to hear the hoped-for clunk from the back but couldn't be sure it had worked. The door was closed softly. The slight scraping of feet on the cement floor sounded like two men. They were moving slowly past the paint locker, now pausing at the mouth of the passage to the rear. Suddenly shafts from two flashlights pierced the darkness. One swept the entry hall, then in a quick step one of the visitors reached up to pull the chain dangling from a ceiling bulb. Simultaneously the cellar entry was flooded with light and a voice barked: 'All right! Police! Who's down here?'

They were two patrolmen, massive in their heavy blue overcoats, revolvers and flashlights in their hands. One whirled as the agent pushed open the paint closet door and stepped out, shotgun laid aside. 'Who the hell are you, mister?' the cop demanded.

There was no time for a reply, for the other officer cried: 'Wait! Look out!' The two agents in the alcove were emerging from the shadows, revolvers in hand. The startled cops crouched, prepared for violence. But a sharp voice rang from the blackness of the boiler room: 'Hold it, f'Chrissake! We're *all* police officers!' In a moment, a light blinked on in the rear of the cellar, and the Narcotics Bureau's Jimmy O'Brien was advancing with his gold shield in hand.

They had to explain to the patrolmen, who had received a radioed complaint from the 41st Precinct about strange men in the basement of 1171 Bryant Avenue, that they were narcotics investigators, without actually revealing details of their mission. It was delicate. The patrolmen were uncertain of what to do at first, but they agreed hesitantly to keep the stakeout quiet.

The following afternoon a uniformed Transit Authority patrolman ventured tentatively into the cellar and was sent packing with the firm admonition to forget that he'd seen them. Within the next forty-eight hours they had two more visits, first by a pair of plainclothesmen from a neighboring precinct whom the desperate house painter had encountered on the street while they were making an arrest several blocks away. He had told them a harrowing tale of a round-the-clock crap game going on in his basement. And then even a green-uniformed Sanitation Department inspector was importuned to come down, the befuddled old man appealing to anybody he could find wearing a uniform. Each time, the men in the cellar had to explain something of what was afoot. 'Security' was coming apart.

Perhaps just as bad, the officers themselves were growing jumpy. One night during this first week, Detective Jimmy O'Brien awoke from a half-sleep in the pitch-black boiler room to see a tiny red glow hovering over him. O'Brien froze: somebody was standing there in the dark, smoking a cigarette! 'Sonny?' he called in a small voice. 'Waters?' He heard only the hum of the boiler. With a loud cry, O'Brien rolled off the mattress onto the cold floor, pulling his revolver in the same motion. There were scuffled footsteps, and then the lights went on. Sonny Grosso, Frank Waters and Jack Ripa crowded the end of the corridor opening into the boiler room, guns drawn.

'What the hell's happening?' Sonny demanded.

'There was somebody in here,' O'Brien said from his prone position. He looked about him, perplexed. The others, crouching, tense, prowled every shadowy corner.

'You must've been dreaming,' Sonny drawled at last, holstering his revolver. 'There's nobody here.'

The lights were switched off. O'Brien crawled back onto the mattress. In a moment he screamed again: 'There he is!' Again the running feet, the lights on, and again no one but four edgy detectives.

Sonny stared at the boiler. He walked over to the square, sooty machine and, looking down at O'Brien, scowled: 'Here's your guy smoking.' He pointed a finger at a small red pilot light at about eye level, an indicator that the mechanism was working.

* * *

Every day the tension thus increased in the dingy basement. The officers had to struggle with themselves to hold tempers in check and, more important, to curb their tendencies to point guns around at strange noises. The shifts were watching eighty-eight pounds of a commodity worth many millions of dollars to the Mafia Dons, and they never knew when a raiding party of Italians might burst into the basement and try to take the heroin.

Occasionally some piece of interesting news would filter in from the outside and give the detectives something to talk about. The most absorbing tidbit came when Lieutenant Vinnie Hawkes paid one of his regular visits to the stakeout. He found Eddie Egan in his accustomed position in the paint locker.

'Hey, Popeye, the machine gun you pulled out of the ceiling at Fuca's? What if it was the same chopper used to kill the guard and wound a cop in that bank job at the Lafayette National on Kings Highway?'

Eddie jumped to his feet in excitement. 'I tailed Patsy there just two days before! I remember at the time thinking he looked like he was casing the place.'

'It seems our boy Patsy was always busy. I wouldn't put it past a bum like him to rent out that machine gun and other weapons too.' The officer smiled cynically at the speculation.

The superintendent of the apartment building wandered into the basement from time to time, but he paid no attention to the stakeout, and the narcotics officers said little to him. In the thickening atmosphere, he almost brought about violent death for himself. One morning he calmly took a plank and rested it on two sawhorses. He stood over the middle of it, breathing heavily, and with a sudden shout, he gave a sharp blow with the edge of his right hand, breaking the board in half with the karate chop.

Frayed nerves reacted instantaneously and five weapons

were brought to bear on him. The startled karate student stared into the barrels of a machine gun, two rifles, and two pistols. Slowly the guns were lowered and that was the last appearance the superintendent made in the basement.

During the long days and nights the detectives sat on the heroin, it was impossible for each of them not to think about the value of the white powder in Tony Fuca's trunk. It would be a simple matter to sell the junk back to the Mafia for a million dollars. It was worth ten times that amount. The heroin hadn't been analyzed yet, but they figured it had to be almost pure. It was a temptation they all were used to; it teased every narcotics officer.

Egan toyed with the fantasy. A life of luxury was within his grasp, he knew. By now Carol Galvin had declared to Egan that she was getting out of his life because she could no longer adjust herself either to his schedule or to his limited income as a cop. He could take this stuff and . . . but his daydreaming ended as it always did: he *was* a cop, and he'd probably always be one, so that was it.

Two weeks went by without any real action or discernible progress toward wrapping up the case. Aside from the visits by other unsuspecting policemen, there were a few occasions when tenants of the building entered the cellar to retrieve some household articles from storage. (At such moments the men on stakeout acted the roles of repairmen, electricians or boiler mechanics, which proved to be welcome breaks in the frustrating monotony.) But there had been no sign whatever of an approach by anybody interested in the cache of heroin. No one had gone into the carriage room at all; the winter cold was keeping babies indoors.

Except for infrequent shopping trips, Peggy Fuca, Tony's wife, had stayed put on the fifth floor with her two small daughters. She had not ventured near the cellar and presumably was unaware of the lawmen holed up there.

It had now become apparent that only the Fuca brothers knew where the treasure was stashed, and evidently there would be no overt move to recover it until such time as one of them was at liberty. Through informers, the police had received indications that agitation among the various vice lords over disposition of the missing junk had noticeably subsided in recent days. This suggested that word had been passed from jail, probably via the prisoners' mother, that the load was safe and would reach the proper hands as soon as one of the principals was released. Chances were small that it would be Patsy, who, with his father and the two Frenchmen, was being held in $100,000 bail. The police felt that such a price would be too high, and too incriminating, for even the Tuminaro organization to front again for Patsy's temporary release.

Tony Fuca also was being held in $100,000 bail for conspiracy and an additional $22,500 for possession of narcotics, and the lawyer hired to represent the Fucas had been vainly pressing for reduction of the bail. Now the police decided that it would be advantageous to allow Tony to get out so they could study his movements. With the consent of the district attorney, the $100,000 for conspiracy was finally waived, and Tony's bail dropped to $22,500.

On Monday, February 19, the Narcotics Bureau was informed that bail had been secured for Tony Fuca and he was about to be set free. Immediately, additional men were dispatched to the stakeout in the Bronx.

That same morning, a police stool telephoned a tip that there might be an attempt by a local mob not affiliated with the Fucas and Tuminaro to intercept Tony and hijack the reputed fortune in 'H' whose existence, at least, by now seemed to be common gossip in 'the street.'

By midmorning on February 19, Detectives Eddie Egan,

Jimmy O'Brien, Jim Gildea and Jim Hurley and Federal Agent Jack Ripa were on duty in the cellar at 1171 Bryant Avenue, the Bronx. A half-dozen other officers watched the house from the street and unobtrusively patrolled the general vicinity. And now two more were positioned on the roof of the building; they had been rehearsing another extemporaneous signal system for the time that Tony actually returned to his top-floor apartment. Henceforth, one officer would remain on the stair landing between the fifth floor and the roof itself, and whenever Tony or his wife left their apartment the detective outside would drop a tin can from the roof down into the alleyway below to warn the men in the cellar to be on the lookout for a possible visit. The dreary basement vigil suddenly became a tense, electric experience.

Egan was stationed in his favorite nook, the paint locker near the entryway. He did not enjoy playing cards, as most of the other officers did, and he wanted to be closest to where the action was liable to take place. This morning four men with him were back in the boiler room, shuffling about, talking in low, nervous tones.

When the door from the alley squeaked open, Egan tensed, put down the book he had been trying to read, and gripped his service pistol. He hoped the others had heard the plaster-filled bucket hit the floor behind the boiler; several times previously they had found that the device was ineffective during daylight hours, when the boiler churned away so loudly that its clanking drowned out the warning thud. Egan edged the closet door open an inch or two, just enough to see out.

His breath caught and icy currents raced across his skin as he saw two swarthy gunmen bent low, creeping silently past his hiding place toward the carriage room. They were grimly intent. He started to nudge the closet door farther ajar, when a third intruder whipped open the door before him and pushed a revolver close to his mouth. A gravelly voice snarled: 'Come out of there, you sonofabitch, or you're dead!'

Egan crouched absolutely still, unable to react, mesmerized by the gun six inches from his face. In a split second a shudder swept his body and he thought about death.

'Drop it!' the harsh voice ordered. The other two men had turned toward them.

Egan looked down at the pistol drooping in his hand. And then his mind started working again. He drew upright and tossed his gun toward the passageway to the boiler room, and as it clattered loudly on the cement floor, he blustered loudly: 'What is this all about? Who the hell are you guys?'

He heard movement from the rear of the cellar, shuffling and quick footsteps. The intruders had heard it, too. His guys would come out shooting. It was going to be war, and he was right in the middle. His eyes darted to the gloomy storage alcove. It was his only chance, however slim. If he could just keep under the machine-gun slugs. Behind, someone new entered the cellar as Egan braced himself to shoulder aside the man next to him and dive for the alcove.

'Hey, lieutenant, don't shoot!' the voice behind him shouted. 'It's Bullets Egan. He's a cop – narcotics squad!'

'A cop? Hold it – police officers!' the man beside Egan yelled into the cellar.

They were all limp when identifications and explanations had been exchanged. The 'gunmen' were detectives of the 41st Squad from the local Simpson Street station. The old painter had marched up to the precinct and related a chilling tale of 'mobs of hooligans and gangsters' occupying his basement work area, 'plotting murder.' It had sounded just improbable enough for there to be something to it. Although some of the precinct's uniformed patrolmen had been aware of the narcotics stakeout almost from the beginning, nobody had passed the word to the detectives. And so five of them had converged on the cellar. They had the windows and exits covered. Although they would have been outgunned, a fire fight probably would have resulted in a massacre of both groups of police.

Egan was unnerved by the near disaster and drained of his normal optimism. When he telephoned his superior, Lieutenant Hawkes, and described the experience, he emphasized that someone was going to get hurt unless they talked more openly with the local police: 'Either we're going to kill somebody, or some of *us* are going to get it,' he said.

Hawkes was sympathetic, but he said: 'We're too close to the payoff to pull out now, Popeye, or even to tip our hand. Now that Tony's out, something has to break soon. Why don't you take a day off? You'll feel better.'

'Hell, I'd kill *myself* if this thing got nailed down while I was beating the sheets,' was Egan's reply.

Tony Fuca seemed to be playing it very cool during the first several days he was at home. Time and time again the augmented force in the cellar tensed when the empty beer can ricocheted in the alleyway, but Tony left the house only to go to neighborhood stores. Thursday of that week he returned to the shape-up on the East Side docks, where he was welcomed back with guarded enthusiasm by his fellow longshoremen. He worked part of the day, and, returning home in midafternoon, he stopped at a grocery store near his house and then went upstairs with a small bundle. But he didn't come near the cellar.

Friday, his movements were about the same. He came home early and remained upstairs with his family. None of the police in the area had seen Tony's wife or children for some days, and after Tony had visited a local pharmacy a couple of times, the speculation was that one of the kids or perhaps Mrs. Fuca herself was sick.

Was it possible that Tony, regarded as the strong-armed, thickheaded link in Little Angie's apparatus, might *not* have been entrusted with the crucial knowledge that the valuable load was hidden in his own building? This question began to nag the waiting police. Yet this seemed too devious even for Patsy and his uncle. Still, they were ending their third week of unremitting surveillance of Tony's house. It had been over five weeks since the first important seizure in Brooklyn, and the Kings County Grand Jury was well into hearings for indictments. But nothing had happened at 1171 Bryant Avenue.

On Saturday, February 24, Sonny Grosso was taking a break. A close friend of his, a fun-loving 'perennial bachelor,' had asked Sonny to be best man at his wedding at St. Patrick's Cathedral. 'I wouldn't miss that if Luciano himself came back to life and offered to sing,' Sonny had said to Egan. Shortly before noon that day, Egan, hunched in the paint locker in Tony Fuca's basement, was daydreaming. He felt so soiled, grimy and lifeless, it was a pleasure to imagine the clean, gay people who would soon be gathering at St. Pat's downtown on handsome Fifth Avenue. He visualized the long, marbled aisle, the bride, pink-faced, in white, flowers on her arm, trailing satin; the smiling faces in the pews, craning eagerly; the groom, standing up front before the altar rail. He tried to picture Sonny, waiting there with his friend, nervous, probably even panicky; scrubbed, shaved, hair neatly brushed, wearing a jacket and pants that matched, shoes shined. Egan could barely remember the last time he had seen Sonny slicked up and fresh – or himself, for that matter . . .

A tin can rattled off the tenement walls outside in the alley. Tony was coming out again. The agents and detectives in the rear scurried to dark recesses of the boiler room and storage alcove. The cellar door opened and squeaked closed. Egan heard a man's steps pause in the entryway. Then they scraped slowly, past the paint closet. Through his door crack Egan saw a squat form in bulky gray sweater and shapeless trousers. Tony!

The detective's heart pounded as he watched Tony halt before the wooden door of the carriage room and peer for several moments to his left, along the dim corridor into the depths of the cellar. Egan bit his lip: Now all we need is for some clown to cough or sneeze back there. Tony looked the dim entry over very deliberately. His face was toward Egan, and enough daylight came through the glass panels of the outside door to enable the hidden officer to study his features. Tony was square-jawed and heavy-lipped, with a wide nose; as with so many unintelligent physical types, his eyes were blank films. Tony turned back toward the carriage room door, unhooked the clasp and disappeared into the darkness.

Egan started hard but could distinguish only vague movements inside. Tony appeared to climb on to something and remain still for a minute or two; he stepped back to floor level and poked around dark corners of the cluttered closet as though searching for something. Then he backed out and closed and latched the door. In one hand he carried what looked like a short crowbar, a tire iron perhaps. He hesitated and glanced again toward the boiler room. Finally he walked past Egan and went out into the alley. He started to whistle a sprightly tune.

'He knows damn well where that stuff is,' Egan told the others after it was reported that Tony had returned to his apartment. 'He was just checking to see if everything was the way they left it. I figure he's getting ready to make the move. We better get some more guys down here.'

Egan called on the portable radiophone to report that they expected someone would pick up the heroin very soon. It was just past 1:00 P.M.

About three-thirty, as the winter afternoon's light began to ebb out of the gray, sooty cellar, four additional men arrived, including Lieutenant Hawkes and Dick Auletta and another pair of Federal agents who stayed up on the street.

By now Egan was concerned over Sonny not being there. His partner *should* be in on this. Egan volunteered to go out for sandwiches. He drove over to 169th Street and a dozen more blocks west until he found a shopping area far enough from the operation. He went into a Jewish delicatessen and ordered ten corned-beef sandwiches on rye, with pickles, and as many Pepsis. While they were being made he went to the telephone booth in the rear.

It took two calls and considerable melodramatic jargon about 'official police business,' but twelve minutes later a quizzical Sonny Grosso picked up an extension phone that had been rushed by a nervous attendant to an alcove behind the great main altar of St. Patrick's Cathedral.

'Is this Detective Grosso of the Narcotics Bureau?' Egan asked cheerily.

'Popeye!'

'Yeah. How's it goin'?' He could hear the hollow rumbling of a giant organ.

'Marty says hello and hang up, we have to get married . . .' Then Sonny lowered his voice and spoke carefully into the mouthpiece. 'What do you want? Anything go wrong?'

'When can you cut out of there?' Egan asked softly, his flippant tone gone.

'Is something happening?'

'It's building. I think it's going to break soon. Tonight maybe. Our boy came down before and checked on his goods. He'll be back.'

'I can't go *now*. Maybe by five o'clock. I'll have to duck the reception. I had a good toast to give, too.'

'You can recite for us. And come as you are. You'll give the place a little class.'

Crumpled waxed paper, empty Pepsi cans and remnants of sandwiches and pickles were piled more or less neatly in a corner of the boiler room. By 5:30 P.M., darkness had fallen outside, and the weak overhead bulb cast a pale, almost sinister illumination over the six men standing around the water heater or leaning against the wall, talking quietly. The passageway to the front was dark, but the entry light was on. Egan had taken his place in the paint locker. Two Federal agents sat in the unlit storage alcove adjacent to the carriage room.

The detectives in the rear all started when the pail filled with plaster clunked behind the boiler. The ceiling light was doused, and they flattened themselves against the walls. A dark figure with a turned-up overcoat collar slunk into view at the corner of the entryway, silhouetted by the glow of the hanging bulb there.

'Popeye?' It was a hoarse stage whisper.

Somebody laughed. The light went on in the boiler room and the men came together to watch Sonny Grosso advance toward them with a sheepish grin on his face. He was still wearing his dress suit.

'Here comes the bride . . .' someone sang.

'I could go for *her* myself,' another lisped.

'I don't know. He don't *look* like a cop.'

'He can't be a regular. He must be one of them private cops.'

Sonny's grin broadened as he looked around at them. 'Well, I can't say it's a pleasure to be back in the dungeon, but at least' – he grimaced and held his nose – 'I'm clean!'

'*That's* who he is,' somebody whooped. 'Mister Clean!'

Their spirits simmered down, however, and three hours later the familiar air of anxious boredom had again settled over the cellar. It was just past 8:30 P.M. when a signal can rattled down the side of the building like a tinny machine gun and hit the alley floor in what sounded like a claxon to the keyed-up squad. They scrambled to hiding places and vantage points. The only light remained in the entryway.

Five minutes ticked by. The boiler had quieted for the night now, and even the sounds of breathing and the smallest scrapes of leather soles seemed exaggerated. Ten minutes. Then they heard footsteps, coming down the inside stairs from the building lobby. The door creaked open. Then silence, as though whoever had come in was frozen, listening. The door closed. The man – it *had* to be Tony – was in. He moved very slowly and quietly. A shadow moved across the entryway. Then the squat silhouette.

Tony paused again at the head of the corridor, motionless, alert, tight as a spring. And then his shoulders sagged as though a tap had been opened and all his suspicion had gushed out, and with swift, easy movements now, he opened the carriage room door. Inside, he even switched on the light. Tony really felt sure of himself.

The moment of truth was approaching, Egan thought; Tony finally was going to lead them to the big guys who had paid for the junk.

Tony opened his lumber jacket and pulled the tire iron from his belt. He climbed onto an overturned baby stroller and from the shelf in the far corner lifted down the well-worn steamer trunk which contained the two suitcases of heroin.

He laid it gently on the floor. As if by reflex, he glanced about him, then, with the tire iron he pried open the lid of the locked case. Egan, watching from the paint locker, prayed that Tony wouldn't notice that the lock had already been forced and refastened.

Tony removed one suitcase from the trunk, then closed it and hefted it back up onto the shelf. Bag in hand, he turned off the light, closed the door behind him and walked easily out to the stairs leading to the floor above. The hidden detectives let him go, prepared to follow in a few moments. It wasn't *him* they wanted as much as his connections.

Meanwhile, Detective Dick Auletta had been on the stair landing above Tony's top-floor apartment, and several minutes after Tony left the flat Auletta had begun to creep silently downstairs after him. Tony was not on the main floor. Auletta went through the vestibule to the front steps. An agent positioned across Bryant Avenue shook his head – Tony had not come out. Auletta stole back toward the door to the basement stairs. Very gently he opened the door and peered down. Below, in the semiblackness, he could hear a faint shuffle of feet. What was happening?

Auletta peeked around the corner. To his shock he found himself staring at the beetle-browed thug, who was only a few steps below, apparently on his way up. He was carrying a bag. Tony recovered quickly from his own surprise. He pulled the tire iron from his belt and charged up at Auletta with a growl. Auletta ducked the iron, but Tony's charge dumped him onto the stairs, and now Tony was scrambling over him and slashing down at his head. This time, twisting away, Auletta caught a heavy blow on a shoulder. The impact sent him reeling down the stairs and into the door, shattering a glass pane.

With a curse, Egan leaped over Auletta and up the steps after the hoodlum. 'Tony!' Egan shouted and fired one round from his .38 past Fuca's ear. The explosion reverberated through the halls. Tony stopped dead at the top of the stairs. The heroin-filled suitcase slid from his hand and tumbled end over end down the stairs to the feet of the advancing officers.

For better or for worse, it was over.

Chapter Twenty-Two

It was not until Monday, April 2, 1962, two and a half months after the Brooklyn arrests, that Kings County Grand Jury No. 1 returned indictments against Patsy and Joe Fuca, François Scaglia and, finally, Jacques Angelvin as well.

A week earlier, on March 26, Angelvin's attorney, Robert Kasanof, who had been secured for him through the joint efforts of the French Consulate and Angelvin's friend Jacques Sallebert of Radio Télévision Française, had attempted to gain a writ of habeas corpus. He demanded that the TV performer be released on the grounds that the state had failed to prosecute and thus the continuance of Angelvin in Civil Prison constituted 'atrocious abuse of legal power.'

Brooklyn Assistant District Attorney Frank DiLalla had persuaded the court that at present Angelvin remained a material witness, that the grand jury would name him in its forthcoming indictment as a defendant. The Frenchman was kept in custody. The grand jury's subsequent action removed any ambiguity about Angelvin's status: he was no longer a key witness, he was a defendant in the conspiracy.

On April 4, the four principals appeared in Kings County Criminal Court, and all pleaded not guilty to charges of possession and/or conspiracy to distribute eleven kilograms of illicit narcotics. Also named in the indictment were two 'John Does,' defendants not present and officially regarded as 'unidentified': the missing Frenchmen, Jean Jehan and J. Mouren.

Tony Fuca, of course, had been jailed in the Bronx and would be tried there on a charge of possession of the other forty kilos of heroin. Nicky Travato meanwhile had already pleaded to a lesser charge of possession and would be sentenced separately from the others in Brooklyn. And the recommended indictment against a now visibly pregnant Barbara Fuca, who had been free on bail since January, was 'held in abeyance' – an indication that the state might not prosecute her at all.

Within a week after the indictment, a bondsman secured Patsy Fuca's release on $100,000 bail. Patsy remained free less than a month. Presumably he had some serious, and possibly unnerving, discussions with his uncle, Angelo Tuminaro, and/or other members of the 'family,' for in early May he contacted the bail bondsman and asked for revocation of the $100,000 bond, and he was returned to the relative safety of a maximum security city jail to await trial.

At about the same time, Little Angie himself – at whose feet lay the ultimate responsibility for his nephew's failure – finally turned up in Florida. At a dog track, he presented himself to a patrolman, a rookie on the job only a few weeks, and surrendered himself for having jumped bail in New York more than two years previously. Extradition was arranged. Having considered all circumstances, apparently Little Angie had become convinced at that point that a couple of years in a secure prison was the best investment he could make in what had to be a dubious future at best.

The legal processes dragged through the summer and into the fall of 1962, without a trial date having been set. In the meantime, the three defense lawyers – Robert Kasanof for Angelvin, Maurice Edelbaum for the Fucas and Henry Lowenberg for Scaglia – undertook a series of legal maneuvers designed to discredit the indictments on technicalities.

First, Kasanof submitted a motion that the indictment handed up by the grand jury was 'faulty' in that it offered no concrete evidence linking Angelvin's automobile with the heroin found in the ceiling of Joe Fuca's basement. If this objection were supported, charges against Angelvin would have to be dismissed, and it could also lead to Scaglia's release as well, inasmuch as the case against the Corsican was so closely tied to Angelvin and his Buick.

On November 1, the district attorney's office was notified that a hearing on Kasanof's motion was set for November 14. Assistant District Attorney Michael Gagliano restudied the indictment at length and decided that the connection of Angelvin's car to the conspiracy was indeed inexactly spelled out – it *was* a faulty indictment. To make the case stick, they needed a superseding indictment, fast. With less than two weeks to act, Gagliano contacted Grand Jury Foreman Jack Champagne, who was on vacation in Arizona. Champagne cut his holiday short and flew back to New York to reconvene Grand Jury No. 1, which had handed up the original indictment.

At 10:00 A.M. of November 14, Angelvin and his attorney appeared confidently at the Supreme Court in Brooklyn. Angelvin, encouraged by Kasanof's enthusiasm over the loophole he'd found, arrived with a small satchel containing his possessions, fully expecting to be on a plane for Paris that night.

As expected, Brooklyn Supreme Court Justice Miles F. McDonald upheld the defense contention that the indictment was faulty, adding that he had no alternative but to dismiss that part of the indictment dealing with the defendant Angelvin.

Even as a joyful Angelvin was picturing himself aboard Air France, Assistant District Attorney Frank DiLalla jumped to his feet and handed the judge a superseding indictment which did contain additional evidence linking the French performer's Buick to the conspiracy.

Justice McDonald spent the next three hours in his chambers studying the new document. At 2:00 P.M., to the consternation of not only Kasanof and Angelvin but all the defendants and their counsel, Judge McDonald denied the motion to dismiss. Jacques carried his satchel back to the Tombs.

Two months later, in January, 1963 – now almost a year to the day after the Brooklyn arrests – Kasanof was trying another last-ditch ploy on behalf of Angelvin. He moved for a so-called 'suppression' hearing, wherein the defense would try to show the court that certain evidence against the accused, however damning, was inadmissible because it had been obtained by arresting officers without authorization. In this instance, Kasanof sought to prove that Angelvin's automobile should be ruled out of evidence on the grounds that, one, the police, who had no search warrant for the Buick at the time, had proceeded illegally when detectives stopped Angelvin and Scaglia on East End Avenue for allegedly passing a stop signal, January 18, 1962; and, two, they had not established the reliability of the unnamed informer who a week after the arrest (as the police had testified) offered the information upon which the search warrant finally was based.

The fact was, of course, that the 'informer' was Detective Sonny Grosso himself, whose deductive reasoning alone had led the police to suspect Angelvin's car following the arrests. Under intensive questioning it was brought out that the informer had tipped off Grosso who in turn had bade Detective Jim Hurley to secure the warrant. The defense attempted to establish that Hurley was acting on secondhand information, while the prosecution maintained that information given to one police officer traditionally was considered firsthand information to all his brother officers.

The suppression hearings before Judge Albert Conway

lasted from January 14 to 16, 1963, and when they came to a close neither side was sure what the sum effect had been upon the court. Again, the police and district attorney's office, despite what they felt was overwhelming evidence against the defendants, were concerned lest one technicality might succeed in causing the judge to rule against use of the Buick as evidence in the trial.

But on April 15, Judge Conway denied the motion to suppress. The trial finally was set for May 14, which would be sixteen months after the arrests of the Fucas and the Frenchmen.

Meanwhile, the district attorney's office had gone ahead preparing the case. At the special request of the district attorney, Detectives Egan and Grosso were relieved of all other duties and specifically assigned to help prepare the prosecution of the entire Fuca case and remain in this capacity until the end of the trial. Assistant District Attorney Frank Bauman, assigned to prosecute, with Egan and Grosso secured a small office in Brooklyn's Municipal Building at Borough Hall and went to work reviewing every detail of the case from the moment they had entered the Copacabana that fateful evening in October of 1961. They lined the walls with maps prepared by Police Department engineers. Every place where Patsy Fuca and his associates had been observed through January 18, 1962, was indicated via the maps and calendars. A recording and playback device was placed in the office and every tape of the recorded conversations during surveillance of the defendants reviewed again and again.

Immediately after Judge Conway's ruling, Assistant District Attorney Frank Bauman left for France to check out in detail all evidence originating there.

Shortly after his departure, toward the end of April, one of the most reliable police 'stools' came up with a startling and, for Egan and Grosso, most vital piece of information: the Mafia had let a 'contract' to eliminate both detectives before the trial. The report even had it that the killer was to be paid $50,000 – half on acceptance of the contract and the rest when the job was done.

The informant advised that a 'specialist' had been chosen for the Egan-Grosso assignment: a vicious Cincinnati hoodlum called 'Tony the Crease,' who was known to be slowly dying of cancer. This, the police knew, was the Mafia's standard operating procedure when it came to picking professional cop killers. Such a man had nothing to lose, and if he did his job successfully, he knew whatever family he might have would henceforth be well cared for.

Guards were posted on Eddie and Sonny around the clock. From that point on, they were not permitted to leave Brooklyn's Municipal Building together nor drive in the same automobile nor visit each other socially without protection.

The information on Tony the Crease had been remarkably good, and so was the cooperation of various police departments between Ohio and New York. The word came that Tony was driving from Cincinnati, and his route was followed fairly accurately. Egan and Grosso and their comrades girded themselves for his anticipated arrival in New York.

But one night early in May, just west of Newark, New Jersey, Tony the Crease met with a fatal automobile accident. His car ran off U.S. Route 1, plunged down an embankment and rolled over, bursting into flames. The imported assassin was incinerated.

Egan and Grosso relaxed. They didn't feel their enemies would try the same thing a second time.

The trial was held in Criminal Term, Part 4, of the Supreme Court in Brooklyn. Judge Samuel Liebowitz presided. This did not please the defense. In the courtooms of New York

City, Liebowitz was referred to as 'the Hanging Judge.' His hatred for hardcore criminals was legend. And very few jurists knew the criminal mind better than Judge Liebowitz: years before he had been one of the country's most famous criminal lawyers, counting among his clients the notorious Al Capone. But like a reformed alcoholic or a religious convert, Liebowitz had dedicated his years on the bench to the most rigid application of the law's penalties to the same type of flagrant violators as he had once defended.

The trial opened at 10 A.M., Tuesday, May 14, 1963. The first, motion was made by Maurice Edelbaum, defense counsel for Patsy Fuca. Edelbaum entered a plea of guilty for Patsy on three felony counts: possession of narcotics, conspiracy to possess narcotics and conspiracy to sell narcotics. Patsy was in court not more than a half-hour. The changed plea was accepted, and he was sent back to jail to await sentence.

Patsy's father, Joe Fuca, next was allowed to plead guilty to a misdemeanor, and he was continued free on bail in his own recognizance.

The Fucas were now severed from the case. Thus began the trial of the two Frenchmen, François Scaglia and Jacques Angelvin.

It was almost no contest. The defense – Henry Lowenberg for Scaglia and Robert Kasanof for Angelvin – had no defense witness to present. For the prosecution, Assistant District Attorney Frank Bauman paraded witness after witness – police technical experts, hotel personnel, detectives who had participated in the long surveillance – knitting the web of complicity about the two accused.

On the morning of the sixth day, Wednesday, May 22, Jacques Angelvin and his counsel, Kasanof, met with Judge Liebowitz and prosecutor Bauman in the judge's robing room. Angelvin wanted to change his plea to guilty.

For almost the entire morning, Liebowitz questioned Angelvin in his chambers, trying to elicit information that might help identify the highest crime lords in the narcotics syndicate and to place Scaglia's role in the heroin ring. Angelvin was plainly terrified. The TV performer indicated that he would be murdered if he talked about Scaglia or others connected with the heroin smuggling to which he had pleaded guilty.

Finally, the judge accepted Angelvin's new plea of guilty with its implication of a lighter sentence and set sentencing for September 13.

Back in court, Liebowitz meticulously charged the jury not to allow the fact that the defendant Angelvin was absent to indicate to them in the slightest degree that Scaglia was guilty or innocent. He made each juror, one by one, repeat the statement: 'The absence of the defendant Angelvin has no bearing on the case against Mr. Scaglia.'

Lowenberg nonetheless made another motion for mistrial on grounds that the severance of the trial of Angelvin from Scaglia was prejudicial. The motion was denied.

The next afternoon, Bauman rested the case for the people. The prosecution had firmly established the skein of conspiracy in which Scaglia was linked with Patsy Fuca, and it had exhibited technical proof that Angelvin's automobile had transported the heroin found in the Fuca basement. The defense had nowhere to go. Lowenberg's plea essentially was for clemency. The trial was recessed until Tuesday, May 28.

That day, Judge Liebowitz charged the jurors, then they were sent out to deliberate.

Within eighty minutes the jury returned its verdict on François Scaglia: Guilty as charged to each of the three counts in the indictment.

The district attorney's office immediately asked that Scaglia be remanded to jail without bail.

Judge Liebowitz agreed. 'A scoundrel of this kind who brings such a load of misery into this country doesn't deserve any consideration. Our country is being flooded by these rats who bring in this insidious drug so that poor unfortunates may be kept on narcotics. This is not some little, petty larceny pusher or addict who is selling a little dope so he can get some for himself. This is a big-time operator. And he can rest assured that he will feel the heavy fist of the law; it will descend upon him in no uncertain terms when he is sentenced.'

Sentencing was set for September 13.

Eddie Egan and Sonny Grosso walked out of the courtroom and into the sunshine, still warm that late spring afternoon. Sonny had just been promoted to first grade detective; the baseball season was underway again – all seemed well with the world.

'What do we do now?' Sonny asked.

'Maybe we ought to celebrate, go popeying around somewhere. What say we go over to the Copa tonight? There's a new hatcheck kid there.

Sonny stopped halfway down the courthouse steps and stared incredulously at his partner. 'The Copa? Are you kidding?'

Epilogue

ON SEPTEMBER 13, 1963, Judge Liebowitz passed sentence on Jacques Angelvin and François Scaglia. Both Kasanof and Lowenberg argued for light sentences. Kasanof reminded the court of Angelvin's two teenage children and his two elderly parents, who had written to the judge: 'We have only this one son. Our life is coming to an end, and we would like to have time to help him remake his life.' He also cited letters received on Angelvin's behalf from such luminaries as Maurice Chevalier, Yves Montand and Simone Signoret.

Lowenberg also asked for clemency, saying that Scaglia had worked in the French underground against the Nazis during World War II. He said that Scaglia 'is contrite and—'

The judge interrupted: 'Oh, he is far from being contrite. He refused to talk to the probation officer, and he has said he would take his chances on appeal.'

Judge Liebowitz sentenced Angelvin to three to six years in Sing Sing and then turned to Scaglia:

'You are one of the most contemptible creatures that ever stood before this criminal bar of justice. You deserve no mercy – none; and let the word go back to France and to the other merchants of death, for that is what you are, that if *they* are caught in this country they too must suffer the full penalty of the law.'

With that, Judge Liebowitz sentenced the Corsican, Scaglia, to Sing Sing, thence to be removed to the Attica State Prison for consecutive terms of seven-and-a-half to fifteen and three-and-a-half to seven years – a maximum twenty-two years all told. It was the harshest penalty levied upon any of the principals in the case.

Three months later, in January 1964, Patsy Fuca finally came up for sentencing. Like his brother Tony, convicted in the Bronx, Patsy drew seven-and-a-half to fifteen years. As for old Joe Fuca, Patsy's father's three-year sentence in the end was suspended, and he was sent home to his bottle and his bitterness.

In May of 1967, the mysterious Jean Jehan finally was apprehended in Paris by the Sûreté. Because of his advanced age, the French police declined requests by the U.S. Federal Bureau of Narcotics for extradition, and as this is written the sinister old boulevardier remains relatively safe in France, presumably under the watchful eye of the National Police.

Probably, Jehan is the only one who could tell what happened to the payoff money – perhaps as much as $500,000 – which never was recovered. He may also be the only one who knows what happened to the single conspirator in the Patsy Fuca case who remains at large, the mysterious J. Mouren.

As for Jacques Angelvin, he was released from prison in the spring of 1968 and returned immediately to France and relative obscurity – although he did succumb to an opportunity to earn some needed cash by writing magazine reminiscences of his experience in American jails. He said that generally he'd found them more comfortable than many French hotels.

An intriguing, if somewhat bizarre, final note:

In August 1968, New York State Police reported finding the bodies of two hoodlums upstate, apparent victims of a gangland execution. Both were known to have been formerly highly placed in Angelo Tuminaro's Brooklyn-based narcotics ring.

One of the corpses was Frank Tuminaro, forty, Angie's younger brother. Following Patsy Fuca's arrest in 1962, Frank Tuminaro had taken over as administrator of his brother's clandestine network. But, in the face of stepped-up pressure from law-enforcement agencies, inspired by leads developed in the Fuca case, Frank's operation proved even more slipshod than his nephew's had been, and in February 1965 he and seventeen others were indicted on narcotics charges. It was another grievous blow to the crumbling Tuminaro organization.

Little Angie, who had remained unobtrusive since his own release from prison in 1966, showed up at his brother's funeral. Detectives who observed the proceedings reported that the narcotics boss, now fifty-eight, looked sad.

A NOTE ON THE AUTHOR

Robin Moore was born in Boston in 1925 and educated at Harvard. In writing *The French Connection*, Moore and his assistant spent many hundreds of hours interviewing the New York and Federal officers involved and listening to recorded conversations, orders and counter-orders. Among other books, he is also the author of the international bestseller, *The Green Berets*.